10⁰⁰

The Vanished Worlds of Jewry

overleaf A member of the Jewish élite of learning.

The Vanished Worlds of Jewry

Raphael Patai

Picture research by Eugene Rosow with Vivian Kleiman

Macmillan Publishing Co., Inc.
New York

Macmillan Publishing Co., Inc.
866 Third Avenue, New York,
N.Y. 10022
Collier Macmillan Canada, Ltd.

Library of Congress Catalog
Card Number: 80-81822
ISBN 0-02-595120-3
First American Edition 1980

Printed in Great Britain

Designed by Allison Waterhouse for
George Weidenfeld and Nicolson Ltd
91 Clapham High Street,
London SW4, England

Contents

Author's Preface

The idea of this volume originated with Lord Weidenfeld and crystallized in the course of two meetings between him, Dr Eugene Rosow, and myself in New York, in 1979. It was agreed that the book should present Jewish life as it developed historically and culminated in the present century, in two types of Jewish communities: those which were subsequently destroyed by the Nazi holocaust, and those which disappeared after World War II because of voluntary or forced mass emigration. It was also decided to include in both categories some of those communities in which a small Jewish remnant survived.

Not all the Jewish communities which suffered either of these fates could be dealt with within the confines of the book. Several which had originally been small in size or whose cultural physiognomy did not differ markedly from that of their neighbours were not included, even though the same events overtook them. However, the eighteen communities which are included comprise most of the Jewish Diasporas which flourished before World War II and subsequently have either disappeared or become greatly diminished in number.

While I am solely responsible for the text, the illustrations accompanying it were provided by Dr Eugene Rosow with Vivian Kleiman, who assembled them from various sources. They asked me to express their indebtedness to the following individuals and institutions: Judith Heller, Irene Lewitt, and Aviva Muller of the Israel Museum, Jerusalem; Shana Abells of Yad waShem, Jerusalem; Ruth Porter and Shayke Weinberg of the Museum of the Diaspora, Tel Aviv; Janet Langmaid of the Wiener Library, London; Alexander Scheiber of the Rabbinical Seminary of Budapest; Sybil Milton and her staff of the Leo Baeck Institute, New York; the YIVO archives, New York; Sylvia Landress and her staff of the Zionist Archives and Library, New York; and the Photographic Collection of the Diaspora Film Project, San Francisco, for their help in locating and providing photographs.

Raphael Patai
Forest Hills, N.Y.
15 February, 1980

Picture Researchers' Preface

One of the most remarkable characteristics of the Jewish people is their historic Dispersion to all parts of the world. Yet there remains a lamentable lack of audio-visual material on the Diaspora experience. The photographs selected for this book are intended to convey a vivid sense of the astonishing diversity that has resulted from the Dispersion of the Jewish people and of the richness and constancy of Jewish traditions that have characterized vanished or dwindled communities.

The photographic research was begun as part of the preparation of a series of documentary films on the Diaspora (the Diaspora Film Project) that is being produced by Cultural Research and Communications Inc with the support of the National Endowment for the Humanities of the United States. We believe that photographs, film and video material can greatly enhance a deep-felt understanding of Jewish historical experiences which in many cases have been neglected or ignored. Thanks to the passionate concern of some individual collectors (like Mr Lazar Ran, whose collection of Lithuanian subjects is represented here) and the all too few archives devoted to such work (like Beth Hatefutsoth, the Museum of the Jewish Diaspora, Tel Aviv), we have access to the visual testimony of Jewish life since the mid-nineteenth century. The preservation of such photographs has been a rather uneven process and the collection of materials has rarely been systematic or thorough. Poland, thanks to the work of YIVO, or Germany, whose Jewish past is documented by the Leo Baeck Institute, are well represented, while other countries, such as Libya or the Yemen, are more difficult to portray visually. In some instances whole collections of photographs have been banished to attics or basements so that even the photographic witnesses of vanished communities have disappeared. We hope that this volume contributes to an understanding of Jewish life in the Diaspora and that the photographs encourage other visual reconstructions of Jewish life past, present and future.

Eugene Rosow and Vivian Kleiman

Introduction

It was in our century that the Jewish people experienced the greatest of upheavals of the four millennia of their history. Prior to our times, the greatest catastrophe that had befallen them was the destruction of Jerusalem by the Romans in 70 CE.[1] But, great as that national calamity was and painful as was the blow it dealt Jewish religious sensibilities everywhere, there was never any question that it could actually endanger the survival of the Jews in their Diaspora, which by that time had embraced the entire Mediterranean area. Nor, for that matter, did the Roman victory terminate the life of the Jews as a national entity in their own country. Quite to the contrary: the loss of the last vestiges of Jewish sovereignty in no way impeded the achievement of the most significant religious development since the great prophetic era of the eighth century BCE[2] – the construction of Talmudic Judaism which took place precisely in the first few centuries of Roman rule over Jewish Palestine.

In contrast, the Nazi holocaust of the twentieth century annihilated not only the largest European Jewish contingents but precisely those with the oldest and richest cultural traditions: the communities of East Europe which, ever since the Enlightenment and the Emancipation, had constituted a great human reservoir from which the less steadfast and less stable Western Jewry could and did replenish its dwindling stock. Thus, from a historical-traditional-cultural point of view, the Nazi genocide did much greater damage to the Jewish people than can be measured even by the millions of its victims.

The second great upheaval that befell the Jewish people in the present century was the disappearance of the millennial Jewish communities from the Muslim lands of the Middle East. Taking place within a few years after the end of World War II and the defeat of Nazi Germany, this had less horrible, but still fateful, consequences for world Jewry. The withdrawal of the Jews from all Arab countries, and to a lesser extent from the other Muslim lands as well, came about in consequence of the achievement of independence by Israel and by a dozen Arab states. It brought to an end thirteen centuries of Muslim-Jewish coexistence, or, more precisely, symbiosis, which had produced the most glorious fruits in all fields of Medieval cultural endeavour. The establishment of Israel and the evacuation of the House of Islam by the voluntary or forced emigration of the Jews to Israel and to hospitable Western countries opened a new era of acute Muslim hostility to the Jews and virulent hatred of the small new polity which they succeeded in establishing in their ancestral homeland in the midst of the huge Muslim world area, nineteen centuries after their defeat by the Romans.

And this, the re-establishment of the historic state of Israel, is, of course, the third great upheaval in the life of the Jewish people that has come to pass in our century. Just as the survival of the Jews in the course of two millennia of Diaspora had been a unique phenomenon in the annals of history, so the re-establishment of the Jewish state after 1,878 years was an entirely unparalleled event in which the Messianic dimension overshadowed the political. Messianic, too, was the fulfilment of the ancient Biblical promise of the Ingathering of the Exiles which had brought together in Israel the remnants of Jewish tribes from the four corners of the earth, estranged brethren whom the long centuries of separation spent in different countries and cultures had rendered so dissimilar that they scarcely recognized one another.

The European destruction, the Afro-Asian evacuation, and the Israeli ingathering have all taken place within an astoundingly short period of time. It all happened in a quarter of a century, from about 1940 to 1965 – a mere moment in the history of Jewry. As a result of these great upheavals, the global distribution of the Jewish people has radically changed. Prior to World War II, the total number of the Jews was about 16,600,000, of which the Diaspora comprised more than 97 per cent, while the *Yishuv* (the Jewish population) of British Mandatory Palestine constituted less than 3 per cent. The Diaspora itself was overwhelmingly European: no less than 57 per cent of all Jews lived in Europe, 33 per cent in America, and 10 per cent in Asia and Africa (including the 450,000 who lived in Palestine). Six years later, the Nazi holocaust had reduced the total number of the Jews to 11,500,000 which, by 1965, after twenty years of gradual growth, had again increased to about 13,500,000. By the mid-1960s, more than one half of all the Jews lived in the Americas, only 29 per cent remained in Europe (two thirds of them in Russia), and 20 per cent lived in Asia and Africa, with most of them (16·6 per cent of the global total, or 2,250,000 in absolute figures) in Israel. To bring the picture up to date, it can be mentioned that in the last fifteen years the number of the American and European Diaspora has gradually decreased, while the proportion of all Jews living in Israel increased, due partly to continuing immigration and partly to natural increase which has been much greater in Israel than in the Diaspora. By 1980, the number of Jews in Israel had reached 3,500,000, or one quarter of the global Jewish total of 14,000,000. The time is not too distant when the Jewish people will comprise two approximately equal moieties: one in Israel, and the other in the Diaspora.

In the course of that fateful quarter of a century hundreds of old Jewish communities, rich in history, tradition, and culture, and vibrant with Jewish folk life, have ceased to exist. Streets which only a generation ago were throbbing with Jewish life, bursting with Jewish activity, brimful of Jewish religious and cultural manifestations, now either stand empty with houses decaying, doorways agape, or else are inhabited by Gentile newcomers. In many cases even the skeletal remains of the Jewish quarter have disappeared: whole sections were destroyed either during or after the war, and new buildings, new streets have risen in their stead, leaving no visible traces of the vanished Jewish worlds.

The ingathering of the exiles in Israel, the building of a new Jewish state, and the psychological transformation of an entire generation of victims, or of their often emotionally damaged children, into a proud, self-confident and strong Israeli people are, of course, magnificent human and national achievements. But ingathering and re-education are inevitably accompanied by a replacement of old cultural and personality traits with new ones, by a melting down of the venerable mosaic-like cultural varieties into a more uniform alloy of a new cultural synthesis which, whatever its human worth and national necessity, must needs appear grey and monotonous when compared to that which it supplanted. Before long, and certainly by the third generation, the Sabras of Israel or, for that matter, the offspring of the newcomers to other countries of Jewish immigration, such as the United States, France, or Canada, will know little or nothing of the life that their grandparents led in Europe or in the Middle East. Then those old worlds of Jewry will not only have vanished, but will be forgotten and irretrievably lost.

The present book is a small-scale attempt to recapture some of that which can still be rescued from oblivion. Its aim is to evoke, in word and picture, the historical development and the life of several great Jewish communities which were wiped out by the holocaust or disappeared as a result of mass emigration. It tries to reconstruct those vanished worlds whose traces can by now be found only in old pictures, in abandoned buildings and empty streets, in written records, and in the memories of old survivors whose numbers diminish from day to day. The Jewish communities which were destroyed or liquidated in the mid-twentieth century were located in five major geographical areas of the Old World: East Europe, Central Europe, South Europe, North Africa, and South-West Asia. A few comments on each will serve as introduction to the more detailed pictures to be presented of them in the body of the book.

The Jews of East Europe made up the bulk of the so-called Ashkenazi division of the Jewish people. They were the descendants of those Jews who in the Middle Ages had lived in German-speaking lands, called Askenaz in Medieval Hebrew. In the fourteenth century, when they were expelled, they settled in Poland and surrounding countries. They brought along with them their Yiddish mother tongue, a German-based language containing many Hebrew culture-words and other elements, which had come into being two centuries earlier and which they were to develop into a juicy Jewish tongue, and in which they were to create a rich sacred and secular literature. They also brought to East Europe their virtuoso devotion to Talmudic studies in which they were to become, by the sixteenth century, the undisputed leaders and masters, and which resulted in their virtually complete intellectual isolation from the Gentile environment. It was East European Jewry which, as a reaction to obsessive Talmudism, brought forth Hasidism in the second half of the eighteenth century, that last great Jewish religious movement which emphasized piety rather than learning, the service of God in joy rather than ascetic self-denial, and the belief in the *Tzaddiq*, the miracle-working rabbi, rather than painstaking adherence to the minutiae of ritual. The Hasidic movement split East European Jewry into two camps between whom for several generations there was no solidarity, no intermarriage, and no consciousness of being one people.

The schism between Hasidism and its opponents (the *Mitnagdim*) was partially healed only in the early nineteenth century, when both found themselves threatened by a new intellectual trend, the Haskala or Jewish Enlightenment, which had penetrated East Europe from German lands. Hasidim and *Mitnagdim* buried the hatchet, or, rather, agreed on swinging it jointly against the *Maskilim* (the 'Enlighteners'). Their united stand against the Enlightenment and all it stood for in modernization and cultural assimilation proved an effective hindrance to the spread of Haskala among East European Jews. Even the subsequent revival of the Hebrew language found among them only limited support, and it was only the *Hibbat Zion* (Love of Zion) movement, and its successor, the political Zionism of Theodor Herzl, which were able to make them budge from their positions of Jewish traditionalism of either the old Talmudistic, or the more recent Hasidic, variety.

In the post-World War I era, the East European Jews translated their age-old traditional conviction of peoplehood into political terms, and insisted on being recognized as a national minority. Until the Nazi onslaught, the typical mode of Jewish existence in Poland and neighbouring countries was that of a nationality, with its own language, religion, culture, schools, institutions, communal organization, and its jealously guarded internal autonomy.

A word is in place here concerning the retention of Yiddish by the East European Jews. This phenomenon was a typical expression of the relationship of the Jews to their Gentile environs. In the fifteenth century the Jews all over the world entered an era of cultural isolation from their Gentile neighbours; its clearest manifestation was that from this time on until the Enlightenment in the nineteenth century they no longer adopted the languages of the Gentile population in whose midst they settled. Prior to that period they had modified the languages of the countries in which they lived, to make them suit their need for a colloquial idiom within their culturally and religiously Jewish-centred society. This is how the Jewish languages known as Judeo-Greek, Judeo-Arabic, Judeo-Persian, Judeo-Spanish (better known as Ladino), Judeo-Italian, and Judeo-German (Yiddish), as well as several other minor Jewish languages, came into being. These Jewish tongues remained alive until the Enlightenment, whether in the countries in which they had arisen or in new linguistic environments.

However, from the fifteenth century on this process of language adoption from the Gentile world ceased. What still took place thereafter was the adoption by one Jewish group of the language spoken by another. This happened with the East

European Slavic-speaking Jews who switched to Yiddish when the Ashkenazi Jews arrived in their lands, with the Sephardi Spanish exiles who, after their settlement in North Africa, gradually adopted the local Judeo-Arabic dialects, and with most of the Greek Jews who assimilated to Ladino after the Sephardim settled in Greece. As a result of the Medieval loss of linguistic flexibility, the largest Jewish communities, settled for centuries in East European countries, never adopted Russian, Polish, Lithuanian, Ukrainian, etc., as their mother tongue, but remained, by and large, Yiddish speaking. Similarly, the Sephardi Jews who lived in Turkey and her Balkan territories never adopted the languages spoken in those lands but retained their Ladino.

The Central European Jews, although Ashkenazim like their brethren to the east, and many of them children of immigrants from Poland, Russia and other East European countries, differed from them in many respects. By the late nineteenth century, their great majority had become Enlighteners, had given up Yiddish for German in German-speaking lands or Hungarian in Hungary, exchanged their traditional Jewish garb for modern fashions, and abandoned their old Jewish isolationism for active, and even intensive, participation in the secular life of their host countries. These changes were facilitated by the fact that anti-Semitism was less prevalent in Central than in East Europe, by the introduction of constitutional emancipatory measures in one Central European country after the other, by the development of Jewish religious reform which put an end to the former exclusively religio-centric orientation, and by the inevitable consequence of all this – assimilation. In all these respects Central European Jews became similar to the Jewish contingents in West Europe, while a widening religious and cultural gap opened up between them and their East European brethren. Ethnically and emotionally, East European Jews remained, until the Communist take-over, emphatically more Jewish than Polish, Russian, Lithuanian, etc.; in Central Europe, on the other hand, Enlightenment, Emancipation and assimilation had, by the beginning of the twentieth century, eliminated Jewish ethnicity and turned the Jews into Germans, Austrians, etc., of the 'Mosaic' or 'Israelite' persuasion, convinced that they differed from their Gentile compatriots in nothing but religion.

At the same time, the Central European Jews, despite their intensive participation in the national life of their host countries, developed organizational frameworks and networks of their own which were not merely equal to, but in fact wider than, those of their Gentile neighbours. Jewish houses of worship, schools, hospitals, orphanages, old peoples' homes, etc., abounded in every Central European country. The number of Jewish organizations, ranging from cultural, educational, and religious, through charitable, economic, and social, to Zionist and anti-Zionist parties, was astounding. In addition, and despite the cultural and religious differences between them and the East European Jews, and despite the often contemptuous attitude they displayed to the *Ostjuden* and other branches of the Jewish people (except those of West Europe), Central European Jews retained enough Jewish solidarity to be prompted to great efforts in support of the politically and economically less fortunate Jewish communities to the east and the south.

Central European Jews, and in particular those who were German-speaking, produced all the great Jewish movements in the late eighteenth and the nineteenth century. Moses Mendelssohn, the father of Jewish Enlightenment, and his early followers and disciples were German Jews. German Jews were in the forefront of the fight for Emancipation. Jewish religious reform began in Germany and was exported from there to the west. The 'Science of Judaism', that is, the scholarly study of Jewish religion, history, literature, sprang up on German soil. The founder of political Zionism, Theodor Herzl, and his first lieutenant, Max Nordau, were both born in Budapest, although the former spent his adult life in Vienna and the latter in Paris, and both spoke and wrote all their works in German. For many decades the official language of the Zionist Congresses was German. This brief list of Central European Jewish initiatives and innovations would not be complete without mentioning that Jewish assimilation, often culminating in conversion to Christianity, was also a movement, albeit unplanned and unorganized, which became more widespread in Central Europe than in any other part of the Diaspora.

As for their participation in the life of their host countries, Central European Jews were among the pioneers in all fields of endeavour. Far beyond their proportion in the general population, they were found among the builders of industries, the developers of commercial enterprises and financial institutions, leaders in all branches of science and scholarship, in the arts and in literature, in journalism and criticism, in politics and diplomacy. With astounding energy and perseverance, they overcame all obstacles placed in their way by official and unofficial anti-Semitism, despite which they came to feel more German, or Austrian, or Hungarian than their Christian compatriots.

Most of the Jews in South Europe, in contrast to their brethren to the north, belonged not to the Ashkenazi but to the Sephardi division of the Jewish people. The Sephardim (the name is derived from the Medieval Hebrew designation for Spain, *Sepharad*) are the descendants of Jews who lived in the Middle Ages in the Iberian Peninsula, and were expelled from Spain in 1492 and from Portugal a few years later. They found refuge in North Africa, in north-west Europe (primarily in the Netherlands), and in the various territories controlled at the time by the Ottoman Empire, including the Balkans. Wherever they settled, they took along with them, and in most cases faithfully preserved, their mother-tongue, Ladino – a form of Medieval Spanish with an admixture of Hebrew – and their interest in cultural matters outside the narrowly religious realm. They also retained their ethnic pride and emphasis on the purity of their descent, two features they had internalized under the influence of the Spanish *grandeza* and of the high valuation the Spaniards put on their own *limpieza de sangre*. Whatever Jewish communities had lived before them in the lands where they settled, the Sephardi Jews managed to make them acknowledge Sephardi superiority, so that before long the Sephardi newcomers became the dominant element in the Jewish population of their countries of refuge. This proved to be the case especially in the Balkans and along the Aegean coast of Turkey where relatively large numbers of Sephardim established themselves within a few decades following the Spanish exile.

In the course of the fourteenth to sixteenth centuries the Turks conquered all of the Balkans, as well as a major part of Hungary. Their rule lasted until the nineteenth century when one Balkan country after the other succeeded in gaining independence. Throughout, the Jews who lived in the European territories of the Ottoman Empire and along the Aegean coast of Asiatic Turkey retained Ladino as their mother-tongue, and it was adopted also by the Italian and Ashkenazi Jews who settled among them. With Ladino went a strong Sephardi consciousness, and assimilation to the Sephardim; before long all the Jews of the Balkans considered themselves Sephardim. In the 1930s, of approximately 247,000 Balkan Jews some 200,000 were Sephardim and only about 47,000 Ashkenazim, most of them concentrated north of the Sava river in that part of Yugoslavia which until 1919 had belonged to Hungary. Apart from the retention of Ladino, the Balkan Sephardim, as the Sephardim everywhere, remained inordinately proud of their Sephardi descent; many of them appended after their signature the two Hebrew letters ST, meaning *S'fardi Tahor*, 'Pure Sephardi', the nearest a Jew could come to hereditary nobility.

Sephardi cultural excellence survived the Spanish exile by less than two centuries. In the seventeenth century, the economic conditions in Greece, where most of the Balkan Jews lived, deteriorated, and the number of Jews prominent in the traditional Jewish intellectual fields dwindled. Depressed conditions create, as a rule, an atmosphere favourable for the upsurge of Messianic expectations and enthusiasm. It is therefore interesting to note that the rabbis of Smyrna banished Shabbatai Zevi, the pseudo-Messiah, in the early 1650s, and the rabbis of Salonika did likewise in 1658, as did those of Constantinople in the following year. On the other hand, Salonika was the centre for the Doenmeh sect, whose members followed Shabbatai Zevi's example and converted to Islam.

As long as the momentum of Sephardi cultural excellence continued, all the important developments in Jewish history were initiated, and all the great achievements attained, by Jews who had been born in Spain or by their descendants. Among these feats can be mentioned the final codification of Jewish law by Joseph Caro, who lived in the Balkans and then in Safed, Palestine; the expansion and popularization of the Kabbala by the mystics of the Safed circle; the greatest pseudo-Messianic movement, which we have just referred to; the most significant advance in philosophy since Maimonides by Baruch Spinoza in Amsterdam; the successful fight for the readmission of the Jews to England by Manasseh ben Israel, also in Amsterdam; the settlement of the first Jews in the New World by Marranos from Spain and Portugal and by Sephardi Jews from Holland, and their crucial role in making Holland a global commercial power.

By the mid-eighteenth century the Sephardi *élan vital* had run its course, and the Sephardi Jewish element lost its importance both demographically and culturally. By the second half of the century, the Ashkenazi Jews were unquestionably the leading element of Jewry.

Across the Mediterranean from South Europe lies North Africa, whose eastern corner, Egypt, was the Biblical birthplace of the Hebrew nation and the site of its first persecution and exile. Some seven centuries after the Exodus, when the first Jerusalem Temple was destroyed (586 BCE), Jews began to return to Egypt, and by the third century BCE they were found also in Cyrenaica to the west, today part of Libya. In the course of the Jewish-Roman war (66–70 CE) many Jewish refugees fled to Cyrenaica, by then under Roman rule. From there they moved on westward, and settled in many places along the northern part of the African continent. These Jews, as well as their brethren who settled in South-West Asia, are usually referred to as 'Oriental' Jews. After the rise of Islam in Arabia (seventh century) this whole area was conquered by the Arabs and, from that time until their large-scale emigration in our own days, the Oriental Jews lived as a religio-national minority in the midst of a Muslim Arab or Arab and Berber majority.

With regard to their cultural ups and downs, the Oriental Jews to a great extent shared the fate of their Muslim neighbours and overlords. When Arab culture flourished, as it did phenomenally from the eighth to the fourteenth centuries, Jewish culture, too, exhibited great vitality, creativity, and originality. The greatest Jewish philosophers, religious authorities, poets, scholars, physicians, scientists, statesmen, and soldiers lived in those centuries in an Arab environment.

By the late fourteenth century, when the first Spanish exiles began to arrive in North Africa (following their 1391 expulsion), the cultural decline had just begun to show its first signs among North African Jewry. By the time the 1492 Sephardi refugees arrived, it was relatively easy for them to claim and establish their cultural supremacy over the indigenous Jews of North Africa. However, the Sephardim themselves were unable to escape for long the influence of the late Medieval complacency and lethargy of the South Mediterranean, so that for the last several centuries the Oriental Jewish-Sephardi cultural mix has had little to boast about, or at least little to show, that would have been comparable to the incipient dynamism of Ashkenazi Jewry. None of the great Ashkenazi developments – Hasidism, the Haskala, Emancipation, the Science of Judaism, assimilation, Zionism, socialism – which originated among European Jews and shaped the course of their history from the eighteenth century on, made any impact on the tradition-bound life of North African Jewry. The first modern influence which reached them emanated from the *Alliance Israélite Universelle* which from the early 1860s established schools in several Muslim countries and made French-inspired education available to Jewish children in the larger cities.

The foregoing brief observations deal, of necessity, in generalities which, however, must not obscure the fact that considerable differences existed between the life and position of the Jews in one North African country and the other, or even between the various segments of the Jewish population in one and the same country. There were differences in occupational structure; in the percentage of the few well-to-do as against the majority of the poor and destitute; in literacy and education; in religious attitudes and practices; in the degree of the absorption of French language and civilization, or, to a lesser extent, of Italian and English; in the relative concentration in cities versus villages; and in the proportion of those who were local citizens as against those who had obtained or retained French or other European citizenships. There were also variations in the attitude of the Muslim majorities to the Jews, and in their reaction to the establishment of Israel which, together with the attainment of their own independence from European colonial rule a few years later, led in some countries to the emigration of 85 to 95 per cent of the Jews, and in others to the evacuation of all but a few families.

The history of the Jews in the Asian part of the Middle East was by and large similar to the experiences which shaped the fate of their brethren in North Africa. Both lived in a Muslim environment; their traditional condition of being *dhimmis*, members of a protected but second-class community, was alike; the cultural stagnation which characterized the South-West Asian countries as much as those of North Africa engulfed the Jews of both continents to the same extent. Both were influenced more or less to the same degree by the mores of the Muslim neighbours, while both considered themselves superior to the Muslims in faith, morality, education – a conviction which was a great psychological support in weathering the rough treatment meted out to them by the Muslims.

Where the Jews of the African and the Asian Middle East differed to a degree was, first of all, in the extent of Sephardi influence they absorbed. In North Africa, Sephardi influence, although it began in different times, was on the whole evenly distributed along the coastline of Morocco, Algeria, Tunisia, and Egypt (in Libya, Italian Jewish rather than Sephardi impact was felt), but the Ladino colloquial of the Sephardim came to be largely replaced by Judeo-Arabic, so that, in effect, the Sephardi immigrants were assimilated into the indigenous Oriental Jewish majority. In the Asiatic Middle East, Sephardi influence was largely confined to a few cities on or near the coast of Turkey, Syria-Lebanon, and Palestine, where it survived undiminished well into the twentieth century. But, the communities of the hinterland, including the Jews of Kurdistan, Iraq, Yemen, Iran, Afghanistan, and India, were untouched by either Sephardi immigration or influence.

The Asian segment of Middle Eastern Jewry differed from the North African in another respect as well. While by the eighteenth century practically all native North African Jews used Judeo-Arabic as their colloquial, in South-West Asia this language was spoken, in varying dialects, only by the Jews of Syria-Lebanon, Iraq, and Yemen. Other large Jewish communities spoke Persian dialects (in Iran and Afghanistan), while yet others spoke Neo-Aramaic (in Kurdistan), and Marathi and Malayalam (in India). This linguistic diversity signified greater cultural differences than existed among the various Judeo-Arabic speaking communities. Except for the Kurdish Jews who spoke Neo-Aramaic (a Semitic language related to Talmudic Aramaic) while the Kurdish majority spoke Kurdish (an Iranian dialect), and the Sephardi Jews in Constantinople and Smyrna who spoke Ladino while their Muslim neighbours spoke Turkish, all other Jewish communities in the Asian and African Middle East spoke languages which differed only in dialect from those of their Muslim neighbours.

A high degree of literacy has always been a Jewish cultural characteristic. In the Middle East, in contrast to their Muslim neighbours who were largely illiterate until the middle of this century, almost all Jewish men were able to read Hebrew, with a good proportion also able to write it. Very few were literate in Arabic or Persian. For Jewish women, literacy in any language was the exception rather than the rule. Since their religious life did not involve reading either the Bible or the prayer book, they were not expected to attend the traditional Tora-school.

Ever since the Middle Ages all literature produced by the Jews in their local colloquials was written in Hebrew characters. Judeo-Arabic and Judeo-Persian works constitute as important a part of Jewish literature as Yiddish and Ladino writings. The Hebrew written characters thus retained, until the Enlightenment, a distribution almost as wide as that of the Diaspora itself.

One of the tragic consequences of the Nazi genocide, perpetrated with the all-too-willing co-operation of Germany's East European war-time satellites, was an inevitable shift in history's judgement of the relationship of the Muslim countries to their Jews. Prior to the holocaust, the position of the Jews in the Muslim world was considered from the point of view of the nineteenth-century European principles of Enlightenment, Emancipation, and equal rights of all citizens irrespective of their religious affiliation. From that angle, Muslim society with its periodic indulgence in violence, murder, rape, plunder, and forced conversion, and the generally scornful attitude of the Muslim populace to the Jews as infidels, could not but be deemed medieval, barbaric, unforgivable. With the holocaust, the perspective changed. In its wake, more and more voices have been raised, proclaiming that, compared to what Germany – one of the most civilized nations of Europe – did to the Jews, the Muslims' treatment of their *dhimmis* was charitable. Tragically, the validity of this comparison cannot be gainsaid. It is a fact that the Muslims, even if they occasionally violated the Jews, *allowed them to live* except for the few outbursts of rage when some Jews were killed. By the same token, the Russian pogroms which flooded over and at times extinguished Jewish life as late as in the early twentieth century, no longer appeared as unspeakable after the Nazi genocide as they did until the beginning of the Hitler era. Greater and later horrors attenuate our revulsion at earlier and lesser crimes.

Both great horrors and lesser crimes combined in bringing about the disappearance of hundreds of historical Jewish communities from the face of the earth. The present book takes a look at some of these historic Jewries, as they worked and rested, laughed and cried, fought and loved, celebrated and mourned, were exiled and called back, in ages which, in retrospect, appear as having been characterized by a balance of joy and sorrow, of pleasures and sufferings, of life and death. The expression 'age of innocence' has become hackneyed when applied to historical periods; but there can be no doubt that the last two decades prior to their uprooting or liquidation represented the nearest to an age of innocence ever experienced by the Jewish communities in the Diaspora who believed or hoped that after the long centuries of troubles they had finally reached the dawn of a better day. In a very few countries – the Western democracies – this hope came true. In the countries discussed in this book it proved to be a vain hope, a false dawn, which was soon to be followed by the dark night of the final cataclysm.

As a Jew I mourn, and shall never cease mourning, the innocent blood of millions of my martyred brethren. I cry over the sufferings of the many more whose countries in which they had trusted and to whose soil they had precariously clung for many generations, suddenly proved to be but the treacherous back of Rabba bar Bar Hana's legendary whale which first had seemed a desirable resting place for the tired seafarers until it suddenly shook and took a dive, spilling the voyagers into the waves. As a lifelong student of folk life, I also bewail the many things that were lost in addition to human lives, the warmth and the intimacy of living within familiar neighbourhoods, the beauty that is gone, the manifold expressions of Jewish talent in vocal and instrumental music, in the creation and transmission of oral folk lore, folk tales, folk songs and poems, in the delicate practice of the minor arts of jewelry, embroidery, weaving and costuming, in the curious folk beliefs and customs, and in more of the many-coloured aspects of folk life which were and are no more.

Let us, for a brief moment, submerge ourselves in the images of those past ages which, despite their trials, tribulations and tragedies, enabled the Jews to survive, to thrive, and to create for themselves their own worlds of many hues, of human warmth, of cultural riches, of Jewish values.

Part One

Eastern Europe
The Yiddish Nation

Jewish clothes merchants in Warsaw, Poland.

Poland

Leaving the synagogue in Lodz after
the service, 1937.

Polish Jewry, this relative late-comer on the global stage of Jewish history, was from the fifteenth to the early twentieth century the bulk and main body of world Jewry, and also, for a major part of this period, the vanguard and the dominant element in most of the essentially Jewish cultural developments. To say that in those five centuries the history of Polish Jewry was *the* history of the Jewry may be a hyperbole, but no more so than a similar statement about Babylonian Jewry in the third to eighth centuries, and the latter has become a commonplace of Jewish historiography.

Since the territory of the Polish state varied greatly throughout history, it is difficult to give a geographical definition of Polish Jewry. Under the Jagellon dynasty (1386–1572), whose two-century rule coincided with the formative period of Polish Jewry, the Polish-Lithuanian kingdom was a great power whose domains included large parts of White Russia and the Ukraine, with boundaries extending from the Baltic in the north to the vicinity of the Black Sea in the south, and from the Oder in the west to the Dnieper in the east. On the other hand, the 1772, 1793, and 1795 partitions of Poland between Prussia, Russia, and Austria first diminished, then entirely eliminated, Poland as a political entity, so that for one century and a quarter, until its re-establishment at the end of World War I, there was no such thing as a Polish state. This, of course, did not mean that the Polish people ceased to exist, nor did the Polish Jews, whether under Prussian, Russian, or Austrian rule, relinquish their separate religio-ethnic identity.

Being different from the Gentile environment, however, did not mean that Polish Jewry constituted a homogeneous ethnic group. In fact the designation 'Polish Jews' was used in two senses: in a narrow sense, it referred to those Jews who were the natives of the historical Great Poland and Lesser Poland, the core area of Poland bounded by East Prussia in the north and Galicia in the south; in the wider sense, the term 'Polish Jews' was applied to all Jews living in the territory which, under the Jagellons constituted the Polish-Lithuanian kingdom, whether they came under Prussian, Austrian or Russian rule after the partition of Poland. This broad usage of the term included Jewish communities which differed greatly in cultural and personality traits, summed up in such Yiddish designations as *Polak* (Polish), *Litvak* (Lithuanian), or *Galizianer*.

The first Jews to reach Poland, about the ninth century, came from the Kingdom of Kiev in south-western Russia, and, farther from the south, from the Byzantine Empire. However, nothing is known of the history of these early visitors or sojourners, nor of their culture. The Jews who laid the foundations of what was to become Polish Jewry arrived considerably later from the opposite direction, from the west. It seems that the first impetus for these Ashkenazi Jews to enter Poland was given them by the persecution of the Bohemian Jews during the First Crusade (in 1098). The second area from which Jews moved eastward was Silesia. By the twelfth century, the Jews had well-established positions in Poland. The coins they minted with Hebrew inscriptions show not only that the Polish kings and princes entrusted the production of their coinage to Jewish mint-masters, but that the Jews were the financial leaders of the country.

In the thirteenth and fourteenth centuries, two factors coincided in bringing to Poland a wave of Jewish immigrants, sizeable for the times, from German lands, Bohemia and Moravia. One was the devastation wrought in Poland by the Mongol invasions from 1241 which motivated the Polish princes to offer inducements to immigrants from Germany and to give them effective help in settling in the depopulated Polish towns and villages. The other was the series of massacres of Jews in Germany, not only by the Crusaders but also by the populace, incited by such leaders as the notorious German nobleman Rindfleisch (in 1298), by the *Armleder* bands of German peasants (1336–9), and by vicious rumours alleging that the Jews desecrated the Host and killed Christian children, to which wide credence was given in Christian Europe. The flight of the Jews from Germany into Poland, triggered by these events, was then followed by their mass expulsions from Germany and other Central European countries in 1348–50 when they were accused of having caused the Black Death by poisoning the wells.

Although it is true that during the frenzied and panicky years of the Black Death the Jews were massacred also in Poland (in 1349), their condition soon improved there while in the west it continued to be extremely hazardous. In these circumstances Poland became a refuge for Jews not only from Germany, Bohemia and Moravia, but also from countries as far away as Italy and Spain. By the end of the fifteenth century there were some twenty to thirty thousand Jews in Poland living in more than sixty communities. In the sixteenth century, looking back upon two centuries of relative quiescence, R. Moses Isserles (1520–72) of Cracow, the famous halakhist, opined that it was preferable for the Jews to live on dry bread and in peace in Poland than in greater affluence in countries where life for them was fraught with danger.[1]

What appeared to Isserles as a poor but peaceful life was, in reality, often disturbed by vexations and tribulations. While the rulers and nobles made use of the financial abilities of the Jews, they remained basically hostile and contemptuous of them. The clergy was implacable in its hatred of the Jews, and church councils frequently issued directives aiming at the isolation of the Jews, their confinement into ghettos, and the repeal of any charters or privileges they were given by the rulers. The business-minded burghers of the cities (many of them Germans) saw in the Jews dangerous competitors and fought them. And as for the peasantry, it considered them hateful exploiters. All elements of the population regarded them as alien infidels.

Yet, withal, despite occasional expulsions such as those of 1495 from Lithuania and Cracow, the Jews of Poland did live in relative peace and prospered until the middle of the seventeenth century. Several cities, it is true, possessed *privilegia de non tolerandis judaeis* ('privileges of not tolerating Jews') and thus could deny Jews the right to dwell in them; still, provided as they were with royal and princely privileges of their own, the Jews could function in all economic fields on an equal footing with the Christians. They controlled the international trade between Christian Europe and the east, and from the late fifteenth century with the Ottoman Empire; provided the nobility with clothing, dyes and luxury items; financed kings, magnates, cities and businesses; managed mines and customs stations; and played a leading part in the periodic fairs which took place in several major cities. In the second half of the sixteenth century began the Polish colonization of the territories of the south-east (Volhynia, Podolia, Kiev, and Bratzlav). The share of the Jews in this settlement activity was considerable: by 1648 there were 115 localities in these areas with more than 50,000 Jews. In the north, i.e., in Poland proper and in Lithuania, the Polish magnates established hundreds of new townships on their vast estates and attracted Jews to them to the extent that in several of these new 'private cities' (as they were called in distinction to the old 'royal cities') the Jews became the majority, and occasionally even the only inhabitants. These developments became the basis for the Jewish *shtetl* (small town) which was to remain a characteristic feature of Jewish life in Poland until its destruction by the Nazis.

The rapid growth of the Jewish population (from 100,000 in 1578 to 300,000 in 1648) and its dispersal over a wide geographical expanse prompted the leadership of Polish Jewry to seek the establishment of countrywide organizations. The most important of these was the 'Council of Four Lands', the central institution of Jewish self-government in Poland, which functioned from the middle of the sixteenth century until 1764 when the Polish Diet ordered general Jewish congresses to be discontinued. While it existed, the Council, which comprised representatives of Great Poland (lead by Poznan), Lesser Poland (Cracow), Polish Russia, i.e., Podolia and Galicia (Lvov), and Volhynia (Ostrag or Kremenetz), met twice annually in Lvov and Yaroslav, on the occasion of the fairs; they issued decisions and decrees, tried civil and criminal cases, imposed penalties, kept records, and, in general, fulfilled the important legislative, administrative, juridical, and spiritual-cultural functions of a Jewish religio-political parliament.

Most important was the role Polish Jewry played in Jewish cultural life. From the sixteenth century on Poland was the undisputed leader in Ashkenazi religious scholarship. For the Ashkenazi Jews, who from 1700 on constituted an increasing majority of the world Jewish population, the *Shulhan ʿArukh* of the Sephardi R. Joseph Caro of Safed, with the emendations of R. Moses Isserles, became the authoritative Jewish law. Polish Talmudic and halakhic expertise was acknowledged by Jews all over Europe, and was highly respected in the Sephardi world as well. By the sixteenth century, Polish Yeshivot, or Talmudic academies, had multiplied to the point where most of the male Jewish population

Scribe repairing a Tora scroll in Annapol in 1912.

was well versed in Rabbinics, which meant that, in addition to their Yiddish vernacular, they knew Hebrew and Aramaic, and were adept at dealing with dialectic problems (the so-called *pilpul*). As the Jewish historian, Heinrich Graetz (1817–91), no admirer of Polish Talmudism, put it:

> Even in small communities of only fifty members there were at least twenty Talmudical scholars, who in turn instructed at least thirty pupils. Everywhere there arose schools with rabbis at their heads as teachers whose chief duty was to deliver lectures, everything else being of secondary importance. Young men crowded to these establishments, where they could live free from care, their maintenance being defrayed out of the treasury of the community, or by wealthy private individuals.[2]

However, East European Jewry was not only a literate, educated, and intellectual element in the midst of a largely illiterate and culturally-deprived general population; it also had higher moral standards that found expression in such forms as mutual aid institutions, charity, a low incidence of criminality, and a markedly better position for women. The inevitable concomitant of these Jewish traits was opposition or even hostility to secular learning, associated in the eyes of the Jews with a Gentile ethos whose manifestations were generally repugnant to them. This attitude contributed to the self-isolation of the Jews from the Gentile environment. In sharp contrast to the Sephardi Jews who in their heyday were among the leading statesmen, diplomatists, philosophers, scientists, mathematicians, astronomers, navigators, physicians, etc., of Spain, North Africa and Egypt, the Polish Jews, with very few exceptions, considered interest in any realm of non-Jewish intellectual endeavour as un-Jewish and therefore prohibited. Even the reading of books other than the Bible, the Talmud, the codes, and the Midrashim was strictly forbidden, and has remained so to this day in those circles in which the East European Yeshiva tradition survives. Woe to the Yeshiva student who was caught reading Maimonides' great work of Jewish religious philosophy, the *Guide of the Perplexed* (which was available in several Hebrew translations from the Arabic original), although the *Mishne Tora* (also known as

Khone Szajfer, an 85-year-old lens grinder, umbrella-maker and folk-doctor in Lomza, 1927.

Yad haHazaqa), the code of religious law written by the same Maimonides, was part of the usual Yeshiva curriculum.

In this atmosphere of concentration on Talmudic learning it was a rare Jew indeed who found in himself the audacity to break out of the 'four cubits of the Halakha' and engage in secular studies or pursuits. There was, however, one great Jewish religious development from which Polish Jewry was unable to shut itself off. This was Kabbalism which, from the early sixteenth century on, has become entrenched in the world of Polish rabbinism. The greatest Polish rabbinical scholars, such as Solomon Luria, R. Moses Isserles and Mordecai Jaffe, studied it and were influenced by it. By the seventeenth century the study of Lurianic Kabbala was considered an organic part of rabbinical training.

The popularity of the Kabbala was one of the two main factors which predisposed East European Jewry to becoming caught up in the pseudo-Messianic movement of Shabbatai Zevi (1625–75). The other was the Cossacks' uprising which culminated in the large-scale persecution, torture, and massacre of the Jews under Bogdan Chmielnicki and other Cossack and Haidamak leaders in the decade of 1648 to 1658. A few years later the news about the Messiah of Smyrna reached the still-smouldering ruins of the East European Diaspora.

According to an old tradition the advent of the Messiah was to be preceded by the 'War of Gog and Magog' in which untold numbers of Jews were to perish. The claim of Shabbatai Zevi that he was the long-awaited Messiah was the more readily accepted by the East European Jews since they could retrospectively interpret the horrors that swept over them as the suffering which the Jewish people had to experience in the Messianic days.

Another outgrowth of Kabbalistic mysticism to cause a serious disruption threatening to lead to a schism the like of which Judaism had never before experienced in the course of its long history was Hasidism. In Poland and in the

adjoining areas Hasidism completely supplanted Kabbalism; there remained almost no Kabbalists who were not Hasidim, so that Kabbalism and Hasidism became synonymous. While Hasidism remained an essentially East European Jewish phenomenon, its emergence and rapid spread is one of the most remarkable chapters in Jewish history.

In the seventeenth and early eighteenth centuries there were in East Europe numerous rabbis, as well as other semi-learned Jews, who catered for the susceptibilities of their more ignorant co-religionists by supplying them with amulets and talismans, administering popular medication, exorcising demons, invoking spirits, and the like. The decline in Talmudic learning, the belief in the so-called 'practical Kabbala', the trauma of the mid-seventeenth century massacres and other horrors, and the despair following the Shabbataian debacle – all this contributed to the proliferation of these magic practitioners. The generic name by which they were referred to was *Ba'al Shem*, 'Master of the Name' (i.e., of God), because they were believed to perform their magic miracles with the help of divine names over which they had acquired mastery.[3]

It was as such a *Ba'al Shem* that the founder of Hasidism, Rabbi Ba'al Shem Tov ('Master of the Good Name' or 'Good Master of the Name', 1700–60), usually referred to by the initials of his name, BeShT, began his career. It was not until he was forty years old that he began to expound his new teachings in Miedzyboz, Podolia. Like a true religious founder, he himself wrote nothing; it was his disciples who memorized, wrote down, and published his sayings, stories, and teachings, as had been the case with Isaac Luria in Safed two centuries earlier. Also, and again as in the case of other religious founders, the key to the phenomenal sweep of his doctrines all over the East European Diaspora must be sought primarily in the personality of the BeShT.

While without the Kabbala there could have been no Hasidism, it is significant

above left A *shulkloper* in Biala in 1926. One of the tasks vital to Jewish community life was that of the men who knocked on shutters to announce the start of prayers.

above A blacksmith in the town of Nowe Miasto in 1925.

that the BeShT was opposed, not only to Shabbataianism, but also to Lurianic Kabbala which emphasized asceticism and mortification of the spirit. In contrast, he stressed the importance of serving God with joy, of loving Him and surrendering oneself to Him with *Hitlahavut* (enthusiasm). His key concept was *D'vequt* (cleaving), a state one achieves when one gives up the consciousness of separate existence and joins oneself to the eternal being of God. In his pantheistic-mystical concept of God, in which we recognize a certain similarity to Buddhist teachings, great importance is attached to the ideal man who, as the BeShT expressed it, 'is to be a revelation himself, and must clearly recognize himself as a manifestation of God'. This man is the *Tzaddiq* (the 'saintly' or 'pious' one), who forms a connecting link between Creator and Creation. It was this centrality of the *Tzaddiq* in Hasidic doctrine that soon led to the breakup of the movement into numerous sub-sects, each centred around a miracle-working saintly rabbi. In the nineteenth century, Hasidism degenerated into *Tzaddiqism*, with competing dynasties of *Tzaddiq*-saints, ensconced in their luxurious 'courts', and with all the overtones of saint-worship as found in the Jewish and Muslim Middle East.

No sooner did Hasidism begin its conquest of the East European Diaspora than opposition to it arose, especially in the north, in Lithuania and its vicinity, inhabited by a Jewry that was more hard-headed, more rational, more logical, sharper of mind and colder of temperament than the Jews of the south, of Poland, Galicia, the Carpathians. Before long East European Jewry was split into two hostile camps, that of the Hasidim, and that of their opponents, the *Mitnagdim*. The complaints of the *Mitnagdim* against the Hasidim were many: the Hasidim played down the importance of Tora study, which was the lifeblood of Ashkenazi Jewry; by negating the value of Talmudic study they also negated, or were

right Parading with the Tora scrolls on Simhat Tora, the 'Rejoicing of the Law', the holiday with which Sukkot ends and on which the annual cycle of Tora reading ends and begins anew.

The fish market at Otwock in the 1920s:
left A merchant pumping water.
above Selling fish.

suspected of negating, the importance of observing all the minutiae of the Law for which painstaking study was a prerequisite. They deviated from old-established custom by importing the 'Sephardi' prayer book of Isaac Luria and following its *nusah* (version) in their services. They attributed superhuman powers to their *Tzaddiqim*, unheard of in Ashkenazi Judaism since the close of the Talmudic period. They emphasized serving God with joy – often helped along by imbibing strong spirits, a most regrettable approximation of the ugly and, to the Jews, frightening Gentile custom of drunkenness. All this made the Hasidim so repugnant to the *Mitnagdim* that, especially in Lithuania, they felt constrained to take firm action, as we shall see in the next chapter.

This twofold division of Polish and East European Jewry soon gave way to a threefold one. The new movement that, from the early nineteenth century, began to make inroads into the ranks of both Hasidim and *Mitnagdim*, was that of the Haskala, the Jewish Enlightenment. The Haskala began in Central Europe in the late eighteenth century and, in general terms, it advocated abandoning Jewish ethnic and cultural isolationism in favour of acquiring the language, culture, manners, clothes, and aspirations of contemporary Europe, and primarily those of German lands.

When the Haskala first penetrated East Europe, both the Hasidim and the *Mitnagdim* sensed the danger it represented to traditional Jewish life, and both engaged in a struggle against it. For a while it seemed as if the Haskala could make no headway in the face of the opposition it encountered. But by the middle of the nineteenth century it had become clear to all that the *Maskilim* had managed to penetrate the strongholds of both *Mitnagdic* conservatism and studiousness and Hasidic enthusiasm and *Tzaddiqism*, and that there were now, not two, but three categories of Jews in East Europe who had to learn to live with one another, if not peacefully, at least without active infighting.[4]

The tripartite division into Hasidim, *Mitnagdim*, and *Maskilim* continued to characterize Polish Jewry until the very end of its existence. The relative strength of the three trends changed with time, the *Maskilim* steadily gaining ground at the expense of the other two, and the character of the 'enlightened' Jews itself

underwent a series of evolutionary changes not unlike those which turned the
German *Maskilim* into assimilated German Jews. After World War I, when Poland
again attained political independence, the major cities with their huge
concentrations of Jewish populations, became ideological battle grounds between
the Jewish groups which adhered to disparate religio-national trends. Many
Hasidim, who were stronger in the small towns than in the big cities, made
common cause with the *Mitnagdim* in rallying around the *Agudat Israel*
(Association of Israel), a Jewish movement and political formation which came into
being on the eve of World War I and which was equally opposed to Zionism and
Jewish secularism. Many *Tzaddiqim* gave their wholehearted support to the
Aguda which, on the political front, participated in the elections to the Polish *Sejm*
(parliament), and, on the educational front, organized and maintained the Horev
network of Talmud Tora schools and Yeshivot, as well as the separate *Bet Ya'aqov*
primary and secondary schools for girls. These schools were attended in 1937 by
71,000 boys and 35,000 girls. In addition, some 40,000 boys attended private
traditional religious schools, the so-called *hadarim* (sing. *heder*).

As against this closing of the ranks in the Orthodox wing of Polish Jewry, the
modern, non-religious, or religiously liberal, Polish Jews were split into two
factions which were sharply opposed to each other. On the one hand there were the
so-called Galuth- (or Diaspora-) nationalists, with the historian Simon Dubnow
(1860–1941) and the Jewish theoretician of socialism Chaim Zhitlowsky
(1865–1943) as its chief ideologists who aimed at strengthening the Jewish
position as a national minority in Poland. Diaspora-nationalism supplied the
theoretical foundations of the programme of Jewish cultural autonomy embraced
by the *Bund* (full name: *Algemeiner Yidisher Arbeterbund fun Russland un Poilen*, or
General Jewish Workers' Federation of Russia and Poland), which considered
Yiddish to be the national language of the Jewish people and was bitterly opposed
to Zionism. The 'Yiddishists', as they were loosely referred to, maintained their

above Workers at the
Brandsteter's clothing factory at
Tarnow in 1910.

top A demonstration in 1905 of
the Polish and Russian Social
democrats with members of the
Jewish *Bund* paying tribute to
those killed in the Vilna pogrom.

own Yiddish-language schools in which the number of pupils enrolled, about 16,000, remained more or less constant throughout the inter-war years. This number is surprisingly small considering the uncontested dominant position Yiddish maintained to the very end of this period. It was the Jewish mother tongue (in fact, it was fondly referred to as *'Mame-loshn'*), the language of the Jewish home and street, the language in which almost all the Jewish papers were published (24 dailies and 140 periodicals, constituting no less than 44 per cent of the world Yiddish press), and which served as the medium for most Polish Jewish authors, including illustrious novelists, poets, essayists, publicists, and scholars.

Yiddish, being an intricate fusion of several stocks – primarily of German, Hebrew, and Slavic – is a language of great riches, has a homespun quality with very many diminutives, and a 'juiciness' which renders it a particularly apt medium for the expression of Jewish cultural specificities. Yiddish meant more to the Jews than, say, German meant to the Germans or Polish to the Poles, because it was a home-language, spoken in the midst of a large other-tongued majority by a small minority for whom it was much more than a medium of communication: it was a cultural treasure, a quasi-religious feature, the language of popular individual prayer (the *t'khine*), the sign of recognition and identification of the Jew, even more reliable than the Jewish garb, or hair and beard style.

Arrayed against the Yiddishists and Bundists were the Zionists, adherents of the

Delivering goods in a Jewish street in Warsaw, 1938.

doctrine of 'negating the Galuth', that is, subscribing to the tenet that the future of the Jewish people in the Diaspora was hopeless and that therefore all efforts must be bent towards the one goal of Zionism, the re-establishment of a Jewish state in the historic land of Israel. Although less numerous than the followers of the other two trends, those of Orthodoxy and the non-Zionist Left, Zionism had unquestionably exerted the greatest influence on Jewish life in Poland in the inter-war years. Much of the Yiddish press was Zionist oriented, and the Zionists themselves had their own papers. They also sponsored and supported an educational network (the *Tarbut* schools) which, founded in 1922, had by the 1930s an attendance of 45,000, and in which the language of tuition was Hebrew – the only large-scale Hebrew school system in the entire Diaspora. Although the

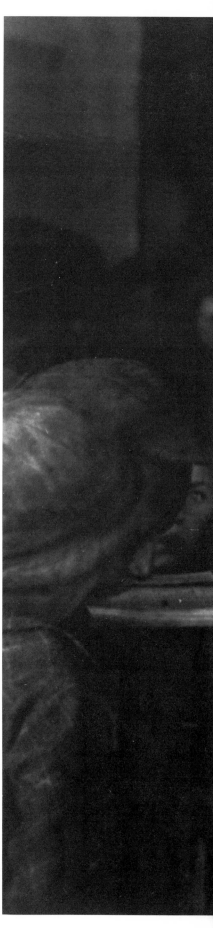

above Two children engrossed in a game of chess.

right Young students at the *heder*, a private traditional religious school, in Lublin in 1924.

The Jewish theatre: a
performance of a play by the
Yiddish writer Sholem Aleichem.

Zionist movement was split up into numerous political parties, each with its own
specific Zionist ideology, youth groups, agricultural training centres preparing
young people for ʿaliya (immigration to Palestine), etc., they all agreed on the
importance of the Hebrew language as the medium of Jewish culture and Zionist
nationalism (while continuing to speak Yiddish); almost all of them were members
of the World Zionist Organization, and all were united in the endeavour to
conquer Polish Jewry for Zionism. The effectiveness of the Zionist work in Poland
and the responsiveness of Polish Jewry to Zionism are indicated by the large
number of Polish-Jewish immigrants who reached the shores of Palestine in the
inter-war years – 137,000, more than the total of all Jewish immigrants from the
rest of the world, including the German Jewish refugees from the Nazi terror.

Despite much Jewish opposition, the Polish language made considerable
headway among the Jews in the inter-war years. While there were few Jews who
produced literary works in Polish prior to World War I, the Jewish contribution to
Polish literature became significant in the period between the two wars. Many
Jewish poets, novelists, playwrights, short-story writers contributed to Polish
belles-lettres; others became influential literary historians and critics, editors and
publishers of important literary reviews, or worked as translators into Polish of
major works from other European languages. Some of these authors wrote for a
Jewish readership, and the very fact that their writings were published in Polish
can be considered an additional indication of the progress the Polish language
made in supplanting Yiddish among widening circles of Polish Jewry. The same
phenomenon was manifested also in the proliferation of Jewish newspapers and
periodicals in Polish.

Polish Jewry was thus, in effect, a trilingual community. There were the Hasidim and other Orthodox Jews and the left-wing Diaspora-nationalists who spoke Yiddish and educated their children in that language; there were the Zionists who also spoke Yiddish but knew Hebrew and gave a Hebrew education to their children; and there were the assimilationists who, while knowing Yiddish, preferred to speak Polish and sent their children to Polish-language schools. The first two groups, while their ideologies divided them, were deeply committed to Judaism. The Jewishness of the third group was lukewarm, and had they been given time to live out their natural span of life they would undoubtedly have developed into a Polish counterpart to the Central and West European assimilationist Jewries.

The opening of the Bezalel Art Exhibition in Lvov in 1909 attended by Boris Schatz, founder of the Bezalel Art School in Jerusalem (seated second from the left).

While its economic position inexorably deteriorated in the inter-war years, Polish Jewry had retained enough strength to continue its Yiddish and Hebrew literary production. Prior to World War I Warsaw had been one of the two great cultural centres of Russo-Polish Jewry (the other was Odessa), the very heart of Jewish creativity, the seat of the greatest Yiddish authors, such as J.L. Peretz (1852–1915), the leading Yiddish and Hebrew poet, whose home in Warsaw was a centre for Yiddish writers, and Sholem Asch (1880–1957), the foremost Yiddish novelist who in 1910 emigrated to America. After the war, with the Soviet suppression of Jewish culture, Poland became the undisputed centre of Yiddish literary activity, and the large Jewish community of its capital, Warsaw, the centre of the centre.

A young generation of Yiddish writers arose, who, building on the work of their predecessors, created new modes and moulds of Jewish expression in poetry and prose, and were read with love and admiration by very wide circles. Only a very few of them can be mentioned here. Uri Zevi Greenberg (born 1894), one of the most original and widely-acclaimed modern Hebrew poets, started writing poetry in Yiddish and Hebrew in Lvov, and soon became one of the leaders of a group of Yiddish expressionist poets. After his immigration to Palestine (1924) he stopped writing in Yiddish and published only in Hebrew. From 1931 to 1934 he lived in Warsaw and edited the Revisionist Yiddish weekly *Di Velt*. Perez Markish (1895–1952), Yiddish poet, one of the founders of the Warsaw *Literarishe Bleter*, lived from 1926 in the Soviet Union, where he was awarded the Order of Stalin in 1939, arrested on charges of Jewish nationalism in 1948, and executed in 1952. Moshe Kulbak (1896–1940) was a Yiddish poet, novelist and dramatist, a teacher in

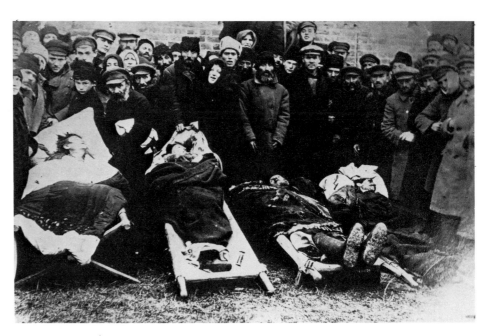

The first victims of the Petlyura pogroms in which over 60,000 Ukrainian Jews perished.

Vilna, then moved to Russia, where in 1937 he was arrested, sentenced to imprisonment for heretical expressionism, and served as a slave labourer until his death in 1940.

Israel Joshua Singer (1893–1944), Yiddish novelist, playwright and journalist, master of the Jewish 'family' novel, spent his formative years and the most creative period in his life (until 1933) in Warsaw. His younger brother, the novelist Isaac Bashevis Singer (1904–   ), grew up in Warsaw, where he developed under the influence of the Yiddish literary atmosphere. He emigrated to America in 1935, and his popularity (in English translation) overshadowed that of his brother. In 1978 he was awarded the Nobel Prize for literature. The only Hebrew author to become a Nobel laureate (in 1966) was Shmuel Yosef Agnon (1888–1970), who was born in Buczacz (or Buchach in Galicia, at that time in Austria, and in the inter-war years in Poland) and whose early writings in Hebrew and Yiddish were published in Cracow. Much of Agnon's later works, written in Germany and, from 1924 on, in Palestine-Israel, are set in the world of the pious Jews in Poland. In the last decade of his life he was generally considered the greatest modern Hebrew novelist.

Modern Yiddish literature as a whole was a new branch on the ancient tree of Yiddish in Poland which still continued to produce fruit of the old flavour in both religious and secular popular works. Yiddish folklore, too, was still alive, which meant that a considerable part of Polish Jewry was, by upbringing and tradition, a so to speak natural audience for what the new Yiddish authors had to say. And not only was it a natural audience but also a most eager one. The Jewish readers considered the new Yiddish literature a vital *Jewish* asset, Jewish not in the religious but in the national sense. They read it, admired it, and discussed it. It was quite literally a part of their everyday life. In this manner Yiddish literature contributed substantially to the intensity of the Jewishness of Polish Jewish life until the very end of the existence of Polish Jewry.

However, all the many-sided and wide-ranging cultural, social, and political, and organizational activities of the Polish Jews were unable to halt, or even to slow, the advance of Polish anti-Semitism. The energetic, often ruthless, Polonization programme, initiated by the government soon after Poland gained independence, proceeded apace. The extent to which the Jews were considered aliens by the Poles became more evident now than it had been while the Poles themselves were subject to Russian, German, and Austrian rule. Polonization for independent Poland meant the systematic and progressive exclusion of the Jews, and it resulted not only in a rapid reduction of the number of Jews in many

Emigrants queuing up at the
Red Star Line shipping office in
Warsaw in 1921.

branches of the economy which were traditional Jewish specialities, but also in a general diminishing of the Jewish population of the cities in which the Jews had concentrated ever since the Middle Ages. In 1921 there were several Polish cities (Bialystock, Grodno, Brest-Litovsk, Pinsk) in which the Jews were the majority; by 1931 they had this position only in Pinsk, and there, too, they were reduced from 74·7 per cent in 1921 to 63·4 in 1931. In addition to the growth of the Christian population in the cities, this reduction was due to Jewish emigration and to a much lower natural increase among Jews (9·5 per thousand) than among Christians (Roman Catholics – 13·1; Greek Catholics – 12·5; Greek Orthodox – 16·7).

The economic enfeeblement (some historians speak of economic 'collapse') of Polish Jewry in the inter-war years was accelerated by the re-emergence of virulent anti-Semitism in the wake of Hitler's accession to power in neighbouring Germany in 1933. There were anti-Jewish boycotts and waves of pogroms. Although the German army which invaded Poland in 1939 was a hated enemy force, the anti-Jewish policies it instituted were received with sympathy and aided by the Polish populace. Had the attitude of the Poles to the Jews been like that of, say, the Italians, the Germans would not have been able to exterminate three million Polish Jews in the five years of the war. But the Poles more than willingly helped the Germans achieve the *Endlösung* (final solution) at least as far as Polish Jewry was concerned, with the result that, at the end of the war, Poland found itself practically *Judenrein*, and the memory of great Polish Jewry with its vibrant Jewish culture and social life and its centuries-old central role in the history of world Jewry survived only in books and in the fading recollections of the few who had escaped in time or miraculously survived the Nazi hell to tell the story of a world that was no more.

Lithuania

Jewish authors with the Yiddish writer Chaim Zhitlowsky, the foremost exponent of Diaspora nationalism.

From the fourteenth century onwards, Lithuania and Poland formed a union which lasted until the third partition of Poland (1795), when ethnic Lithuania was divided between Prussia and Russia. An independent Lithuania was established after World War I, and at the start of World War II the Russians transferred to Lithuania the city of Vilnius (Vilna), which became the capital, as well as the surrounding territory which they had seized from Poland. In 1940 Lithuania was incorporated into the Soviet Union as one of the republics of the USSR.

Just as the history of Lithuania was for centuries closely bound up with that of Poland, so the history of the Lithuanian and the Polish Jews had strong affinities. For one thing, organizationally and institutionally, Lithuanian Jewry closely resembled the Jews of Poland. For another, Gentile-Jewish relations were similar, the Jews of both lands being taxed and otherwise treated in the same manner by the noblemen, churchmen, and kings. Incidentally, from the tax assessment of Sigismund III in 1613 we learn that in that period the number of Jews in Lithuania was 29 per cent higher than in Poland. When the Jews of Poland set up their country-wide council, the Lithuanian Jews participated in it, and organized their own council, termed 'Council of the Lands of Lithuania', which united the communities of three large areas, headed by Brest-Litovsk, Kovno, and Pinsk. This Lithuanian Jewish council was, at most times, subordinate to, and co-operated with, the Polish Council of Four Lands.

Lithuanian Jewry also adopted the educational methods of Talmudic study from the Polish Jews, and its first prominent rabbis, such as Mordecai ben

Abraham Jaffe (c. 1535–1612) and Joel Sirkes (1561–1640), were either Polish Jews or products of Polish Yeshivot. In the seventeenth century, Lithuanian Talmudic scholarship came into its own, and in the eighteenth, the Gaon of Vilna, Elijah ben Solomon Zalman (1720–97), developed his own method of study, which rejected *pilpul* (casuistry), and insisted on accurate interpretation of the Talmudic text, close scrutiny of all the sources, and knowledge and utilization of grammar. The approach of the 'Vilnaer Gaon' determined the character of Lithuanian Talmudism and made it pre-eminent for several generations. It was also, partly at least, due to his influence and to that of his disciples that for quite some time neither Hasidism nor Haskala was able to make much headway in Lithuania. The great Lithuanian Yeshivot, such as those of Mir, Telz and Slobodka, became in the nineteenth century the most important centres of Jewish learning, combining a profound study of the Talmud with the study of *Musar* (ethical literature); they attracted talented students from all over Russia and other Diasporas, and produced many of the most outstanding rabbis. Also, several of the leading Jewish scholars, authors and poets (e.g., Hayyim Nahman Bialik) received their early education in Lithuanian Yeshivot.

These intellectual influences of Lithuanian Talmudism left their mark on the character of Lithuanian Jews in general. They were intensely religious, and scrupulous in observing the Law as laid down in the *Shulhan 'Arukh* and its commentaries, of which a very high proportion of the men had a thorough first-hand knowledge. The term 'Litvak' came to mean a person possessing a profound familiarity with the Talmud and halakhic literature, a man of sharp intellect, in whom logical thinking rather than emotions predominated, who was quick-witted, and of a cool and dry temperament. The character of the Litvak, it was felt, contrasted with the emotional warmth and heartiness of the Polish Jew. The Litvak was also considered to be stubborn to the point of obstinacy, and, with all his meticulous observance of the Law, was held to be lacking in true, internal piety.

The language of the Lithuanian Jews, like that of the other East European Jews, was Yiddish, but a Yiddish spoken in a special dialect. Not only did the Lithuanian Jews pronounce the vowels differently from the Polish Jews – such differences existed in many regions of the widespread Yiddish language area – but, in certain parts of Lithuania, there was a unique deviation from the standard pronunciation of a consonant: the *shin* (sh) was pronounced as 's': e.g., they said 'Sabes' for 'Shabes' (Sabbath). This gave rise to the jocular comment that the Litvaks must be the descendants of the Biblical Ephraimites who suffered from the same inability, and pronounced 'shibboleth' as 'sibboleth' (Judges 12:6).

Despite the power of Lithuanian Talmudism, it could not for long stem the tide of Jewish Enlightenment which penetrated from neighbouring Prussia. However, the kind of Haskala which in the nineteenth century gained many adherents in Lithuania was of a specifically 'Litvak' type. It did not involve, as it did in Germany and other Central European countries, a switching from Yiddish and Hebrew to German, nor was it accompanied by an alienation from Judaism. The Lithuanian *Maskilim* remained faithful to the Jewish community, and continued to speak Yiddish. Most of the authors among them wrote either in Yiddish or in Hebrew, producing not only novels, short stories, poetry, and criticism, but also scholarly Jewish studies and popular works of general history, geography, and the natural sciences. Some of the greatest names in early modern Hebrew literature are those of Lithuanian Jews: Abraham Dov Lebensohn, Micah Joseph Lebensohn, J.L.

Gordon, Abraham Mapu, Peretz Smolenskin, Mendele Mokher Seforim. True, several of the *Maskilim* helped the Russian government in spreading Russian culture among the Jews, opening Jewish state schools, and establishing a governmental rabbinical seminary in Vilna, and some of them wrote in Russian. But the great majority of Lithuanian Jews remained faithful to Yiddish and, even as recently as in 1959 when only a few thousand Jews were left in Lithuania, 70 per cent of them declared Yiddish as their mother tongue in the official census.

The struggle between the socialists and the Zionists in the inter-war decades in Lithuania bore a close resemblance to that which took place in Poland in the same period. In this era Lithuanian Jewry found itself divided among three states: the Belorussian SSR with some 400,000 Jews; Poland, which controlled Vilna and a large strip of territory to the south-east of Lithuania; and independent Lithuania with a Jewish population of some 160,000.

The most important Jewish city in Lithuania was Vilna. Externally, the history of the Jews in Vilna differed in no way from that of the other Jewish communities in the major East European cities. They, like the others, had their share of privileges, restrictions, oppressive tax burdens, devastations by arson, mob attacks, expulsions, escapes from enemy armies, readmissions, periods of growth alternating with periods of shrinkage, eras of peace and prosperity, and many times seven lean years. As in other East European cities, the Jews made a living, despite all the tribulations they had to endure, in petty trading and in crafts not

subject to guild organizations. They were millers, bakers, tailors, harness makers, plasterers, glaziers, blacksmiths, waggoners, porters, distillers of alcoholic beverages, and the like. In the late eighteenth century, the Jews of Vilna put up strong resistance to the establishment of Hasidic congregations in their midst. The antagonism between Hasidim and *Mitnagdim* reached such intensity that in 1795 both sides turned to the Russian authorities for intervention, again, as was done in several other East European Jewish communities.

Where Vilna differed from other great East European centres of Jewish life was in its emphasis on Jewish scholarship. Other cities too had their Yeshivot and their learned men, but the scholarly individuals in every other community constituted a small minority in the midst of an ignorant or semi-educated majority. In Vilna, the average level of Jewish learning was exceptionally high. It was this scholarliness of the ordinary Vilna Jew which earned the city the accolade of 'Jerusalem of Lithuania'. In no other Jewish community did scholarship command such respect as in Vilna, and in Lithuania in general. The whole country, as one of the Lithuanian Jewish writers put it, was much more the kingdom of the *Shulhan 'Arukh* than that of the Tsar. The spiritual and intellectual world the Jews developed for themselves enveloped them like a natural environment, a self-contained habitat almost entirely free of alien influences. They were a community imbued with the prophetic ideal of 'All thy children are learned of the Lord.'

The scholars of Vilna are too numerous to list, but the Gaon of Vilna, Elijah ben

far left The ceremonial laying of the cornerstone of a building for the society 'Mishmeret Holim (Care of the Sick) in Vilna.

left The Villbig choir.

below left A Yiddish marionette theatre, the 'Maydem', in Vilna.

below The Vilna Jewish Central Committee.

Solomon Zalman, to whom reference has already been made earlier (see above, p. 35), was too great a figure to be passed over in silence. No other Jewish scholar since the Babylonian Geonim of the Middle Ages has been endowed by popular consensus with the title Gaon ('genius'). The Gaon of Vilna was one of the greatest spiritual and intellectual leaders of Jewry. An infant prodigy, the Gaon (as he is usually referred to) acquired most of what he knew by his own independent efforts, and spent all his life in relentless study, constantly widening his circle of interest until it included the Bible, the Talmud, Halakha, Midrash, the Zohar and other sources of the Kabbala, Hebrew grammar, as well as secular sciences such as geometry, measurements, astronomy, medicine, and even music. He repeatedly stated that a full understanding of the Bible and subsequent traditional Jewish literature is possible only if one is familiar with the various secular fields of human knowledge. He encouraged Jewish scholars to translate important works from other languages into Hebrew, wrote prodigiously on an astounding variety of fields, and held that the widespread lack of interest in secular sciences which characterized East European Jewry was a degradation of Israel among the nations who could with justification disparage the Jews for their lack of knowledge.

The Gaon was a bitter opponent of Hasidism, and was instrumental in placing the Hasidim under a ban. He had one of the basic books of Hasidism, *The Testament of R. Israel Ba'al Shem Tov*, publicly burned in Vilna. His stand against the Haskala was no less severe, but because of the cautious position of the early *Maskilim* he had little opportunity of fighting them. The Gaon left behind a vast amount of writings, only part of which was published, while several of his treaties were lost. With his books, and perhaps even more so with the courses he gave to selected disciples, he exerted a profound influence, especially on Lithuanian Jewry whose intellectual physiognomy was once and for all marked by his stamp.

above Abba Kovner, commandant of the Partisan camp 'Avenger' in World War II.

opposite: above The market at Novigorod.

left Jewish raftsmen transporting logs, Vilna, c. 1930s.

Once the Haskala began to spread to Lithuania (in the 1840s), Vilna, of course, became its centre. Most of the scholars and writers mentioned above lived in Vilna. In 1860 a Hebrew weekly, *HaKarmel*, began to appear, with Russian supplements. Since the Russian government barred Jews from living in villages, many rural Jews had to move to Vilna whose Jewish population in 1897 reached 64,000, or two-fifths of the total population. Before the end of the century, the congested conditions in Vilna prompted many Jews to emigrate, most of them going to the United States and South Africa.

Jewish social and cultural life flourished in the inter-war years in Vilna, now a part of Poland. A network of Hebrew elementary and secondary schools was established, as well as Hebrew and Yiddish teachers' seminaries and trade schools. Several Yiddish daily and weekly papers were published, and there was a profusion of Yiddish political, scientific, literary, and educational magazines. In 1919 a museum and archive were established by the Vilna Jewish historical and ethnographic society, founded by S. An-Ski, the author of *The Dybbuk*. In 1925 was founded the YIVO (abbreviation for *Yidisher Visenshaftlikher Institut* or Institute for Jewish Research), with headquarters in Vilna and branches in Berlin, Warsaw, and New York. YIVO concentrated on research in Yiddish language, culture, and folklore, attracted a large number of Yiddish scholars and authors, and issued important publications in Yiddish. It also initiated a training programme for young scholars in Vilna in 1935, and collected a rich specialized library and valuable manuscript archives.

For one hundred and forty years Vilna was one of the most important centres of Hebrew printing. The Hebrew printers of Vilna were, at one and the same time, also publishers. Especially outstanding was the work of the Romm family whose edition of the Talmud became famous all over the Jewish world as the 'Vilna ShaS'. They printed many other standard texts, employing in 1866 no less than a hundred typesetters and printers and fourteen proof-readers. The Romm press continued to function until 1940.

While the workaday existence of the Jews was filled with a relentless struggle to make ends meet, yet their life was an essentially Jewish life, due to the almost exclusive use of Yiddish as the colloquial, and the through-and-through Jewish consciousness which permeated every moment of their waking hours and even their dreams. And when, after the long hours of daily work, the precious minutes of leisure were reached, they were spent in the synagogue, or the *Bet haMidrash*, the House of Study, where they would congregate to pray, gossip, and, above all, study. Most men belonged to one or more of the religious societies: the *Hevra Kadisha*, through which they fulfilled the commandments of charity and loving-kindness, the *Hevra ShaS* for the study of the Talmud, the *Hevra Mishnayot* for the study of the Mishna, and so forth. As for the women, while not many knew Hebrew, most of them could read the Hebrew alphabet and thus were able to read the prayers and the Yiddish favourites of the women folk, such as the famous *Tzene-Rene*. Despite the inroads made by Enlightenment and secularization especially after World War I, this remained the dominant atmosphere of Lithuanian Jewish life until the holocaust.

At the outbreak of World War II, the Jewish population of Lithuania, including the Vilna area, numbered 260,000. During the war Lithuania was first (1940–1) under Soviet rule, then in 1941 the Germans occupied it. The systematic extermination of the Jews was immediately initiated by the German *Einsatzgruppen* (Action Units), aided by local anti-Semitic groups. Until the end of 1941, more than 136,000 Jews were killed. By the time Lithuania was re-occupied by the Soviet army (summer 1944) only a few Jewish families and children, who had been hidden by Gentiles, and a few hundred Jewish partisan fighters, were still alive. A few thousand more, who had escaped to Soviet Asia, and some hundreds who were found in various concentration camps, made their way back to Lithuania. According to the 1959 census, there were 24,672 Jews in the Lithuanian SSR.

Rumania

Jewish workers in a lumberyard at Sighet in the Maramures regions in 1925.

Jewish history in Rumania begins with 101–6 CE when the Roman Emperor Trajan conquered the territory known at the time as Dacia, and made it a province of the Roman Empire. Jewish tombstones found in various Roman towns in Dacia show that Jews had come, probably as merchants, with the Roman legions. After this early testimony history keeps silent about the Jews of Rumania until the fourteenth century when Jewish exiles from Hungary arrived in Walachia, a principality in the south of modern Rumania, founded in 1290 and freed from Hungarian vassalage in 1330. By the sixteenth century there were Jewish communities in Moldavia, the second of the two Rumanian principalities, to the north of Walachia, including those of the cities of Siret (Sereth), Suceava (Suczawa), Botosani, and Iasi between the Carpathian Mountains and the river Prut. Moldavia at the time was a province of the Ottoman Empire, and remained under Turkish rule until its north-western region, Bukovina, was acquired by Austria (1775), and its eastern region, Bessarabia, by Russia (1812). In 1918 both provinces were incorporated into Rumania; however, in 1940 Bessarabia and the northern part of Bukovina were annexed by Russia.

Under Turkish rule the Jews of Walachia and Moldavia were well off: they were treated tolerantly, as were the Jews in other parts of the Ottoman Empire, had internal autonomy, and were headed, from 1719, by a hereditary *Hakham Bashi* (see below) whose seat was in Iasi. They could engage freely in commerce along the trade routes connecting the Ottoman territories in the south with Poland in the north. The Cossack massacres of 1648–9, led by Bogdan Chmielnicki and resulting in the destruction of hundreds of Jewish communities in the Ukraine, prompted many Jews to seek refuge in the hospitable lands under Turkish dominion, and thus Moldavian Jewry acquired a Polish-Ashkenazi majority, with the Sephardi element reduced to a small minority. In the eighteenth century, the Moldavian rulers, interested in rebuilding or enlarging their towns, granted special privileges to Jews so as to induce them to settle in the country. The success of this policy was shown by the increase of the Jewish population in the towns of Bukovina and Bessarabia.

However, such manifestations of a friendly attitude to the Jews were rare and confined to a few rulers. The general attitude of the population was mostly anti-Semitic.

Despite persecutions, the Jews themselves could not close ranks in the defence of their interests. They were organized, under a governmental system, into a guild, headed by a Jewish *staroste* (elder), whose Hebrew title was *rosh m'dina* or 'head of the country', and who apportioned the collective tax the Jews had to pay the government. This he did by imposing a tax on the kosher meat, from which revenue he paid the collective tax, while using whatever was left over to defray the expenses of the Jewish schools, cemeteries, and other institutions. The spiritual head of the Jews in Rumania was the *Hakham Bashi* (lit. 'chief Hakham', 'Hakham' being the title of a rabbi among Sephardi Jews), first appointed for Walachia and Moldavia by the Sultan in 1719. However, the Russian and Galician Jews, who were respectively Russian and Austrian subjects, were mostly adherents of Hasidism, followers of their own *Tzaddiqim*, rabbis in whose miraculous powers they had unshakeable faith. Consequently they were opposed to the person and office of the *Hakham Bashi*, in whom they saw an instrument of government oppression. They asked their consuls to intercede and complained to the authorities, with the result that first the jurisdiction of the *Hakham Bashi* was restricted to 'native' Jews (1819), and then, while strife among the diverse Jewish groups was growing in intensity, his office was abolished altogether (1834). This meant also the end of the Jewish guild, and signalled the disintegration of the Jewish communities.

The emancipation of the Jews was a slow, hesitant process, imposed from the outside on the local governments rather than being granted by them through any spontaneous recognition that all their subject groups, including the Jews, should enjoy equal rights. Although the revolutionary forces, which staged uprisings against the Ottoman-appointed rulers, and again in 1848 against Russia, proclaimed civil equality for the Jews whose support they needed, it never came to a test because their revolts were put down without bearing fruit. The 1856 treaty of Paris provided that all inhabitants of Walachia and Moldavia, irrespective of religion, should enjoy religious and civic liberties, and, after the unification of the two principalities in 1859 under Alexander Ioan Cuza, certain limited rights were indeed granted to the Jews. However, even this small improvement was nullified in 1866 when the anti-liberal Prince Carol of Hohenzollern-Sigmaringen was elected sovereign, and new anti-Jewish measures

above Young Jewish
blacksmiths in the town of
Bender in 1920.

were adopted: the Jews were excluded from citizenship, and within a year there
began the expulsion of the Jews from the villages, and of Jews who were non-
citizens from the country. These measures were accompanied by outbreaks of anti-
Jewish violence: the Choir Temple of Bucharest was demolished and the Jewish
quarter plundered.

Bribery had for long been an established feature of contact with authorities and,
made vital by the new anti-Jewish measures, it now assumed the character and
dimensions of large-scale official extortion. Foreign intervention in favour of the
Jews by the governments of Great Britain, France, Holland, and Germany, or by
influential individuals such as Adolphe Crémieux and Sir Moses Montefiore,
were of no avail. At the Congress of Berlin (1878), despite the opposition of the
Russian and Rumanian delegates, the granting of full independence to Rumania by
the great powers was made conditional on Rumania's grant of civil rights to the
Jews. Yet in defiance of this provision, the Rumanian Government naturalized

only 2,000 Jews, including 883 who had taken part in the 1877 war against Turkey, and went on to introduce a number of new anti-Jewish measures and embark on an openly anti-Jewish campaign on the Russian model. Added to all this was Prince Carol's declaration to the effect that the Jews were a harmful economic influence, especially on the peasants. Even those Jews who had formerly been considered Rumanian subjects, albeit with narrowly limited rights, were now declared foreigners, while on the other hand the Rumanian government prevailed upon Austria and Germany to deprive those Austrian and German Jews who lived in Rumania of their citizenship. A large number of occupations were outlawed for Jews – they could not be lawyers, chemists, teachers, railway officials, army officers, stockbrokers or dealers in government-controlled monopolies such as salt, tobacco, alcohol, etc. In 1893 they were excluded from public schools, and Jewish leaders who participated in the struggle for emancipation were expelled from the country.

A remote Jewish village in Rumania, c. 1900.

Little wonder that these circumstances produced a steady, ample, and increasing flow of Jewish emigration from Rumania to the United States and other western countries: from 1900 to 1914 about 70,000 Jews left the country – had they been able to defray the travel expenses, probably three times as many would have left. However, due to their high birth rate, most of this demographic deficit was made up by natural increase, so that in the same period the total number of Jews in Rumania decreased by only 26,000 (from 266,000 to 240,000).

After World War I Rumania gained control over Transylvania, which had been part of Hungary, thereby more than doubling its area and gaining an additional population of about five million. Of these, some 1,600,000 were Hungarians, including 180,000 Jews. In 1930 Rumania had a Jewish population of 756,000 of whom 263,000 were in the so-called Old Kingdom, 207,000 in Bessarabia, 93,000 in Bukovina, and 193,000 in Transylvania.

The first Jews to arrive in Transylvania were Turkish Sephardim, who, however, were soon outnumbered by Ashkenazi Jews moving in from Hungary in the west and from the Slavic countries to the north-east. Typical of the multiplicity of Jewish ethnic groups in Transylvania was the community of Alba Julia (Hungarian Gyulafehérvár), the old princely capital of the state, whose extant minute-book (*pinkas*) covering the years 1736–1835, is written in a mixture of Hebrew, Yiddish, Ladino, German, and Hungarian. While the Jews did not enjoy full civil rights their position was infinitely better than in Rumania and Russia. In

right Members of a Jewish
youth movement.

fact, Jewish religion made a strong impact on the Hungarians and Szeklers, and in
the 1580s a Judaizing sect, called *Szombatosok* (Sabbatarians) was founded.

At the time when Transylvania was incorporated into Rumania, its Jewish
population, comprising 110 communities, consisted of several greatly disparate
elements. The Orthodox Jews of the north of Transylvania were culturally and
religiously part of the great East European Yiddish-speaking, tradition-bound,
partly Hasidic and partly *Mitnagdic*, branch of the Jewish people. Typical of this
part were the Jewish communities of Szatmár (Satu-Mare) and Munkács
(Mukachevo). Farther to the south, in the west-central part of Transylvania,
Hungarian-speaking Jews were dominant and modern trends prevailed. The
communities of Arad, Nagyvárad (Oradea) and Kolozsvár (Cluj) were typical of this
area. In southern Transylvania German cultural influences vied with Hungarian,
as in the communities of Temesvár (Timisoara) and Brassó (Brasov).

In 1910, of all Transylvanian Jews, 73·3 per cent stated that their mother tongue
was Hungarian. They were emphatically Hungarian also in patriotic and
nationalistic sentiments, and had an important role in spreading Hungarian
language and culture among the Rumanian and other non-Hungarian population
elements in the province. Most remarkable was the combination of their

A village woman carding wool in the region of Bessarabia.

Magyarism with the Jewish-nationalistic and Zionist fervour they displayed after Transylvania became part of Rumania in 1918. In post-World War I Rumania the Jews were considered officially a national minority enjoying, theoretically at least, the right to have their own schools in their own language, and protected, again theoretically, by the minority treaties worked out at the Versailles Peace Conference and signed by the newly-created or defeated states, including Rumania. In contrast to the situation in Hungary where the official Jewish position had been, and remained so after World War I, that the Jews were Hungarians by nationality and Jews by religion, the Jews who from 1918 found themselves under Rumanian rule suddenly discovered that they were Jewish nationals, and founded, as early as in November of that year, the Transylvanian Jewish National Federation, which affiliated in 1920 with the World Zionist Organization. Characteristic of the differences between Hungarian and Transylvanian Jewry in this respect was the fact that in Hungary the National Bureau of Hungarian Jews and the other official Jewish organizations opposed Zionism, while in Transylvania (as in the rest of Rumania) most of the Jewish congregations, especially those of the Neolog and Status Quo trends, were sponsors of Zionist activities and organizations.

Another manifestation of the differences between the two Jewries was the absence in Hungary of any educational institution with Hebrew as the language of tuition, as against the existence of several Hebrew secondary schools in the major Transylvanian cities. That is to say, for Hungarian Jewry Hebrew remained the sacred language of the Bible, the prayers, and Jewish religion, while for Transylvanian Jewry it became the medium and vehicle of a new Jewish national consciousness. A third difference was that while in Hungary the Jews would have reacted with horror to the idea of establishing a Jewish political party in connection with either national or local elections, in Transylvania the Jews did in fact organize a national Jewish party, campaigned on a large scale in municipal and parliamentary elections, and succeeded in seating candidates who used their positions in the various elective bodies to fight for Jewish rights and against anti-Jewish discrimination.

Thus, what the annexation of Transylvania by Rumania meant for the Jews was, on the one hand, a transition from the relatively liberal Hungarian regime to the much more repressive and hostile Rumanian rule, while on the other it meant their passing from the typical Central and West European Jewish self-view as a purely denominational group to the typical East European Jewish position of a national minority with its concomitant upsurge of interest in Hebrew culture, participation in Zionist work, and activities in Jewish-national politics.

It is a remarkable thing that despite the oppression and persecution, despite being considered aliens and excluded from citizenship, the Jews of Rumania produced, even before the end of the nineteenth century, numerous outstanding individuals who made significant contributions to Rumanian literature and scholarship. One of the first of these was Julius Barasch, MD (1815–63), who was not only a Jewish historian and an energetic Jewish community leader, but also the first writer to publish scientific works in Rumanian, including writings on hygiene, botany, zoology, and forestry, creating a Rumanian terminology for these sciences which, prior to his work, had not existed in Rumanian. Moses Gaster (1856–1939), a native of Bucharest, who in 1885 was expelled from Rumania because he protested against the treatment of the Jews, and settled in England where he became a leading figure in Jewish and comparative folklore and an early supporter of Herzl, wrote, while still in Rumania, the standard history, and compiled a great chrestomathy, of Rumanian literature. The most prominent Rumanian philologist, author of a four-volume standard Rumanian dictionary and a three-volume study on Oriental influences in Rumanian language and culture, was a Jew, Lazar Saineanu (Schein, 1859–1934) who, although he converted to Christianity, was still denied Rumanian citizenship, and in 1901 emigrated to Paris. Heinrich Tiktin (who also converted) wrote a two-volume scientific Rumanian grammar, and was another celebrated Rumanian philologist. Moise Roman-Ronetti (1847–1908) was a leading Rumanian poet whose Jewish-inspired play *Manasse* (1900) was performed before the royal family but then driven off the stage of the Rumanian National Theatre by anti-Semitic demonstrators.

These comments give some idea of the Jewish contribution to Rumanian literature, culture, and science. They must be supplemented by a few brief remarks about Jewish cultural and literary life. Jewish life in Moldavia and northern Transylvania was strongly influenced by Hasidism. The Jewish colloquial was Yiddish, which was only gradually supplemented by Rumanian. In the late nineteenth century several histories of Rumanian Jews and other books of Jewish content appeared in Hebrew, but soon Rumanian became the language of Jewish writers, except in Transylvania where Jewish poets, novelists and dramatists wrote in Hungarian.

The Rumanian Jewish press, too, was multilingual. There were Jewish papers in Rumanian, Yiddish, Hebrew, German, Hungarian, and some were bilingual (Rumanian and Yiddish or Rumanian and French). From 1919 to 1923 a Zionist daily in Rumanian was published in Bucharest. In the inter-war years several

Elderly men in the Jewish cemetery in Sadagora.

Jewish journalists served as editors-in-chief of the major Rumanian papers, while continuing to contribute to the Jewish press.

Disciples greeting the 'Sepinker' Rabbi in Upper Viseul in the Maramures region.

Thus the overall picture one gains of Rumanian Jewry is that of a heterogeneous community, always oppressed and occasionally persecuted by the authorities, living an intensive Jewish life of many hues, often torn by internal strife, sharply divided along religious lines, but, on the whole, with the exception of the extreme Hasidic wing, imbued by a Zionist conviction.

The liquidation of Rumanian Jewry began in January 1941 when the Rumanian Iron Guard carried out a pogrom among the Jews of Bucharest. In June the German soldiers slaughtered the Jewish population of Iasi, and in August the deportations commenced. By September half of the 320,000 Jews who lived in Bessarabia, Bukovina, and the Dorohoi district of northern Moldavia had been exterminated. To the credit of the Rumanian government it must be stated that, despite German pressure, it refused to deport its Jews to the 'east'. On the other hand, it undertook severe anti-Jewish measures, including forced labour. The post-war balance showed that 'only' 43 per cent of the Jews who lived under Rumanian rule in the war years (that is, including those of Bessarabia and northern Bukovina) perished in the holocaust period, in massacres, in the death-camps and ghettos, or in epidemics, famine, and exposure. Most of those who survived, estimated at 428,000, were left without a livelihood. This number was sharply reduced by emigration in 1944–7, and at an even more rapid rate after the establishment of Israel when 200,000 Rumanian Jews made their ʿaliya (immigration). By the end of the 1960s no more than 100,000 Jews were left in Rumania, and in 1978 – 60,000.

Part Two

Central Europe
Stepchildren of the Heartland

The Altneuschul in Prague (on the left of the picture), the oldest
extant synagogue in Europe, built in the thirteenth century.

Germany

Employees of the Oppenheimer woollens factory at Bruchsal in Baden, in 1913.

The German lands had a special place in Jewish history. It was after Germany – *Ashkenaz* in Hebrew – that the name *Ashkenazim* was applied to all but a fraction of the Jews of Europe and their descendants in other parts of the world. It was here that the language destined to become the mother tongue of the great majority of the Jews originated in the twelfth century. Here, in the eighteenth century, arose the Haskala, the Jewish Enlightenment, which transformed the whole character of the Jewish people. It was here, in the nineteenth century, that Jewish religious reform began, that the 'Science of Judaism' was created, that assimilation and desertion of the ranks reached their greatest height. It was German Jewry which became the bastion of Jewish neo-orthodoxy on the one hand, and of Zionism on the other. It was the German language which, until World War II, was the lingua franca of modern Judaism all over the world and the language of international Jewish gatherings, such as the congresses of the World Zionist Organization. And it was in Germany that the diabolical idea of annihilating world Jewry was hatched by the latter-day Armilus, that the plan of the *Endlösung* was first carried out, and it was from Germany that it was exported to all the parts of Europe (and North Africa) which fell to Hitler's armies.

Until the rise of Nazism the history of Jews in Germany did not differ substantially from their history in neighbouring lands. Jews first reached Germany with the Roman armies, and settled in the Roman-founded towns along the Rhine. In the early fourth century the Jewish community of Cologne is mentioned in Roman decrees, and thereafter sporadic references are found to Jews in other cities. By the tenth century Jews lived in Mainz, Worms, and Regensburg, and by the thirteenth in all major German cities, from the Rhineland in the west to Breslau, Vienna and Prague in the east. From the eleventh century a number of leading Jewish scholars lived in Germany, e.g., Gershom ben Judah (960–1028) the famous Talmudist, known as *M'or haGola*, or 'Light of the Exile', whose ban against polygamy became a milestone in the development of Ashkenazi Jewish life. Rashi (1040–1105), the greatest commentator on the Bible and the Talmud, lived in the French city of Troyes, just west of Germany, but studied in the German Yeshivot of Mainz and Worms.

In the early eleventh century, Jewish persecutions and expulsions began. The Jews of Mainz had the sad distinction, in 1012, of being the first to suffer this fate. In 1096 large-scale massacres were perpetrated by the knights and soldiers of the First Crusade in many Jewish communities on the Rhine. These events acted as a precedent to be turned into a pattern by German mobs in times of social unrest or religious ferment which usually signalled a devastation of many a Jewish community. However, the Jews were protected by the nobility which profited from their commerce and money-lending, and thus, when the troops of the Second Crusade swept over the Rhineland (1146), the Jews were allowed to take refuge in the castles and fortresses of the noblemen and thus escaped a repetition of the first major disaster.

One form of Jewish reaction to the bloodshed and martyrdom they suffered was to turn to pietism and mysticism. The twelfth century saw the rise of the *Haside Ashkenaz* (The Pious of Germany, not to be confused with the eighteenth-century Hasidism of East Europe), who lived a life of asceticism, reliance on God, abstention from pleasures and sexual temptation, and concentration on religious learning as the foremost value. But even those who did not follow this difficult pietistic path led a deeply devout life in which religious scholars were the recognized leaders and the observance of Talmudic law, as interpreted by them, was the basis of everyday conduct.

In the thirteenth to fifteenth centuries the life of the Jews in the German lands was made miserable by restrictive decrees, blood libels, accusations of desecrations of the Holy Host, increasing tax burdens. Occasionally entire communities were massacred or expelled, as happened in the wake of the Black Death (1348–50), and the accusations of well-poisoning made by agitators and by the credulous mob. That the Jews were soon after invited back to the cities which could not function without money-lenders ironically accentuated the instability of the Jewish condition. Moratoriums or cancellations of debts owed to Jews were frequently resorted to by local feudal lords, whose will or whim was law in the absence of a central authority. Exorbitant and extortionist taxes were imposed on the Jews by money-hungry rulers. It is truly nothing short of remarkable that despite these circumstances Jewish scholarship continued to flourish, and important halakhic works, including those of the Tosaphists, were produced on both sides of the French-German border. Equally remarkable is the fact that in the fifteenth century, when the Jews were successively and repeatedly expelled from one German city after the other, when every year attacks took place on the Jews in one locality of another, they nevertheless managed to penetrate new fields of commercial activity, in addition to money-lending. Thus, when forced out of the cities and into small towns and villages, they established themselves as middle-men between the agricultural producers and the urban wholesalers. On the other hand, this was the period of large-scale Jewish migration out of German lands to the east which resulted in the numerical and intellectual growth of Polish Jewry, destined, as we have seen, to become the leading Jewish community in the world.

It has been the way of religious founders and reformers to first try to win the Jews over to their movement, and then, failing in this effort, to turn against them with a vehement hatred. This is what the young Christian church did in the Roman Empire, what Muhammad did in the Arabia of the seventh century, and what Luther (1493–1546) repeated in the Germany of the sixteenth century. The difference between the founder of Islam and the initiator of the Reformation was that Muhammad preached only the subjection and humbling of the Jews as the price of their toleration by the Muslims, while Luther applauded everything that could be done to persecute them, and thus became the spiritual father of German anti-Semitism which in turn made the Nazi genocide possible. As far as anti-Jewish attitudes and acts were concerned, the German Catholics and Protestants remained one.

Another development in the sixteenth century which caused great hardships to the Jews was that they became pawns in the sharpening struggle between the cities, where guilds gradually gained the upper hand over the patrician class and the landed gentry, including the ruling princes. Both sides tried to maintain, or establish, their control over the Jews, which essentially meant the power to tax them. This competition for Jewish taxes often resulted in the Jews having to pay taxes to two, or even three, authorities. The one advantage in this situation was that when the Jews were expelled from the cities they were allowed to settle in villages owned by the gentry, so that expulsion often meant nothing more than taking up new residence a few miles away.

The mercantile system, which spread in Germany in the seventeenth century, also worked to the benefit of the Jews. Money gained by trading became the basic instrument of state power, and the Jews, with their commercial experience, their capital and their taxes, were recognized as an important asset, and invited to settle in the German cities. At the same time there began a reversal in the direction of Jewish migration: instead of moving from west to east, that is, from Germany to Poland, Jews fleeing from the 1648 Chmielnicki massacres, now came from the east to Germany. Among them were rabbis, teachers, and scholars whose presence soon became felt in the religious and intellectual life of German Jewry.

In the late seventeenth century, the Messianic fervour created by Shabbatai Zevi

below left In the streets of Berlin, 1928.

below The synagogue on the Zirkusgasse in Vienna, 1930.

(1625–75), the Turkish pseudo-Messiah, had strong repercussions among German Jews. That the popular belief in the coming of the Messiah did not diminish among the simple Jewish folk in Germany after Shabbatai Zevi's conversion to Islam (1666), we know from, among other sources, the satiric account of Hans Jakob Christoffel von Grimmelshausen (1622?–76), the most important German novelist of the age, who in his novel, *The Enchanted Bird's Nest* (1672), describes how an amorous Christian rogue exploits the Messianic beliefs of a foolish Jewish maiden in order to seduce her. On the other hand, Glueckel of Hameln's (1645–1724) Yiddish memoirs, begun in 1691, show the strength of the Messianic fervour evoked by Shabbatai Zevi in the Jewish patrician circles of which she was a member. The veneration of Shabbatai Zevi continued even among the leading German rabbinical scholars, such as Jair Hayyim Bacharach (1638–1702). As late as the eighteenth century German Jewry was shaken by the fierce controversy between the pro-Shabbataian Jonathan Eybeschutz (1690/95–1764) and his opponent, Jacob Emden (1697–1776); both had much support in Jewish scholarly and leading circles.

The seventeenth and eighteenth centuries were the time when the position of the Court Jews reached its zenith. The Court Jews were contractors, suppliers, bankers, and financial agents for the courts of kings and princes, especially in German lands. They served as tax farmers, empowered by the rulers to organize and carry out the collection of taxes – which, of course, did much to increase the hatred for the Jews in general in the eyes of the populace – and arranged large loans for the princes whose revenues could never keep pace with their expenditures on their armies and their luxuries. Some Court Jews served simultaneously as heads of the Jewish community; others kept their distance from the Jews and assimilated in clothing, hair style, language, and manners to the prevalent fashion of the court in which they fulfilled their important function. In either case, their position was precarious. The prince's death, or even his whim, could abruptly end their careers and cost them all their fortune and even their

below right The interior of the Tietz Department Store in Cologne.

A class reunion in 1909.

lives. Thus Joseph Suess Oppenheimer (1698/99–1738), Court Jew and confidential financial adviser to Duke Charles Alexander of Wurttemberg, after serving the duke for five years during which he was, next to his master, the most powerful man in the duchy, was publicly hanged after the death of the duke.

The annexation by Prussia of large parts of Poland (in 1772, 1793, and 1795) brought many Jews under German rule, with the result that the German Jewish movement of Enlightenment, the so-called Haskala, reached directly a much larger number of Jews than it could have within Prussia's old boundaries. The Haskala movement, although it had its antecedents among the Jews of Italy and Holland in the seventeenth century, began in the second half of the eighteenth century with the work of Moses Mendelssohn (1729–86) in Berlin. Its basic tenet was that in order to achieve Emancipation the Jews must acquire intellectual, cultural and social conformity with the Gentile population, and reform, that is, modernise, their religion. All three goals, Enlightenment, religious reform, and Emancipation (which was doled out to German Jews beginning in 1807) were achieved within a few decades of the movement's inception. One outcome, both unforeseen and unwelcomed by the Jewish leadership, was assimilation, in its milder form taking the shape of indifference to and ignorance of Jewish religion, history and values, while in its extreme form leading, despite the most intensive efforts by the leading rabbis of the period, to conversion to Christianity which in the early nineteenth century assumed the dimensions of a mass movement.

Despite the eagerness of many Jews to become 'German citizens of the Jewish faith', anti-Semitism was again on the rise in the early 1800s, nurtured by several factors. There was a reaction to the ideals of equality of the French revolution, a reaction expressed in the conservative concepts of the 'German-Christian' state. There was a rising bitterness at the appearance and increasing visibility of the new 'upstart' class of Jewish financiers, bankers, merchants, and entrepreneurs, and at the heavy indebtedness of the peasants to Jewish livestock traders and money lenders. And there was also considerable direct anti-Semitic agitation by German nationalist politicians. In any case, in 1819, the so-called 'Hep hep riots' broke out all over Germany causing widespread damage before being suppressed by troops.

Jewish reaction to the new anti-Semitism manifested itself in two opposite directions: on the one hand, there was an upsurge of conversions to Christianity (as Heine cynically put it, 'The certificate of baptism was the passport to Europe'), and, on the other, efforts were made to re-cast Judaism into a modern shape. The latter endeavour brought about religious reform aimed at 'liberating' Jews from the 'yoke of the commandments' which had effectively barred Jews from social contact with Gentiles, emphasising instead the spiritual, ethical, and universal-human aspects of Jewish religious teachings, and thereby transforming the traditional 'am Yisrael (people of Israel) into 'Germans of the Mosaic faith'. The aims of reform also included the launching of a scholarly scrutiny of the history of the Jews and Judaism, and especially the history of Jewish religion, of Jewish literature, beginning with the Bible, of Jewish philosophy, and of other aspects of Judaism. In this manner were laid the foundations of the Wissenschaft des Judentums (Science of Judaism) of which Germany became the undisputed centre in the late nineteenth and early twentieth centuries.

A visible expression of German-Jewish interest and leadership in Jewish scholarship was the foundation of three rabbinical seminaries: in 1854 of the Jüdisch-theologisches Seminar in Breslau (representing a liberal-conservative trend) and in 1872 of two schools in Berlin, the Reform Hochschule für die Wissenschaft des Judentums (College for the Science of Judaism) and the Orthodox Rabbinerseminar für das orthodoxe Judentum.

Soon after the full emancipation of the Jews a law was passed in Prussia (in 1876) which permitted individuals to secede from the Jewish community for religious reasons. Thereby the way was opened for the establishment of separate Orthodox congregations by traditional Jews who objected to the modernizing trend of the

above Albert Einstein, the most famous scientist of the modern world. He won the Nobel Prize for Physics in 1921.

Gottlieb Magnus, a marine engineer in the German army; he died in Auschwitz in 1942.

majority. On the other hand, the same law enabled individual Jews who wished to sever all connection between themselves and the Jewish community to do so without formally converting to Christianity. Thus a considerable body of Jews came into being who imposed upon themselves this kind of clandestine self-excommunication, and felt secure in the twilight zone outside all religious affiliation, until Hitler's Nuremberg Laws caught up with them (or their descendants) and forced them back into the ranks of Judaism which they had wished to escape.

While this was happening on the Jewish religious front, the German Jews, whose emancipation had become incorporated into the constitution of the newly-formed German Reich (1869 and 1871), made great strides in all fields of economic, political, social, and cultural life. By the end of the century, they numbered close to 600,000, were a prosperous community, all German-speaking and German-feeling, with more than half of them in commerce, one-fifth in industry and trade, and about 6 per cent in liberal professions and public services. The only positions which remained closed to them, due to the persistence of anti-Semitic prejudices and usages, were officerships in the army, government posts, and full professorships at the universities. On the other hand, the Jewish share in literature, the press, the theatre, the arts, sciences and technology was disproportionately high. Zionism, although it attracted only a minority among the Jews, was a strong and well-organized movement, and after the death of Theodor Herzl (1904), the headquarters of the World Zionist Organization moved from Vienna to Germany (Cologne and Berlin) where it remained until the end of World War I.

Jewish participation in World War I was considerable. Of the 100,000 Jewish soldiers in the German army, 12,000 fell in battle. The brief period of fourteen years between the end of the war and the beginning of Nazi rule in Germany was 'the finest hour' in the history of German Jewry. In the liberal Weimar Republic Jews enjoyed fully equal rights in both theory and practice. Their share in the literary, artistic, scientific, and cultural life of the country increased, and even in government and politics they played a leading role. As an illustration, it can be mentioned that of the sixty Nobel Prizes which went to Germany from 1901 to 1975, sixteen (or 26·6 per cent) were won by Jews. These were also the years of the great flowering of Jewish culture in Germany, which had become a safe haven for Jewish refugees from the east, primarily from Russia. Among them were the foremost Hebrew poets and writers, whose works were published by Hebrew publishing houses. The number of books published in German on Jewish subjects, including Judaism and Zionism, was larger than it had ever been in any non-Jewish language. Zionist and other Jewish educational institutions were active, and German Jewry in general was the most highly cultured Jewish community in the entire Diaspora.

On the eve of World War II, although the Jews constituted less than 1 per cent of the population, as many as 16 per cent of all lawyers were Jews, as were 10 per cent of the doctors and dentists, 17 per cent of the bankers, 25 per cent in the retail trade, 30 per cent in the clothing trade, and 70 per cent in department stores. On the other end of the economic scale, poverty was widespread among the Jews: one-quarter of the Jews of Berlin, for instance, were on charity.

To turn to cultural activity: apart from such early isolated phenomena as the thirteenth-century Jewish *Minnesänger* (minstrel) Süsskind von Trimberg, Jewish participation in German literature began with the Jewish Enlightenment in the eighteenth century. Its initiator, Moses Mendelssohn, was the first modern Jew to write in literary German, and his works made a considerable impact on the German public. The late eighteenth century saw the beginnings of the Jewish salons in Berlin, which became important places of literary gatherings and discussions, and the launching pads of many a distinguished literary career. In the nineteenth century, two names stand out: Heinrich Heine (1797/99–1856) the greatest German lyricist of all time who had himself baptized in 1825 but remained a Jew not only in heart but also in his writings; and the social philosopher who was destined to become the patron saint of Communism, Karl Marx (1819–83), who was baptized by his parents when he was six, studied at German universities and, though from the age of twenty-five he lived in Paris, Brussels and London, wrote in German all his life. In the twentieth century, the number of outstanding German–Jewish authors was so great that the German nationalists could easily demonstrate the *Verjüdung* (judaization) of German literature. There was Paul Heyse (Nobel Prize for literature in 1910), Stefan Zweig, Arnold Zweig, Arthur Schnitzler, Franz Kafka, Jakob Wassermann, Franz Werfel, Karl Kraus, Kurt Tucholsky, Ernst Toller, Alfred Doeblin, Lion Feuchtwanger, Max Brod; and the poets Else Lasker-Schueler and Nelly Sachs (Nobel Prize for literature, 1966).

Modern Jewish philosophy was almost entirely the domain of German Jews, beginning with Moses Mendelssohn and Solomon Maimon in the eighteenth century, Solomon Formstecher, Samuel Hirsch, Solomon Ludwig Steinheim, and Moritz Lazarus in the nineteenth, and Hermann Cohen, Martin Buber, and Franz Rosenzweig in the twentieth. Most of these writers and philosophers lived in Germany, some in other places such as Vienna, Prague or, later, in Palestine-Israel, but all of them wrote in German and were the product of a unique combination of German and Jewish intellectual culture. Equally important was the role of Jews as German critics, literary historians, and historians of philosophy.

The 1920s were the period of intensive integration of the Jews into German life and of the insidious disintegration of German Jewry. On the one hand, one-third or more of all doctors and lawyers in the major cities were Jews and all German Jews, even the most orthodox, felt totally German; on the other, 45 per cent of all Jewish men and women who entered matrimony in 1921–7 married Christians, and every year a thousand Jews converted to Christianity or left the Jewish community without affiliating with another religion. The total number of Jews in Germany, despite the sizeable Jewish immigration from the east, diminished from 615,000 in 1910 to 564,000 in 1925. The extent of defection from the ranks of Jewry, and the magnitude of demographic loss sustained by it became evident with the passing of the Nuremberg Laws of 1935 which deprived all Jews and persons of partly Jewish descent of German citizenship: the number of Jews in Germany at the time had further diminished to 503,000, but more than two million were stigmatized as 'non-Aryans', which drove many ex-Jews to utter despair and even suicide.

The tragedy of being thoroughly assimilated into a culture and a society, of considering oneself an integral part of it, and of contributing to it significantly, and then being suddenly excluded from it and stigmatized as a parasitic and inferior alien, an evil subhuman being who does not deserve to live, is too great to be expressed in words. The 'German citizens of Jewish faith' were designated 'Jews in Germany', forbidden even to term themselves 'German Jews'. Emigration of Jews from Germany began in 1933, but it was hampered by the reluctance of all countries to receive them. The largest number of German Jews admitted to any single country in the crucial years from 1933 to 1939 when escape was still possible was 63,000 – this was the number of those who were allowed into the United States. The British let 55,000 into Palestine and 40,000 into Great Britain. All the countries of the world accepted some 315,000 German Jews in those six fateful years, leaving 214,000 to wait in Germany for their deportation and extermination.

The remarkable thing was that, while all or most of the German Jews tried to escape, they had enough spirit left to engage simultaneously in intensive Jewish social and cultural activities. Zionist work expanded, schools were opened for trades and languages (in preparation for emigration), adult education flourished, agricultural training centres were founded, the readership of the Jewish press increased dramatically, a Jewish cultural union was organized – in brief, for the first time since the beginnings of the Enlightenment, the German Jews lived a full Jewish life while the shadow of death was falling upon them.

above The champion long-distance swimmer, Leo Ledermann, who swam the English Channel in 1895.

Max Lieberman, celebrated painter of portraits and landscapes. In 1920 he became president of the Berlin Academy of Art – a position he lost when the Nazis came to power.

Czechoslovakia

A deal between a Jew and a Huzul in Carpatho-Russia, a region which
formed part of Czechoslovakia after World War I.

The state of Czechoslovakia as it exists today came into being after World War I
when territories formerly under Austrian and Hungarian rule were detached by
the victorious allies from the Habsburg Empire and recognized as the independent
Czechoslovak republic. Thus the so-called 'Historic Lands' of Bohemia, Moravia
and part of Silesia which were under Austrian rule, and Slovakia and Carpatho-
Russia (or Sub-Carpathian Ruthenia), which were parts of Hungary, came to form a
new country in which two closely related Slavic tongues, Czech, spoken in the
west, and Slovak, spoken in the east, became the official languages.

Until 1918, the history of the Jews in Bohemia, Moravia, and Silesia was part of
the history of Austrian Jews, while the Jews of Slovakia and Carpatho-Russia
shared their history with the Jews of Hungary and Transylvania. In the Historic
Lands, German was the prevalent language of the Jews, although after the
independence of Czechoslovakia more and more Jews spoke Czech; in Slovakia
and Carpatho-Russia they spoke Yiddish and Hungarian.

After the establishment of the Czechoslovak republic its Jewish community was

A Hasid and a young Jewish farmer
in Carpatho-Russia *c*. 1930.

recognized as a national minority in accordance with the minority treaty signed by Czechoslovakia at the Versailles Peace Conference in 1919. The two decades that elapsed between independence and the outbreak of World War II were too short a period to enable a common cultural basis to develop between the disparate Jewish elements of the new state. Apart from the religio-cultural differences which existed between the Jews of the eastern and the western parts of Czechoslovakia in general, the Jews of Carpatho-Russia were exceptional in that two-thirds of them lived in villages (in 1930) – the highest proportion of rural Jews in any European country. The Jewish communities of Slovakia, and especially those of its western part which adjoined Moravia, bore a greater resemblance to the Moravian communities their ancestors had come from several centuries earlier.

The Jewish community of Bratislava (Hungarian Pozsony, German Pressburg), the capital city of Slovakia, was one of the oldest and most important Jewish centres in Central Europe. Since, among the Jews, the city was always known as Pressburg, we shall refer to it by that name. From the eighteenth century on

above Two members of the Jewish Central Milk Co-operative in Bilka, 1925.

left A dry-goods merchant in Carpatho-Russia in the 1930s.

top A Jew in Munkács (Mukachevo) in Carpatho-Russia.

Pressburg served as the meeting place for Hungarian Jews; in the early twentieth century, both the Hungarian Zionist Organization (in 1902) and the World Mizrahi Organization (in 1904) were founded there.

The proximity of Pressburg to Vienna made it a favoured dwelling place for Court Jews whose business took them frequently to the Viennese imperial court. The most outstanding among them was Koppel Theben (d. 1799), who represented Jewish interests energetically and successfully *vis-à-vis* the emperor and the Hungarian magnates and authorities.

Under Rabbi Moses Sofer (1763–1839), who was rabbi of the Pressburg community and the leading Talmudic authority of his age, the 'Pressburger Yeshiva', founded in the fifteenth century, became the foremost institution of Jewish learning (with 400 students at its peak period), and the city a centre of Orthodoxy for the whole of European Jewry. The Sofer dynasty, which for four generations served as rabbis of Pressburg from 1807 to 1940, was largely responsible for preventing Jewish religious reform from having more than limited response in Austria and Hungary. Not until 1872 was a Neolog congregation (similar in religious orientation to the Conservative trend in America) founded in Pressburg. The city became the seat of the Orthodox provincial office, which later put up a bitter fight against Zionism, and also the centre of the *Agudat Israel* of Czechoslovakia.

In the inter-war years both the large Orthodox and the smaller Neolog congregations maintained numerous educational, charitable, and social institutions, and twenty synagogues. The Jews of Pressburg, although they numbered only 15,000 in 1930, had a surprisingly large number of associations and club-like organizations, each dedicated to one particular purpose. They were either charitable (such as supplying kosher food for Jewish patients in hospitals, aiding poor women, providing dowries for poor girls, helping poor bed-ridden patients and poor mourners, providing for the needs of poor Jews in the winter, supplying them with wood and coal, distributing cash and clothing, supporting poor pupils), or else cultural-religious (such as the *Hevras HaShaS* which held Talmudic lectures every evening; the *Toras Hesed* in which Talmudic scholars lectured every day; the *Mehadre haTalmud*, whose members studied in their homes various tractates of the Talmud and gathered for an annual joint *siyyum*, that is, 'conclusion' of their studies; numerous other such societies which held lectures on Biblical subjects every evening). Thus the Jews of Pressburg lived an intensive Jewish religious and intellectual life which was not surpassed by any other Jewish community. Pressburg was also an important centre of Hebrew printing from 1789.

Early during the Nazi rule (1939–45) many 'illegal' transports of immigrants to Palestine were organized in Pressburg. Almost all those who remained in the city were deported by the Nazis and killed. After the liberation, Pressburg became the centre of forty-two reconstituted Jewish communities of Slovakia, and a semblance of the pre-war Jewish life began to be rebuilt. However, with the establishment of the Communist regime in 1948 these attempts had to be given up and most of the remaining Jews emigrated.

The intensive, almost exclusive, Jewishness of the Pressburg community contrasted sharply with the highly Europeanized cultural atmosphere which pervaded the Jewish community of Prague, the old historic capital of Bohemia, and, from 1919, that of Czechoslovakia. Of all the Czechoslovak Jewish communities the most important by far was unquestionably that of Prague. By the time the *Altneuschul* (Old-New Synagogue) – the oldest extant synagogue in Europe – was completed in 1270, the Jewish community of Prague was several hundred years old, and boasted of generations of outstanding halakhists who had their rabbinical seat in the city.

The trials which the Prague Jews had to endure in the course of the centuries were nothing exceptional in European Jewish history. The Jews were repeatedly attacked, pillaged, expelled, allowed to return. Of the numerous anti-Jewish

above Hasidic Jews in the town of Munkács.

right A square in the Jewish quarter in Prague, *c.* 1900.

measures directed against them, the so-called Familiants Laws of Charles VI, issued in 1726–7, were particularly oppressive and painful, given the traditional value put by Jewish religion on early marriage. These laws set a fixed limit on the number of Jewish families in Bohemia (8,451), Moravia (5,106), and Silesia (119), which meant that a Jew could marry, and thus found a new family, only upon the death of his father, and that a younger brother could marry only if his elder brother died. These measures forced many Jews to marry in secret, in which case their children were considered illegitimate by the government, and had to bear their mothers' names, and the offending father was severely punished by flogging and expulsion. Many young men, and especially younger sons, chose emigration, and became the founders of new communities, mostly in Slovakia which was under Hungarian rule and in which the Austrian Familiants Laws did not apply.

Of all the great Jewish historic personalities of Prague none became more of a legend than Rabbi Judah Loew ben Bezalel (*c.* 1525–1609), whose impressive statue (the work of a Gentile sculptor) adorns the entrance of the Prague town hall to this day. It shows a tall, severe figure of a man with a high cylindrical hat and a long, flowing beard, fending off with his raised left arm a naked woman clinging to him. Rabbi Judah Loew, known as *'der hohe Rabbi Loew'* (The High Rabbi Loew), spent most of his life in Prague, where he was teacher, rabbi, and chief rabbi. He was a

great scholar, outstanding not only in the traditional Jewish studies, including the Kabbala, but also in the secular sciences, especially mathematics. The astronomer Tycho Brahe was his friend and it seems that he had contact also with the Emperor Rudolph II, perhaps on account of their joint interest in alchemy. He was a prolific writer who dealt with a wide range of halakhic, exegetic, and ethical subjects. His fame in later generations, however, was due not to his writings but to the legend that he was the creator of the famous Prague Golem, a clay figure of a man which he allegedly made and brought to life with the help of a magic name of God. The legend has it that Rabbi Loew's purpose in making the Golem was to use him as a servant, and, according to one version, to have him defend the Jews; but then the Golem ran amok and the rabbi was forced to destroy him by removing the magic name from under his tongue.

Towards the end of the nineteenth century Prague developed into one of the most important centres of Jewish literary and intellectual activity. The language which the Prague Jews spoke and in which they created works of great significance was primarily German, and secondarily Czech. The German 'Prague circle' of Jewish authors comprised many who achieved international renown, including Franz Kafka, Max Brod, Franz Werfel, Oskar Baum, Leo Perutz, Egon Erwin Kisch, Willy Haas. These authors made Prague a German literary centre rivalling Berlin and Vienna. The group of Jewish authors who wrote in Czech remained less known, because of the language barrier, but it too included important figures such as the poet Siegfried Kapper, the novelist Eduard Leda (Lederer), the humourist Vojtech Rakous (Oesterreicher), the philosopher Jindrich Kohn, the brothers Frantisek and Jiri Langer. There were also a few Jewish writers who contributed to Slovak literature, and published Slovak translations from the Yiddish. Almost none of the writings of these authors is available in translations in any of the major European languages. As in other European centres in which Jews played an important role, in Prague too Jewish participation in the cultural life of the city extended also to various sciences, philosophy, music (Gustav Mahler spent several years in Prague as a conductor), the theatre (both German and Czech), political life and journalism.

Although from 1900 on the majority of the Prague Jews declared themselves to be Czech (in 1930, 55 per cent as against 18 per cent who declared themselves German, and 27 per cent who declared themselves Jews), the attraction of German culture remained much stronger for them than that of Czech culture. In addition to the literary scene, this could be seen from the fact that in 1925 30 per cent of the students of the German university in Prague were Jews, while their number among the students of the Czech university was less than 10 per cent. Of course, considering that the 35,000 Jews of Prague (in 1930) constituted little more than 4 per cent of the total population of the city, both proportions were quite high.

The total number of Jews in Czechoslovakia in 1930 was 357,000, of whom 137,000 lived in Slovakia, 103,000 in Carpatho-Russia, 76,000 in Bohemia, and 41,000 in Moravia-Silesia. Characteristic of the strong Jewish consciousness of the Czechoslovak Jews as a whole was that 57 per cent of them declared their nationality as Jewish. In the same census (1930), 25 per cent declared themselves as being Czechoslovak, 12 per cent as German, 5 per cent as Hungarian, and 1 per cent as other.

Jewish emigration began immediately after the annexation of the Sudetenland (the westernmost belt of Bohemia) by Nazi Germany, with some 15,000 Jews leaving the country for Palestine either legally or with 'illegal' transports. By October 1941, when emigration was banned, a total of 27,000 had succeeded in escaping. Between November of that year and March 1945, 277,000 Czechoslovak Jews became victims of the Nazi holocaust. On the day Czechoslovak national sovereignty was restored in Prague (5 May 1945), only 2,800 Jews were alive in Bohemia and Moravia. In 1948 when the Communists came to power, the total number of Jews in Czechoslovakia was about 55,000. Emigration to Israel and other countries again reduced this number to 18,000 by 1950, and to about 12,000 by 1968.

Hungary

The chief rabbi of Pressburg blesses King Karl IV and Queen Zita of Hungary, 1918.

Inscriptions on Jewish tombstones and sarcophagi found in various Roman settlements in Hungary, including Aquincum on the outskirts of present-day Budapest, testify to the presence of Jews in what was then the Roman province of Pannonia from the early third century CE at the latest. Then follows the usual lacuna of the post-Roman age – usual, that is, for early Jewish history – which ends only well after the conquest of Hungary by the Magyars which took place in 897.

The first Medieval documentary evidence pertaining to the Jews in Hungary clearly indicates that by the eleventh century they must have been present in considerable numbers to prompt the issuance of anti-Jewish regulations. In 1092, less than a century after the Hungarians had converted to Christianity, the council of Szabolcs forbade the Jews to marry Christians, to work on Sundays and Christian holidays, or to own Christian slaves. In the twelfth to fourteenth centuries, repeated decrees limiting the rights of the Jews to hold governmental and fiscal office and own landed property alternated with letters patent which assured them of equal rights with the Christian Hungarians. In 1360 the Jews were expelled from the country altogether, but financial exigencies led to their recall within four years. In 1365, Louis the Great (1342–82) created a special office headed by the 'Judge of the Jews', who was elected from among Hungarian

(Christian) nobility, and entrusted with the task of collecting the taxes from the Jews, watching over their privileges, and dealing with their complaints. In general, the king and the nobles (who in many parts of the country were virtually autonomous rulers) tolerated and protected the Jews as long as they found them financially useful. Thus King Sigmund (1387–1437) admitted the Jews expelled from Austria in 1421, but five years later annulled all the debts the city of Pozsony (Pressburg, modern Bratislava) owed the Jews.

When the Hungarian Renaissance king Matthias Corvinus (r. 1458–90) ascended the throne, he abolished the office of the 'Judge of the Jews', and appointed instead a Jew to serve as *praefectus Judaeorum*; on the other hand, he too annulled the debts several cities owed the Jews. His successor, Vladislav (Ulászló) Jagellon of Bohemia, imprisoned Jews in Pressburg and set them free only after they paid him a ransom of 400 guilders, and allowed fourteen Jews of Nagyszombat (Tyrnau, Trnava, today in Czechoslovakia), against whom a blood-accusation was levelled, to be burnt to death in 1494. In order to protect the interests of his treasury he forced the city of Sopron (Odenburg) to cancel the taxes it had imposed upon the Jews, but then in 1503 he annulled the debts owed to the Jews all over Hungary. While a few individual Jews reached high positions in the early sixteenth century – one was the director of the royal mint, another (a converted Jew) was royal treasurer – the financial operations of these men only increased the people's hatred of the Jews which expressed itself in attacks and plunder (e.g., in Buda).

The defeat of the Hungarians by the Turks in 1526 was blamed on the Jews, who were consequently expelled from several cities which remained in Hungarian control. Many Jews were captured and released only against the payment of exorbitant ransom. The wearing of a yellow badge was made obligatory (1551). As a result many Jews sought and found refuge in Buda and in other places in the central part of Hungary which remained under Turkish rule until 1686. In 1670, Count Eszterházy admitted the Jews expelled from Vienna into the cities which were part of his huge estates in western Hungary. The so-called 'seven communities' of Burgenland, which absorbed this Jewish influx, gained considerable importance and remained centres of Jewish life until the holocaust. The defeat of the Turks was followed by a renewed wave of persecution of the Jews, who were expelled from the royal cities (including Buda), excluded from the guilds, and confined to hawking and money lending.

That the number of Jews in Hungary grew despite these conditions was due to the fact that in neighbouring countries their situation was even worse. In Austria, for instance, the laws in force in the first half of the eighteenth century severely limited the number of Jews allowed to marry, which resulted in a migration of Austrian Jews to Hungary where this law did not apply. Many Jews also came from Poland, among them rabbis and scholars of renown who developed the cities of Pressburg and Eisenstadt into important centres of Jewish learning. According to a 1735 head count, there were at that time 11,621 Jews in Hungary.

In 1744 the empress Maria Theresa (r. 1740–80) introduced the collective 'tolerance tax', which bitter Jewish humour termed 'Malke geld', i.e., 'queen money', and which was increased gradually (from 20,000 to 160,000 guilders), until the Jews were financially squeezed dry. Under her son, Joseph II (r. 1780–90), the situation of the Jews improved. This enlightened monarch set about making the Jews useful citizens of the state; he insisted upon such external signs of assimilation as the cutting off of their beards and sidelocks; decreed that they

בית המדרש
הגדול דפאקש זצ"ל

Students of the Talmudic
academy, Paks Yeshiva, in 1915.

must speak the language of the country and assume family names; and eased the
Jewish tax burden. His 1783 decree opened most of the cities to Jewish settlement,
allowed the Jews to found primary schools, and gave them the right to study. Within
a few years the first Jewish MD graduated from the University of Buda.

The death of Joseph II was followed by a reaction but the Jews, emboldened by
the first taste of freedom and prompted by the ideas of the Haskala, began to
bombard the Hungarian Diet and the king-emperor with petitions for various
rights, including full Emancipation. Gradually a liberal trend made itself felt in the
Hungarian governmental and parliamentary circles, and more and more rights
were actually granted to the Jews.

By 1840 the number of Jews in Hungary had grown to 200,000 and their
penetration into the scientific, medical, and economic life of the country was well
on the way. In 1844 the Jews of Pest (later part of Budapest) founded a
'Magyarizing Society' which maintained a Hungarian kindergarten and a
Hungarian-language school, and played an important role in the publication of a
Hungarian-Jewish periodical, a calendar (1848), a translation of the prayer book in
Hungarian, etc. As the Hungarian *Jewish Lexicon*, published in Budapest in 1929,
states, 'By 1867, when the nation pronounced the Emancipation of Jewry, its new
generation was totally Hungarian not only in its feelings, but also in its language.'
From 1840 to 1848 an impressive number of books was published by Hungarian
Jews in Hungarian, about Jews, Judaism, equal rights, Emancipation, Jewish

apologetics, and patriotism. A typical example was an 1848 book entitled *We Won't Go to America, But Shall Stay Home!* Liberal rabbis, such as Leopold Löw in Szeged and Aaron Chorin in Arad, began to preach in Hungarian, and placed themselves at the head of the struggle for Emancipation.

The Hungarian uprising of 1848 against the Austrian rule had the enthusiastic support of the Hungarian Jews, who enlisted in the revolutionary forces in numbers far surpassing their proportion in the population. Ironically, at the same time mobs inflamed by the fire of rebellion engaged in Jew-baiting in Pest and Pressburg. When the revolution was put down by the superior Austrian forces in 1849, the Jews of Hungary were fined 2,300,000 guilders for their part in it. The fine was subsequently reduced to 1,000,000 and the money was actually used in 1856 to set up a fund for the establishment of a rabbinical seminary – which is still

left Ignaz Goldziher (1850–1921), Hungarian Jewish Islamologist of world renown.

far left Mrs Goldziher and her two sons.

functioning in 1980 as a Hungarian state school – and other Jewish educational and charitable institutions.

In the eighteen years of absolute Austrian rule (1849–67) the position of the Jews gradually improved and they inched their way towards full Emancipation, which was granted by the Hungarian Parliament in 1867, the same year in which Austria and Hungary reached a 'Compromise'. Emperor Francis Joseph I of Austria was crowned king of Hungary, and the Austro-Hungarian dual monarchy, which was to survive until the end of World War I, was established. By 1869, the number of Jews in Hungary had greatly increased, due to both natural increase and the inflow of immigrants, especially from Galicia (then part of Austria), so that the census carried out that year enumerated no fewer than 542,000 Jewish inhabitants.

The same year witnessed the country-wide organization of Hungarian Jewry. The Jewish congress, convoked at the initiative of Baron Joseph Eötvös, Hungarian minister of culture, resulted in the setting up of a union of Jewish congregations in which the liberals (corresponding in religious orientation to the Conservative wing of American Judaism) were in the majority. Dissatisfaction among the more tradition-minded led in 1871 to the organization of a second union, that of the Orthodox congregations. Those remaining congregations for whom the Neolog trend was too liberal, while the Orthodox was too observant, remained outside both unions and became known as the Status Quo congregations.

Thus, until the very end, Hungarian Jewry was officially organized into three separate religious bodies.

After Emancipation there followed decades during which Hungarian Jews of all the three persuasions threw themselves into the economic, political, social, cultural, literary, and artistic life of the country. They were soon among the leaders in all endeavours, and felt as Hungarian as the oldest Magyar elements, and as far as patriotic feelings were concerned – a most conspicuous feature in the Hungarian national character – they even outdid them. They flocked to high schools and universities, especially in the capital, Budapest, where, in 1910, the Jews constituted more than half of all medical students and physicians and almost half among students of the technical college and among lawyers and journalists. They had no less a share in literature, music, the arts; they were leaders in the process of industrialization which reached Hungary belatedly in the second half of the nineteenth century; and they achieved high positions in the government, the municipalities, and even in the army. In recognition of their services to the country, the king, on the recommendation of his government, ennobled hundreds of Jews, made dozens of them barons, and awarded the titles 'royal councillor' or 'court councillor' to many others. Total assimilation into Magyardom was so irresistible to these Jewish nobles and councillors that many of them converted to Christianity. The Hungarian Jews' complete identification with the society and culture of the Christian majority which, in no small measure, they helped shape, and, more than that, with its thinking and feeling, had no parallel in any other European country.

However, the love-affair – there is no better name for it – between the Jews and Hungary was not, could not be, entirely undisturbed. Anti-Semitic outbreaks began in the 1880s, and in 1882–3 a blood-libel took place in Tiszaeszlár which, although it ended with the acquittal of the accused Jews, triggered anti-Semitic manifestations even years later. On the other side of the balance was the legal recognition of Judaism in 1895 as an 'accepted' religion, enjoying the same status as the other (Catholic and Protestant) denominations. This meant that not only the individual Jew but Jewish religion as a whole was given full and equal rights.

Little wonder that in this super-patriotic atmosphere Zionism could barely strike roots. Although both Theodor Herzl (1860–1904), the creator of modern political Zionism, and his first lieutenant, Max Nordau (1849–1923), were born and spent their youth in Budapest, Herzl until he was eighteen, Nordau until he was thirty; although the man who introduced Herzl to the Turkish Sultan was a Hungarian ex-Jew, Arminius Vámbéry; and although a Zionist organization was founded in Hungary as early as in 1897 – only a very small minority of Hungarian Jews joined the movement which was opposed by the majority and especially by the official Hungarian Jewish organizations. Herzl himself considered Hungarian Jews 'a withered branch on the tree of Jewry'. Feelings among Hungarian Jews against the handful of Zionists among them often ran high.

But, to return to an earlier period, in World War I, as in the revolutionary struggle of 1848–9, the Jews had a share much greater than their numerical proportion in the population. Ten thousand Hungarian Jews fell on the battlefields. After the war, which ended not only with the defeat of Hungary (one of the Central Powers) but with the loss of two-thirds of the country's territory, and especially after the short-lived Communist regime of 1919 headed by Béla Kun, himself a Jew, anti-Semitism boiled over for a while and continued to simmer thereafter. With the inauguration of the new government under Adm. Nicholas Horthy as regent in 1919, the ultra-nationalists who called themselves 'Awakening Hungarians', embarked upon a series of anti-Jewish excesses known as the 'White Terror' which cost 3,000 Jews their lives. Sporadic attacks continued until 1923, and in 1920 the law of *numerus clausus* was introduced which provided that, since the Jews constituted 5 per cent of the total population, their proportion among the university students must not exceed that percentage.

Although all this came as a terrible shock for the Jews, their sentimental

The Jewish Béla Kun (left), head of the short-lived 'People's Republic' communist dictatorship in Hungary in 1919.

commitment to Hungarian patriotism weakened neither within the reduced boundaries of Hungary nor in the territories annexed by Czechoslovakia, Rumania, and Yugoslavia, where the Jews remained more Hungarian than the Christian Magyars. In Hungary itself, the Jews took solace in such sops as the law of 1928 which gave them, as a religious denomination, representation in the Upper House of the parliament: a Neolog rabbi became the representative of the Neolog Jewry, and an Orthodox one the delegate of the Orthodox Jews. While Zionist activities were brought to a standstill after the war, from 1927 on the Zionist organization was again allowed to function, although most Hungarian Jews and the official Hungarian Jewish bodies did not support it. At the same time, in order to create an organization through which those Jews unwilling to commit themselves politically to Zionism would be able to participate in the upbuilding of the *Yishuv* and further its cultural development, Joseph Patai took the initiative of organizing the 'Pro-Palestine Union of Hungarian Jews', with Baron Adolf Kohner and other leading Jews in the praesidium.

Latent Hungarian anti-Semitism became again virulent with the rise of Nazism in Germany. Anti-Jewish laws were passed in 1938 and 1939 restricting Jewish economic and professional activities and political rights, and cutting off more than one half (or 250,000) of all Jews in Hungary from their sources of livelihood. Jewish reaction to this turn of events was mixed. While thousands converted to Christianity, other thousands returned to Jewish values or joined the Zionist movement. Many made their ʿaliya to Palestine.

Despite the painful and occasionally bloody rebuffs the Jews suffered at the hand of Hungarian anti-Semites, the first third of the twentieth century saw the most intensive participation of Jews in Hungarian literary and artistic life. The *Encyclopaedia Judaica* (1972) contains the biographies of no less than ninety Hungarian-Jewish novelists, poets, playwrights, critics, journalists, and editors, as against 120 German-Jewish authors who lived in the same period in Germany, Austria, Switzerland and Czechoslovakia, a much larger language area with twice as many Jews. In no other country was the share of Jewish authors in the national literature as great as in Hungary. They also dominated the theatre and the press. With one or two exceptions, all the editors and contributors of *Nyugat* ('West'), the most influential modern Hungarian literary magazine (launched in 1907), were Jews. Many of the painters and the performing artists on the concert stage, in the opera and in the legitimate theatre were Jews. An extremely high proportion of the patrons of literature and the arts were Jews, and it was primarily Jews who filled the auditoriums of the theatre, the opera, and the concert halls.

The tragedy of Hungarian Jews was that the great majority completely identified itself with Magyardom, not only in political outlook and socially and culturally, but also emotionally, in the fullest and deepest sense, to the extent of turning away from Judaism and from any contact with local or international Jewish bodies. Since the Hungarians were great patriots, the Jews felt an urge to manifest an even more fervid Magyar patriotism, which feeling was engendered and fostered during the fifty years of Hungarian liberalism from the Emancipation of the Jews to the end of World War I. The greater was the shock and, for many, the tragedy after World War I, and even more inevitably on the eve of World War II, when they were forced to recognize that they had been living in a fools' paradise, and that they were considered strangers, unwanted and hated aliens, by the Hungarian Government and people alike. After a period of increasingly painful and danger-fraught existence in the twilight years of Armageddon, the physical annihilation by the German and Hungarian Nazis of four-fifths of Hungarian Jewry in the very last year of the war was but the death of a body that still sheltered a mortally wounded soul.

Part Three
Western and Southern Europe
Sephardi Pride and Prejudice

Ya῾akov Meir, chief rabbi of Salonika, *c.* 1913.

The Netherlands

A Jewish family celebration in Amsterdam.

Following sporadic indications of Jewish presence in earlier centuries, the history proper of the Jews in the Netherlands begins with the arrival in Amsterdam of Portuguese Marranos (crypto-Jews) about 1590. This followed the 1579 Union of Utrecht which gave complete religious freedom to all inhabitants of Holland. In 1619, when the provinces of Holland and West Vriesland decided to let each city adopt its own policy toward the Jews, there were already in existence Jewish communities in several Dutch cities. Holland thus became one of the very few countries in the world where the Jews never experienced persecutions – until the Nazi occupation, that is – and the first to free them from all legal disabilities. This was one of the three great attractions the Netherlands held for the Marranos. The second comprised the great economic opportunities available to all inhabitants of the country which in the seventeenth century became the foremost commercial state and maritime power in the world. And the third was the cultural flowering which accompanied the material prosperity.

The Portuguese Marranos participated intensively in all Dutch activities, cultural endeavours, international commerce, and overseas colonization. Their interests had always embraced both Jewish and secular culture. They had experience in maritime trade, and for them to settle in a new country, even if located in a different hemisphere, was not strange. Together with these abilities and inclinations they had also brought to Holland their Spanish or Portuguese mother tongue which they continued to cultivate, and their *grandeza* which made Jew and Gentile alike relate to them with respect.

Before long, the Dutch Sephardim, although their number was never to become large, rivalled in cultural attainments those of their ancestors in the Golden Age of Spain. There were among them outstanding statesmen, physicians, surgeons, and pharmacists. Many of them were artists, illuminators and engravers, poets and playwrights in Spanish and Portuguese. Others were gem merchants, wholesale traders, brokers. They established various industries. They took an active part in the stock market and the export trade. They led in the establishment of commercial relations with the Barbary States of North Africa, and with Turkey which at that time dominated the entire eastern Mediterranean. They owned one quarter of the shares in the Dutch East India Company, took part in setting up the Dutch West India Company, and settled in large numbers in Brazil whose north-eastern parts were under Dutch control from 1624 to 1654. By 1640, fully one half of the civilian European population of Dutch Brazil was Jewish. The first twenty-three Jews to arrive in New Amsterdam (later New York) in 1654 were Dutch Sephardim who fled from Portuguese reprisals in Brazil.

The two greatest figures among the seventeenth-century Dutch Jews were Manasseh ben Israel (1604–57), the learned statesman, who was instrumental in obtaining the re-admission of Jews to England, and Baruch Spinoza (1632–77) who is generally recognized as one of the greatest, if not *the* greatest, of modern philosophers, and whose influence on Western thought continues undiminished to this day.

Equally remarkable is the achievement of the Dutch Sephardim in Jewish studies. Within a generation they transformed themselves from Marranos, most of whom were totally ignorant of Hebrew, into Jewish scholars who founded, and taught in, Yeshivot, who wrote important Hebrew books on literature, theology, and other scholarly subjects, and who made Holland into the foremost centre of Hebrew printing and of Jewish life in general in the whole of Western Europe. Characteristic of the high cultural attainments of the Dutch Sephardim and of their broad view of Jewish education was that in their Amsterdam Talmud Tora school Hebrew grammar and poetry were included in the curriculum, and in the upper grades only Hebrew was spoken. Its graduates became rabbis in many Sephardi congregations in Western Europe and the Mediterranean countries, and achieved renown as Hebrew writers and poets. It was in keeping with the intensity of their Jewish feelings that one of the European Jewish communities, in which the reaction to Shabbatai Zevi's appearance was most enthusiastic, was that of the Dutch Jews.

The early seventeenth century marked the beginning of the decline of the Dutch Sephardim. In 1620, barely one generation after the arrival of the first Sephardim, began the immigration of German Jews from the Rhineland and South Germany. In 1648–9, after the Chmielnicki massacres, and in 1655, after the Swedish invasion of Poland, came the impoverished Polish Jewish refugees in much larger numbers. In 1673, a municipal ordinance of Amsterdam forced the German and Polish Jews to unite into one congregation. Although these Ashkenazi Jews remained in a subservient position until the end of the seventeenth century, they quickly outnumbered the Sephardim who gradually lost influence and had to find consolation in their communal and genealogical pride. By 1780, of the 30,000 Jews in Holland, only 3,000, or 10 per cent, were Sephardim, and although their number increased to over 6,000 by the early twentieth century, the increase of the Ashkenazim was much greater, so that the proportion of the Sephardim was reduced to a mere 6 per cent.

In contrast to the Sephardim, the Yiddish-speaking Ashkenazim were poor (although there were a few rich families among them), and, as in other Ashkenazi communities, they eked out a meagre livelihood as peddlers, butchers, cattle dealers, diamond workers, printers, dealers in second-hand goods, foodstuffs, and the like. Their intellectual horizon remained confined to traditional Jewish studies. Still, in 1795, they participated in the founding of the patriotic *Felix Libertate* society which strove for full civil rights for the Jews. In 1796 the Batavian National Assembly proclaimed their complete emancipation.

However, after the French conquest of the Netherlands (1794) the Dutch Jews became impoverished, and in 1799 no less than 54 per cent of the Sephardim and 87 per cent of the Ashkenazim in Amsterdam were on relief.

In the early nineteenth century the Dutch Jews were especially hard hit by the decline of the economic conditions in the Netherlands. By 1849 the proportion of the Portuguese paupers in Amsterdam exceeded that of the Ashkenazim: 63 per cent of the former, as against 55 per cent of the latter subsisted on Jewish dole. The situation improved in the second half of the century when the development of the diamond industry (in Amsterdam), and the rise of cotton mills (in eastern Holland) led to an increase in the average income of the Jews, and Dutch Jewry became more urbanized. A law of 1857 made education in public schools obligatory, and this in

A family in Amsterdam in front of their *sukka*, the temporary booth used during the Feast of Tabernacles.

turn resulted in the gradual replacement of the old Jewish tongues (Portuguese, Ladino and Yiddish) by Dutch, energetically promoted by many leaders of the Ashkenazi community.

By the late nineteenth century the integration of Dutch Jews into Dutch life was complete, and their participation in all aspects of Dutch culture was remarkable. The leader of Dutch painters was Jozef Israels (1824–1911), many of whose finest canvases deal with Jewish subjects. The jurist Tobias M.C. Asser (1838–1913), a scion of an old Jewish family of lawyers and public workers, won the Nobel Peace Prize in 1911. Among the outstanding Dutch writers was Israel Querido (1872–1932) whose novels and plays deal with Biblical themes or depict the life of the workers and of the Sephardim in Amsterdam. His younger contemporary, Carry van Bruggen (1881–1932) presented in her novels the joys and sorrows of the religious family in which she grew up, and also wrote philosophical studies. The bibliographer and historian Sigmund Seligmann (1873–1940) founded the Society for the Science of Judaism in the Netherlands. Others excelled as historians and scientists. The communal consciousness among the Dutch Jews was strong, and they maintained a large number of public institutions, such as hospitals, clinics, homes for invalids and the mentally disturbed, orphanages, old peoples' homes, and charities for the support of the poor.

Houses in the Jewish quarter of Amsterdam.

The Jewish section in Amsterdam on a Sunday morning.

Jews took an active part also in Dutch economic and political life. They were among the industrialists, bankers, financiers, statesmen, and representatives in international forums. Although their number never reached even 1 per cent of the total population of the country, their share in all these fields was much greater, due to their concentration in the major cities and the attraction these occupations had for them. On the eve of the German occupation of Holland the 100,000 Dutch Jews owned no less than 22,000 businesses.

Urbanization, increasing prosperity, the acquisition of the language of the country, and intensifying contact with the Dutch population were among the factors which made for an increase in inter-marriages, and a decreasing birthrate, which all but wiped out whatever demographic gain would have accrued to Dutch Jewry due to immigration from the east. These trends could not be counteracted by the relatively small Orthodox wing, although the strongly Orthodox character of the *kehillot*, the Jewish congregations, was maintained. Zionism became a factor in Dutch Jewish life only in the early twentieth century, but encountered the opposition of most Dutch rabbis. During and after World War I, under the influence of the many refugees who came from Belgium to Holland, the Zionist movement gained, Zionist youth groups were organized, a Zionist press was established, modern Hebrew studies were introduced, and Holland became the base for the training of East European *halutz* youth. When the Nazis rose to power in neighbouring Germany, a steady stream of refugees reached Holland, and the Zionist leadership became a foremost factor in Jewish community life.

In the inter-war years Dutch Jews suffered, like the much larger Jewish community across the German border, from the effects of assimilation. Having enjoyed for more than a century equal rights, a relative prosperity, and an open attitude on the part of the friendly Dutch people, many of the Jews lost all consciousness of Jewish peoplehood, and considered themselves purely a religious denomination. On the eve of Hitler's rise to power the modal personality of the Dutch Jew presented a picture of staid solidity, of identification with the Gentile majority and its interests, with a no more than marginal concern for Jewish affairs, expressed mainly in works of charity. With the appearance of Nazism all this underwent a radical, even traumatic, change.

A group of Jewish soldiers in the Dutch army during World War I.

In the six years from 1933, when Hitler took control of Germany, to 1939 when World War II began, the life of Dutch Jewry stood in the shadow of Nazism and the impending doom it spelled for Jews. In 1933, when German Jewish refugees began to arrive, a Committee for Special Jewish Affairs was established by Dutch Jewish leaders. Its major task was to provide for the Jewish refugees who, by 1939, numbered 30,000, while the number of the Dutch Jews was at the time 110,000. In 1939, the refugees who crossed into Holland illegally from Germany were placed by the Dutch government in a camp at Westerbork, with the financial burden falling on Dutch Jewry. The Committee also facilitated the absorption of the refugees and aided their emigration to other countries. These great tasks absorbed much of the energies of Dutch Jewry in the pre-war years, and strengthened its Jewish consciousness.

Holland capitulated to Germany on 14 May 1940, and a few months later the Germans began to introduce their anti-Jewish measures. Of the 106,000 Jews transported from Holland to death camps only some 5,000 survived. Of the 22,000 Jews who were hidden by friendly Dutch Gentiles, at great risk to themselves, about 10,000 survived. Among those helped by the Gentiles to hide in Amsterdam was Anne Frank (1929–45); an act of betrayal led to her discovery, deportation, and death. All of the 10,000 Jews who were married to non-Jews survived. Some 2,000 managed to escape in time to other countries. After the war, about one fifth of the pre-war Jewish population re-emerged in Holland. Subsequent emigration counterbalanced the low natural increase, so that the number of the Jews in Holland in the last forty-five years has remained constant, about 30,000.

Yugoslavia

The Jewish National Committee in Belgrade, *c.* 1920.

The kingdom of the Serbs, Croats and Slovenes was founded in 1918, following the Allied victory in World War I. In 1929 it assumed its present name of Socialist Federal Republic of Yugoslavia. It comprises three major republics, Croatia, Bosnia-Hercegovina, and Serbia, and three smaller ones, Slovenia, Montenegro, and Macedonia. Prior to the establishment of Yugoslavia, each of these six constituent units had a history of its own – mostly under foreign rule – and the events and circumstances of Jewish life differed accordingly. This being the case, the history of the Jews of Yugoslavia lends itself to a state-by-state treatment rather than to a country-wide overview. In this chapter we shall confine ourselves to briefly sketching Jewish history and life in the three major republics, although Jews also lived in Ljubliana (formerly Laibach), capital of Slovenia (a few dozen families in 1940), Skopje, capital of Macedonia (4,000 in 1940), and elsewhere in the three smaller republics.

The oldest evidence of Jewish presence in what is today Yugoslavia dates from Roman times, when Jews arrived in Dalmatia (today part of Croatia), established a community in Salona (now Solin), in the vicinity of Split (Spalato) on the Adriatic coast, and left behind their cemetery with tombstones dating from the third century CE. The Salona community existed until 641 when it was destroyed by the Avars. The survivors fled to the nearby large and fortified palace of Diocletian which subsequently became the town of Split. From the twelfth to the fifteenth century Split belonged in turn to Hungary, Venice, Hungary again, Bosnia, and Venice again, which then maintained its rule over the city from 1420 to 1797. Then, after a brief spell of French rule (1805–13), Split and the rest of Dalmatia were ruled by Austria until after World War I.

From the sixteenth century on two groups of Sephardi Jews lived in Split: a Ponentine (western) group which had come from Italy, probably originally from Spain; and a Levantine, or eastern group, which had issued from the Ottoman possessions in the Balkans. The distinction between the two remained so pronounced, even as late as the eighteenth century, that the Venetian law of 1738, regulating the rights and duties of the Jews, provided among other things that the Levantine Jews had to wear a yellow hat-covering and the western Jews (including the few Ashkenazim) a red one.

The Jews of Split constituted an important link in the trade between Venice and the Ottoman Empire. Because their services were important to Venice, the republic protected them from the Inquisition, exempted from the residence tax all Jewish merchants who hailed from the Ottoman Empire and wished to settle in the city, and granted immunity of person and capital to Jewish merchants travelling to Venice via Split. Some of the Jews made a fortune in the Venetian-Ottoman trade, and one of them, Daniel Rodriguez by name, established a free port in Split with the authorization of the Venetian senate. Other Jewish specializations in Split were medicine and tailoring.

When the Turks attacked Split (1657), the Jews were assigned the defence of one of the towers in the city wall which later became known as the *posto degl' Ebrei* (Position of the Jews). In the eighteenth century a series of anti-Jewish measures were passed by the Venetian authorities, among them attempts to exclude the Jews from the food trade and tailoring. The 1738 law mentioned earlier also prohibited the Jews from leaving the ghetto between midnight and sunrise, and all day on Thursday and Friday of holy week; it provided that the shops in the ghetto must remain closed on Christian holidays; and forbade the employment of Christians by Jews. Further anti-Jewish laws were promulgated in 1779, which, coupled with the decline of Venice, prompted many Jews to emigrate, so that in 1796 there were only 173 Jews left in the city. Under the Napoleonic regime the ghetto was abolished, but in 1814 when Split came under Austrian rule, restrictions on Jews in force in Austria were introduced. During the nineteenth century many more Jews left Split for Italy, while, on the other hand, there was an influx of Jews from Croatia and Bosnia with the result that Croatian became the dominant language of the community.

In 1873 full Emancipation was granted to the Jews. Their position consequently improved, then remained unchanged until World War II. During the war, as long as Italy was in control, the Jews suffered relatively little. Just before the Germans entered the city, several hundreds of Jews were able to cross the Adriatic in small boats to Italy and partisan-held islands, while others joined the partisans on the mainland. All the Jewish men, women and children who remained in Split were arrested by the Germans and sent to concentration camps where they perished.

The data pertaining to the history of the Jews in the rest of Croatia (which includes Slavonia) are fragmented until the eighteenth century, although Jewish presence is attested by a few, widely-scattered, historical documents and references. The earliest of these is the famous letter sent in the tenth century by Hasdai ibn Shaprut, the Spanish-Jewish statesman, to the king of the Khazars, in which Hasdai mentions that 'the king of the Gebalim, the Slavs' – who was none other than King Krešimir of Croatia – sent a deputation to the Caliph of Cordoba which included two Jews, Mar Saul and Mar Joseph by name.

From 1102 to 1526 Croatia was united with Hungary in the person of a common monarch. In the thirteenth century Jews from France, Malta and Albania settled in Zagreb (today the capital of Croatia), and the city's chronicles from the fifteenth century refer to a *domus Judaeorum*, or 'house (probably synagogue) of the Jews' and to a *magistratus Judaeorum*, or 'magister (or chief) of the Jews'. Also, in the same period, Jews from Hungary and Moravia arrived in Zagreb and in the area between the Sava, Drava, and Danube rivers comprising most of Croatia. In 1526, when most of Crotia came under Ottoman rule, while the rest became associated with the Austrian Empire, the Jews were expelled from Zagreb. Thereafter, no Jews lived in Croatia until the eighteenth century, when, after the defeat of the Turks (1718) and the extension of Austrian control over all Croatia, they re-immigrated from Burgenland, Hungary, Bohemia, and Moravia, all provinces under Hapsburg control. Thus, from this time on, the Jews of Croatia were Ashkenazim. In 1815, at the Congress of Vienna, Austria annexed Dalmatia, but the two other Croatian lands, Croatia and Slavonia, remained within the kingdom of Hungary. In 1867, when the so-called 'Compromise' was concluded between Austria and Hungary which resulted in the creation of the dual Austro-Hungarian monarchy, Croatia became a 'land of the Hungarian crown', and the Budapest government embarked upon a policy of intensive Magyarization of the population. Hungarian Jews who settled in Croatia, as well as in Vojvodina (the northern part of Serbia, also under Hungarian rule), were enthusiastic supporters of this policy, as a result of which most Jews in both northern Croatia and northern Serbia remained Hungarian-speaking even after World War I when both areas became parts of Yugoslavia.

In the nineteenth century, the Jewish community of Zagreb, which gradually became the largest in Croatia, developed all the typical Ashkenazi institutions. It had a large Jewish congregation (founded in 1806) similar in religious orientation to that of Conservative Judaism, and a small Orthodox one (founded in 1841). Rabbis from Hungary were invited to serve as spiritual leaders, and in 1867 a beautiful new synagogue was inaugurated in Zagreb, built in a pseudo-Moorish style not unlike the huge synagogue of the Neolog congregation in Pest (later Budapest) completed only eight years previously. A Jewish primary school and a Talmud Tora were established; a union of Jewish high school students was organized (1898); a Hevra Kadisha and a Jewish home for the aged were founded; a new cemetery was laid out; and an Association for Humanism, the first public assistance society in Croatia, was set up. In 1873 the Jews of Croatia were granted full civil rights, and they repeatedly had occasion to appeal to the Hungarian capital or to Vienna for safeguards and protection against anti-Semitic attacks.

In the inter-war period Zionism had a strong following among the Jews of Croatia, and especially of Zagreb, which became the headquarters of the Yugoslavian Zionist Federation. There was a full complement of Jewish organizations: of women, of Jewish employees, and of youth; there were Maccabi sports clubs, choirs, Jewish journals; and there was an active Jewish participation in the social, artistic, literary, scholarly, scientific, industrial, and commercial life of the city. Among the Jews there were prominent painters and sculptors, musicians, physicians, librarians.

Emblematic of the extent to which some Jews in Croatia broke out from the narrow confines of traditional Jewish life as early as in the second half of the nineteenth century was the tragic figure of David Schwarz (1845–97), a Zagreb timber merchant, who invented, and devoted the last ten years of his life to the

A performance by the musical group 'David' at the celebration of the Day of Peace in Belgrade, 1935.

construction of, an aluminium-framed rigid airship, and who died of a heart attack when he received a telegram informing him of the German government's willingness to finance the test flights of his dirigible. Incidentally, Count Zeppelin, who was present when Schwarz's airship was flown from Tempelhof airfield and crashed, bought all his plans from Schwarz's widow, and rebuilt the airship with his own modification, calling it 'Zeppelin'.

Bosnia (full name: People's Republic of Bosnia and Hercegovina), although one of six constituent republics of the Federal People's Republic of Yugoslavia, is very different from the other five. When Bosnia was taken by the Ottoman forces (late fifteenth century) most of the nobles and those of the peasantry who belonged to the Bogomil heresy accepted Islam, while the other parts of present-day Yugoslavia were either never under Turkish rule, or if they were, their population remained Christian. Thus, although Ottoman domination over Bosnia and Hercegovina came to an end in 1878 when they came under Austro-Hungarian protection, 35 per cent of the population, including most of the leading elements, were Muslims until the outbreak of World War II.

The Jews of Bosnia and Hercegovina differed at least as much from their co-religionists in Croatia as did their Gentile population from its neighbours. The first evidence of Jewish presence in Bosnia is supplied by a Turkish document mentioning Jewish merchants in present-day Sarajevo in 1541, and by tombstones dating from 1551 – unusually late dates for the Balkans. A special Jewish quarter was built in 1577, and a synagogue called *Il Cal Grande* was erected in 1581. The merchants referred to had come from Salonika, and in the early seventeenth century more Jews arrived from the Ottoman Empire. The community grew apace, and in 1686 was augmented by the arrival of Jewish refugees from Buda (Ofen; later Budapest), among them the famous halakhist, Rabbi Zevi Hirsh Ashkenazi (1660–1718), better known as Hakham Zevi, of East European extraction, who had become Sephardized in the course of his studies in Salonika. Upon his arrival in Sarajevo Hakham Zevi was appointed *hakham* (i.e., rabbi) of the Sephardi community, which post he filled until 1689 when he moved to Germany. The Ashkenazi Jews who, fleeing Christian persecution in Central and East Europe, arrived in Sarajevo in the seventeenth century founded their own community, which remained a separate body until the holocaust.

In Sarajevo relations between the Jews and the Muslims were, on the whole, satisfactory. Characteristic of the rights enjoyed by the Jews was that they could even appear before the Muslim religious courts in civil cases, which contrasts with the inadmissibility of Jewish evidence in other Muslim countries. Nor were there legal restrictions preventing Jews from moving outside the Jewish quarter, so that before long Jews lived in various parts of the city, and established themselves in other localities of Bosnia and Hercegovina as well. In their internal affairs the Jews enjoyed the autonomy usually accorded to them in the Ottoman Empire, and if the rabbinical court so requested, its decisions were enforced by the Ottoman authorities. However, again as usual all over the Ottoman Empire, the Jews had to pay the poll tax, were subject to various extortions, and had to bribe the Turkish officials at every step.

While the Jews were the earliest physicians and pharmacists in Bosnia – by the middle of the nineteenth century all doctors in Bosnia were Jews – most of them were artisans and merchants. They were blacksmiths, tailors, shoemakers, joiners, metal workers, and butchers. They operated saw-mills, sold lumber, and traded in iron, chemicals, textiles, furs, glass and dyes. In addition, they engaged in trading with all parts of the Ottoman Empire and with Italy.

In the nineteenth century the Sarajevo community continued to grow, and in 1840 its rabbi, Moses Pereira, was appointed by imperial *firman Hakham Bashi*, or chief rabbi, of Bosnia and Hercegovina.

Upon the annexation of Bosnia by the Austro-Hungarian empire in 1878, the new authorities demanded that the Jews of Sarajevo pay a levy of 100,000 ducats; this was a huge sum which the Jews could defray only in several instalments. New Jewish immigrants, Ashkenazim from the north, arrived and participated in the development of commercial and industrial enterprises, and of trade with Budapest, Vienna, and Prague. A testimony to the wealth of these newcomers was the palatial synagogue they build themselves. The new Sephardi synagogue, the largest in the Balkans, was not completed until 1931. By the end of the nineteenth century the two communities of Sarajevo (the Ashkenazi and the Sephardi) numbered a total of about 10,000 Jews, which figure remained constant until the holocaust.

On the eve of World War II there were about 14,000 Jews in all Bosnia, of whom about 10,000 were Sephardim. They constituted less than 1 per cent of the total population, but their share in the economic, cultural, literary, and artistic life of the country was considerable. In 1928 the federation of Jewish communities opened an educational institution in Sarajevo which was a combination of high school and rabbinical seminary. Social and benevolent organizations thrived, among them *La Benevolencia*, a mutual aid society (founded in 1894); two other societies *Melacha* and *Geula*, served the needs of artisans; a choir society, *Lyra* (founded 1901), fostered Judeo-Spanish singing; and several Zionist organizations were active, as well as an organization with Sephardi separatist tendencies. Several Jewish weeklies were published from 1898 to 1941, the first of these, *La Alborada* (1898–1902) in Ladino, the rest in Croatian.

Serbia, the third of the three major constituent republics of Yugoslavia, was until 1876 a vassal state of Turkey. Sporadic traces of a Jewish population date from Roman times, but Jews seem to have settled in Belgrade only in the thirteenth century, coming from Italy and Hungary. After the Turkish conquest of Belgrade in 1521 Sephardi Jews began to arrive, Don Joseph Nasi having obtained privileges for them from the Sultan. The Jews had their own quarter, and, as in neighbouring Bosnia, they were physicians and merchants, as well as weapon-smiths and tanners, and were allowed to own land. In the sixteenth and seventeenth centuries all was well with the Jews of Belgrade, who numbered 800 in 1663. They maintained a Yeshiva which, in the seventeenth century, became well known due to its outstanding rabbis. There was also a Hebrew printing press.

With the weakening of the Ottoman Empire in the late seventeenth century the position of the Jews became difficult. As happened in many places, when an enemy force – in this case the Austrians – approached the city in 1688, its defenders, the Janissaries, vented their anger on the local Jews. Possibly they suspected the Jews of sympathizing with the enemy, or, more probably, they masked their fear of the coming onslaught with an attack on the helpless Jews over whom their 'victory' was an assured thing. In any case, they plundered and burned the Jewish quarter. When the Austrians captured the city, they took their turn in the burning, looting, and murdering of Jews and Turks indiscriminately. Most of the surviving Jews were captured and taken to Austria to be sold as slaves, or offered to Jewish communities for ransom. Only a few Jews made their escape, fleeing to Bulgaria. When they were allowed to return to Belgrade, they rebuilt their synagogue.

During the ensuing century the city was grabbed back and forth three times between the Austrians and the Turks, and each time the Jews suffered massacre and plunder. In the early nineteenth century as well Belgrade changed hands several times, the forces contending for it being Serbs and local Turkish despots. For Jews this made little if any difference. They were expelled and readmitted several times. It is a phenomenal testimony to Jewish resilience that, despite these frequent catastrophes, the Jews were able to maintain their number which in 1831 was 1,300, of whom 1,100 were Sephardim and 200 Ashkenazim. Finally, in 1867, the Serbs managed to drive out the Turks for good, and made Belgrade their capital, with the Sava and Danube rivers as borders between Serbia and Hungary.

The territory north of the two rivers, today the Vojvodina province of Serbia, remained in the possession of Hungary until the end of World War I. All the major towns in this territory had Jewish communities, most of them founded in the 1840s by Hungarian Jews. The most important communities were those of Subotica (Hungarian Szabadka) with 6,000 Jews in 1940; Novi Sad (Ujvidék) with 4,000; Veliki bečkerek (Nagybecskerek) with 1,250; Sombor (Zombor) with 1,200, and Sente (Zenta) with 1,000. The total number of Jews in Vojvodina was 22,000 in 1928 and 19,200 in 1941, before the holocaust. Most of them were Hungarian-speaking Ashkenazi Jews while the Jews of Serbia, south of the Sava and Danube, were Ladino-speaking Sephardim.

The Jews of Vojvodina, together with all the Jews of Hungary, were emancipated in 1867; those of the rest of Serbia were granted full rights in 1878. By that time the Jews of Vojvodina were quite advanced in their assimilation to Hungarian culture, and formed an integral part of Hungarian life in the major towns of the province. South of the Sava assimilation into Serbian society began only after 1878, and only among the wealthier Jews. They sent their children to state schools and to the university of Belgrade (founded in 1863), and gradually penetrated academic professions, medicine, the civil service, banking, etc.

The writer Hajim Davitscho in Belgrade.

A presentation at the Jewish Children's Home in Zagreb in 1945.

This development was accompanied by a movement out of the ghetto and into the modern parts of Belgrade.

While the Jews of the north – let us use the terms north and south for the sake of brevity – were thus ahead of their southern co-religionists in assimilating to the culture of their environment, they were behind them in absorbing the Zionist idea and participating in the Zionist movement. In the south, Zionism had become an important factor of Jewish life within a few years after the foundation of the movement by Theodor Herzl in 1897, and by the time of World War I most of the Jews were Zionists. In the north the intense Hungarian patriotism, which the Jews all over Hungary shared with their Christian countrymen after their emancipation in 1867, kept them away from Zionism, which was able to make headway among them only after they came under Yugoslav rule. In the inter-war years, the Yugoslavian Zionist Federation had local groups in all the Jewish communities in the country, whether in the south or in the north, with the exception of the seven Orthodox congregations in the north which sympathized with the anti-Zionist *Agudat Israel*.

Another development in the inter-war years came about as a result of the deterioration of the economic circumstances of the Jewish communities. Until World War I all the larger Jewish communities had their own elementary schools, in which the language of tuition in the north was Hungarian, and both Jewish and general subjects were taught. After the annexation of the north by Yugoslavia, the communities, no longer able to maintain these schools, ceded them to the state, which introduced Serbo-Croatian as the language of tuition while retaining their Jewish curriculum, including the teaching of the Hebrew language. The activities of the Jewish organizations continued undisturbed: in each community there was a Hevra Kadisha taking care of burials and general charity; a ladies' auxiliary with varied cultural activities; some had, in addition, orphanages, poor people's homes, and soup kitchens. The Jewish community of Subotica maintained the only Jewish hospital in Yugoslavia. There were numerous Jewish sports organizations and boy scout groups which were affiliated with the Federation of Jewish Youth Organizations (headquarters in Zagreb).

Economically, the Jews of the north, mostly small merchants whose narrow economic base was shaken by the new tax laws and other drastic changes, suffered more than those of the south from the birth pangs of the new federal Yugoslavia. In the south, where most of the Jews, as we shall recall, were Sephardim, their circumstances changed little as a result of the unification of Serbia and Bosnia-Hercegovina and the expansion of the new Yugoslavia to the north. In the north, on the other hand, the Hungarian Jews suddenly found themselves under a new power, inimical to their beloved Hungary with which for two or more generations they had identified linguistically, culturally, and, above all, emotionally.

In 1917, the government of the aged King Peter I Karageorgevich of Serbia recognized the Balfour Declaration (that memorable instrument in which the British government undertook to facilitate the establishment of a Jewish national home in Palestine), and addressed on the occasion an official greeting to the Jews of Serbia. This event was symptomatic of the difference in the position of the Jews under the old Hungarian and the new Yugoslavian regime: in Hungary they were Hungarians of the Jewish persuasion and in Yugoslavia members of an officially recognized national minority. In fact, whatever distrust the Hungarian Jews encountered in Yugoslavia was evoked not so much by their Jewishness as by their Magyarness.

Both in the north and in the south the Jews participated in literary and artistic life. In the north, a Jewish journalist edited the largest Hungarian daily paper in Yugoslavia (in Subotica), and there were dozens of Jewish writers, novelists, poets, publicists, authors of studies in various scholarly fields and of Zionist writings, all writing in Hungarian. There were also Jewish painters and other artists. In the south, there were a few Jewish poets and authors who wrote in Ladino. A remarkable development was the appearance of studies in Serbo-Croatian dealing with Ladino *romances* (ballads) and culture, and with Sephardi life in Bosnia. Most of the poets, writers and translators in the south wrote in Serbo-Croatian, and devoted themselves to general (that is, non Jewish) themes. Most of the writers, both of the north and of the south, perished in the holocaust; the few who survived gave literary expression to their experiences, either in Hungarian or in Serbo-Croatian.

In 1926 the total number of Jews in Yugoslavia was 73,000. Of them, 30,000 were Sephardim and 43,000 Ashkenazim. Of the latter, 22,000 were Hungarian Jews. By 1939, as a result of the low birthrate, conversions to Christianity, and emigration, their number had decreased to 71,000. In 1941–3, the Nazis, with the help of their local Christian and Muslim supporters, either massacred or deported most of the Jews, except for those who escaped to Italy or to the mountains where they joined the partisans, or who managed to go into hiding otherwise. After 1944, those who were still alive and those who survived in the prison camps returned to the cities. Their total number was 14,000. Of these, about 8,000 emigrated to Israel between 1948 and 1952, leaving a diminished community of some 6,000 to 7,000, half of them Ashkenazim, half Sephardim, and with a 57 per cent to 43 per cent preponderance of females over males. Subsequent censuses and estimates reveal no increase in this number.

Peter I, King of Serbia, attends the ceremony of laying the cornerstone of the new synagogue 'Beth Israel' in Belgrade.

Greece

A demonstration of the Jewish bootmakers' guild at Salonika, 1925.

The history of Jews in Greece begins with scattered references to Jewish slaves. The first Jews to step on Greek soil were Judean captives in the fifth century BCE who were sold into slavery by Tyre and Zidon, as we learn from a reference by the prophet Joel (4:6). Two centuries later, the name of a Jew crops up the first time in Greece: he was 'Moschos the Jew', a slave. From the second century BCE we have inscriptions from Delphi referring to Jewish slaves. However, at that time Jews already resided in various parts of the Greek mainland and isles, and after the Jewish-Roman war (66–70 CE) their number increased considerably. In the early second century CE the Jews of Cyprus staged an uprising, and laid waste its capital, Salamis, before they were banished from the island. The Jews who settled in Greece adopted the Greek language and forgot Hebrew, so that it became necessary for them to resort to a Greek translation of the Bible, the Septuagint, which was prepared in the third and second centuries BCE in Alexandria, Egypt, at the time the greatest Hellenistic cultural centre.

Hellenization, both linguistic and cultural, was the first example of large-scale Jewish adaptation to a foreign culture, and, as was to happen with subsequent assimilatory waves, it resulted in the production by the Jews of important religious, literary, and historical works written in Greek, especially in the first and second centuries CE, although not in Greece itself but in Alexandria.

A difficult period for the Jews of Greece began with the onset of Byzantine rule (330 CE). The emperors periodically issued laws which either increasingly limited Jewish rights or decreed that all Jews must convert to Christianity. The very fact that these laws and decrees were repeated from time to time shows that the efforts to convert the Jews were unsuccessful. Despite their legal and civic disabilities, the periodic attacks on them and the orders for their expulsion, the Jews were most of the time able to continue in their occupations as physicians, artisans, weavers, dyers, makers of silk garments, or in commerce and farming. However, the almost total absence of any Jewish scholarly and literary activity throughout the Byzantine period is a clear indication of the restrictive quality of the life imposed upon the Jews by Byzantium. Neither did the numerous invasions from the north and the west, which swept over Greece from the fourth to the twelfth century, contribute to the well-being of the Jews. The eleventh and twelfth centuries were a relatively tranquil period for them, and the two Jewish travellers, Benjamin of Tudela and Petahia of Regensburg, both of whom visited Greece about 1170, reported that they found a large number of Jews in many localities both on the mainland and the isles, who were, on the whole, quite well off, and 200 of whom were farmers on Mount Parnassus. That silk weaving was an important Jewish speciality is mentioned in several sources, and is borne out by the transfer of Greek-Jewish silk weavers to Sicily by Roger II.

In the thirteenth century, Greek rulers as well as foreign conquerors established numerous kingdoms in Greece, some of considerable duration. Their policy toward the Jews ranged from harsh to cruel. They were all absorbed by the Ottoman Turks who began their conquest of the Balkans in 1365.

In the course of the fourteenth to sixteenth centuries Jewish exiles from Spain and Portugal arrived in Greece. The Hungarian Jewish refugees who came in 1376 and 1525 became, within a few generations, assimilated to the Sephardim. Also Polish Jews, fleeing from the persecutions of 1648, found refuge in Turkish-ruled Greece.

A high point in the history of the Jews in Greece was the appointment by Sultan Selim II of Don Joseph Nasi (c. 1524–79) as duke of the island of Naxos and the surrounding isles. Joseph was born a Marrano in Portugal, and at the age of thirty went to Constantinople where he had himself circumcised, became influential in the Sublime Porte and befriended Selim, son of Suleiman I. Even before his appointment as Duke of Naxos, Joseph Nasi obtained from the Sultan plenary authority over Tiberias and seven nearby villages, and had the city's walls restored. He invited Italian Jews to settle in Tiberias, and seems to have attempted to establish some sort of Jewish political entity there.

There is little to be said about the history of the Jews in Greece in the seventeenth and eighteenth centuries. As in earlier times, many Jews were engaged in silk making, wool weaving, and cloth manufacturing. They played an important role in commerce, money lending, and tax leasing. Jewish wholesale merchants had connections with other parts of the Ottoman Empire, as well as with Italy, France, Holland, Germany, and England. Most of the Jews, however, lived in great poverty, and many eked out a living as pedlars and tinsmiths.

The Greek revolt against Turkish rule, which broke out in 1821, had dire consequences for those Jews who were loyal to the Turks. The rebels vented their anger against them, massacred 5,000 Jews in the Peloponnesus, and forced others to flee to Corfu. Further attacks, blood libels, and anti-Jewish riots led to Jewish emigration to Turkey, Egypt, and Italy. On the positive side was the granting by the

Greek state of civic and political equality to the Jews (in 1821) and of a legal status to the Jewish communities (in 1882). Economically, too, the situation of the Jews was satisfactory. Still, emigration brought about a reduction in their number, from about 100,000 in 1913 to about 77,000 in 1939. In World War II 13,000 Jews served in the Greek army.

Although, as we have just seen, many waves of Jewish immigrants reached the shores of Greece, the one which imposed its own character on all the rest, as well as upon most of the old-established Greek Jewish communities, was that of the Sephardim. In fact, only a few Jewish communities retained their Greek tongue, notably those of Ioannina and Preveza in Epirus (numbering 4,500 in 1900); Xanthe (Zante, 175); Arta (300); and Khalkis (Chalcis) on the island of Euboea (200), or fewer than 5,000 in a total of some 100,000 Greek Jews. Another 5,000 on the Ionian island of Corfu, which was long under Venetian rule (until 1797), adopted the Italian dialect of Apulia, from where many of the Jewish immigrants had come. (By 1939 the number of Jews on Corfu had diminished to 2,000, almost all of whom were deported to Auschwitz in 1944.) The rest of the Jews in Greece, whether originally Greek-, Portuguese-, Italian-, or Yiddish-speaking, adopted Ladino, and assimilated to the Sephardi Jews in both ritual and culture.

Among the cultural traits the Sephardi Jews had brought with them from Spain to Greece was their love of merriment and luxury. These foibles were emulated by all those who could afford them, and were carried to such extremes that the rabbis of Salonika felt constrained to issue a decree forbidding women to wear any jewellery or ornament of gold or silver, except for one simple ring on a finger, prohibiting nocturnal wedding processions and the employment of male musicians at festivities, and interdicting participation in games of hazard and the dancing together of men and women.

More importantly, the Sephardi immigrants served as examples for the other Greek Jews in manners and comportment. The Spanish Jews had acquired from the Christian Spaniards pride in noble ancestry, valuation of purity of descent (the well-known Spanish *limpieza de sangre*), a dignified pattern of behaviour, and a disdain for people outside and beneath – the two were practically identical – their ranks. After living for one or two generations in the shadow of the proud newcomers, the other Jewish groups in Greece assimilated to them to such an extent that only their names remained to attest to their non-Sephardi origins.

The extent to which Sephardi self-importance and self-assurance remained part of Sephardi Jewish consciousness right down to the last years prior to the annihilation of Greek Jewry by the Nazis is remarkably illustrated by the portrait of the Castilian Jews in Salonika penned by one of them, Joseph Nehama, in 1935. Although Nehama purports to describe the relationship and differences between the Castilians and the other Jews in Salonika in objective terms, his own identification with the Castilians cannot remain hidden. After arriving in Salonika,

. . . the Castilians were soon giving the tone to everything, to the entire population, their customs and their manners. The task was easy for them. They were by far the most numerous and they exercised a considerable ascendancy in all domains. Who could have contested their superiority? These proud hidalgos were versed in all the sciences. Munificent, of the grand manner, they had been admitted into the entourage of the Court and the grandees of Spain, and they had preserved their sentiments and demeanour. They themselves had often worn the cape and the sword, they had occupied the most eminent positions. They had known honours and dignities. They looked down from above on other people and had the habit of command. Imbued with the sentiment of honour, perquisite of the Spanish feudal aristocracy, they were courteous, brave, respectful of the given word, and persevering in their enterprises. The contrast between them and the other people was all too manifest. The Aragonese, Catalans, Majorcans bowed and let themselves be eclipsed. The Portuguese themselves were, in their great majority, of Castilian origin, and it was not for them, however rich and lettered, to deny a supremacy in which they had a share. Italians, Sicilians, Calabrians, Apulians put up some resistance. They even tried to

Rabbi Asseó in Salonika. Salonika was the largest and most important Jewish community in Greece.

combat the Castilians' influence. Above all those of Otranto had pride in their origin. For a long time they married only among themselves and followed meticulously their own customs.

Next, Nehama describes the relationship between the Sephardim and the Ashkenazim:

The last to yield were the Askenazim. They did not mingle with the Sephardim, nor married their daughters who, in any case, would have been refused to them as if they belonged to another race. Sephardim and Ashkenazim did not eat at the same table, they did not touch each other's dishes, for they each considered impure the meat prepared according to the other's rites, and eating such meat would be a grave sin. Customs, prayers, liturgies, everything differentiated them. The Sephardi looked down from on high upon the poor little Jew from the north, accustomed to misery and oppression, who cowered, made himself humble and hugged the wall, who had always lived with doors and windows closed, shut up in the *Judengassen* [Jewish streets] in sullen isolation, who shunned all social contact, all friendship with the non-Jew; who, always despised and unwanted, lived here and there as a veritable nomad, always ready to take off, with his bundle and his wanderer's staff.

The Ashkenazi, in turn, regarded the Sephardi with distrust. He did not contest his superiority, but considered him some sort of miscreant. He did not want to let himself be subjugated, he bridled and kicked.

After ten centuries of separation, these two brothers in Israel had ceased to recognize each other. Their encounter did not take place without hurt. They were not far from considering each other strangers.

The Sephardi superiority expressed itself, among other ways, in the linguistic assimilation of the other Jews to the 'Castilian', i.e., Ladino, colloquial of the Sephardim:

The proud Castilian witnessed this rapid triumph with real pleasure. Was there in the world, in their eyes, a language more harmonious and nobler than theirs? It was honoured

left A gathering in the synagogue in Salonika with Rabbi Haim Haviv.

all over Spain, where an army of writers and of scholars, sustained by the princes, had raised it to literary dignity. The Sephardim who established themselves, in a period of 150 years, in all the vital points of the earth, adopted it, as they did in Salonika. This is how it happened that Tunis, Nice, Amsterdam, London, Hamburg preserved for a long time the Spanish of Castile, this one living relic of the lost fatherland. . . .

As one can see, the influx of the first waves of immigrants, among whom the Castilian refugees dominated, changed the aspect of the old city of Salonika within twenty years, and imparted to it a clearly Jewish and Spanish character.[1]

What is psychologically remarkable in these pride-filled paragraphs is that they were written at a time when all claims for Sephardi excellence lay in the distant past. The only feature the Sephardim retained intact from the great days of the Spanish Golden Age was their language, Ladino, the Spanish element in which had remained practically unchanged since their expulsion from Spain in 1492. As far as the other Sephardi attainments were concerned – the originality in producing the

above A wealthy Jewish family in Salonika, 1920s.

greatest Hebrew poetry of all times, making great strides in Jewish law and religious philosophy, striking out into the *terra incognita* of mysticism and Kabbala, creating an entirely new science of Hebrew linguistics, making great contributions to medicine, mathematics, geometry, astronomy, as well as astrology and alchemy, while at the same time serving as leading statesmen and commanders of armies – all activities whose sum total made the Spanish Golden Age unique in Jewish history – of all this little survived into the seventeenth century. For about 150 years after the Spanish exile, the momentum of excellence which was theirs, coupled with the typically Spanish trait of pride and the equally typically Spanish inquisitorial severity in controlling congregational life carried them forward in all the countries in which they found refuge, and even elevated them everywhere to positions of pre-eminence. Then the cultural momentum began to give out, the *élan* was spent, and Sephardi creativity gradually ground to a standstill. What remained was pride and self-importance which became greater as the true basis for them receded into the past. They continued to express themselves in such vain gestures as appending the abbreviation ST standing for *Sefardi Tahor*, or Pure Sephardi, after their signatures, whether by hand or in print, refusing intermarriage with non-Sephardim, and finding vicarious satisfaction in recounting, as Joseph Nehama did, the glories of the Castilian past.

With the annihilation of Greek Jewry by the Germans the once great and unique Sephardi division of the Jewish people was brought to the end of its historic road. The small remnants which survive are in the process of merging, both culturally and biologically, into either the European and American Ashkenazi majority of Jewry, or the Oriental division of the Jewish people which in Israel attained absolute majority several years ago.

The largest and most important Jewish community in Greece was that of Salonika. Its origins go back to the second century BCE. The apostle Paul preached in the synagogue of Salonika for three consecutive Sabbaths in about 50 CE. In Byzantine times and under the Latin Empire the Jews of Salonika suffered persecutions, as did those of other Greek towns. Nevertheless, they managed to make a living, and even to prosper in commerce, and especially in the silk trade which was a Jewish monopoly.

far left A group in the poor Jewish section of Salonika in the 1920s.

left Jewish women working in Salonika's tobacco factory.

A student dramatic club,
Salomika, *c.* 1920s.

In 1376 Hungarian Jewish immigrants came, followed, after the Turkish conquest of the city in 1430, by Bavarian Jews, and later in the fifteenth and sixteenth centuries by Jews from Spain, Portugal, Italy, Sicily, France, and North Africa. It has been estimated that in 1553 there were 20,000 Jews in Salonika. They were divided into some thirty independent congregations, each with its own communal institutions, including a *Hevra Qadisha* (lit. 'Holy Society') which took care of burials, and several philanthropic organizations. They had a *Bet Din* (law court) and a Yeshiva. This Yeshiva, incidentally, was such an outstanding institution of Jewish learning that Isaac Abrabanel chose to send his son Samuel there. There were also Jewish societies for the study of poetry, singing, medicine, sciences, astronomy, and other secular subjects. In the sixteenth century, several prominent rabbis and authors lived in Salonika, among them Sh'lomo Alqabetz, author of the Sabbath hymn *L'kha Dodi*, and scholars who wrote important rabbinic and halakhic works.

As already stated, the Sephardi Jews from Spain and Portugal became the dominant element of the immigrant groups, imposing their language, culture, and ritual upon the others. One of the activities in which the Spanish and Portuguese Jewish refugees engaged in Salonika, and which significantly furthered Jewish cultural life in the city and in Greece as a whole, was the establishment of Hebrew printing presses. The most outstanding among the Jewish printers happened to be not a Sephardi, but an Italian Jew, Gershom Soncino (d. 1534), a member of the famous Jewish printers' family of German Jewish origin who took their name from the town of Soncino near Cremona where they had settled in 1454. This Gershom Soncino was perhaps the first international printer: at various times in his life he printed books – many of them from manuscripts which he obtained in the course of his travels in different countries – in ten different Italian cities, as well as in Salonika and Istanbul. His son Moses, too, printed a number of books in Salonika from 1521 to 1527.

Although in the seventeenth century the city suffered from frequent plagues and fires, which prompted some Jews to move away, the number of Jews in Salonika increased to 30,000, or half of the city's total population. The city continued to be prominent as a centre of rabbinic and Kabbalistic studies, and as the seat of leading halakhic authorities. When Shabbatai Zevi arrived in Salonika (in 1657) and declared himself the Messiah, he was summarily expelled by the leading rabbis of the city. However, several years after Shabbatai Zevi's death, a group of his followers emulated him in converting to Islam, and established the Doenmeh sect with Salonika as its centre. Other, positive, results of the Shabbataian upheaval were that in 1680 the numerous separate congregations merged into one, headed by a council of three rabbis and seven communal leaders, and that the rabbinical courts were reorganized into three bodies, each composed of three rabbis and each with a clearly defined jurisdictional authority.

In the eighteenth century, as the power of the Ottoman Empire declined, the economic conditions of the Jews in Salonika worsened. In the second half of the nineteenth century began the modernization, that is, Westernization, of the city and of Jewish life in it. A new port was built; Western culture and technology knocked at the gates of the city; the *Alliance Israélite Universelle* opened a school (in 1873), and two years later the influential Allatini family founded two more modern Jewish schools. Western medicine eliminated the epidemics which formerly had periodically decimated the population; liberalization in religious matters spread in the community, while, on the other hand, a society for the propagation of the Hebrew language was founded (in 1899). In 1900 there were 80,000 Jews in Salonika in a total population of 173,000. The importance of the Jews in the economic life of the city was indicated by the fact that on the Sabbath the port, in which most stevedores were Jewish, closed down, and business in the city came to a standstill.

Turkish rule continued in Salonika much longer than in other parts of Greece; the Greeks succeeded in capturing it only in 1912, at which time King George of Greece

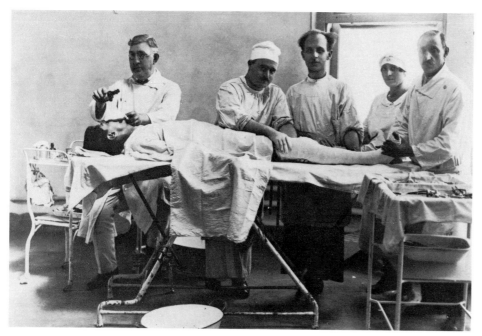

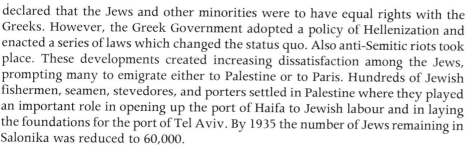

declared that the Jews and other minorities were to have equal rights with the Greeks. However, the Greek Government adopted a policy of Hellenization and enacted a series of laws which changed the status quo. Also anti-Semitic riots took place. These developments created increasing dissatisfaction among the Jews, prompting many to emigrate either to Palestine or to Paris. Hundreds of Jewish fishermen, seamen, stevedores, and porters settled in Palestine where they played an important role in opening up the port of Haifa to Jewish labour and in laying the foundations for the port of Tel Aviv. By 1935 the number of Jews remaining in Salonika was reduced to 60,000.

Salonika was the centre of Greek-Jewish journalism in Ladino. The short-lived journal *Salonik* (appeared 1869–70) was published as a multilingual paper in Ladino, Turkish, and Greek, with a Bulgarian supplement edited in Sofia. More important was *La Epoca*, which appeared from 1875 to 1912, first as a weekly, then as a bi-weekly, and finally as a daily. *La Solidaridad Ouvradera* (Workers Solidarity), which, as its title shows, was a socialist-oriented paper, was launched in 1911 and soon changed its title to *Avante* (Forward); it was first a bi-weekly, and then, during the Balkan Wars (1912–13), appeared as a daily. In 1923 it became the mouthpiece of the Jewish Communists, and continued to be published until 1935. From 1916 to 1920 the Zionist Federation of Greece published the weekly *La Esperanza* (The Hope), and another Zionist weekly, *Lemaʿan Yisrael—Pro Israel*, was published partly in French and partly in Ladino from 1917. A Ladino satirical journal, *El Kirbatj* (The Whip) was launched in the early 1900s, and was followed from 1918 to 1923 by *El Nuevo Kirbatj* (The New Whip). In 1923, yet another satirical paper, *La Gata* (The Cat), began to appear. It might be mentioned here that between 1846 and 1939 no less than 296 Ladino journals were published, most of them in the Balkans, and the Middle East. Salonika was the undisputed centre of this journalistic activity which in toto is an eloquent testimony to the vitality of Ladino until World War II. After the war, Ladino was no longer a medium for Jewish journalism.

The German invasion of Greece in World War II spelled the end of Greek Jewry, including that of Salonika. In 1943 the Germans deported 43,850 Jews, or 95 per cent of the total Jewish population of the city, to Poland, where all but a handful were killed. Most of the 5,000 who had remained in Salonika died of maltreatment in forced labour, or escaped to the mountains, or to Athens. After the war, in the whole of Greece, no more than 11,000 Jews, or 15 per cent of their 1939 number, remained alive.

above Rabbi Herman Keretz, Chief Rabbi, with King George of Greece and Prime Minister Metaxes. Rabbi Keretz died in Bergen Belsen in 1945.

above left The operating theatre in the Hirsch Hospital in Salonika.

Part Four
North Africa
Between Arabs and Berbers

A rabbi in the Sorrerro Synagogue, Fez, Morocco.

Morocco

Jewish village girls adorned with jewels and colourful head-dresses typical of Morocco.

According to legend, still heard until recently in the *mellahs* of Morocco, the Jews settled in the west of North Africa even before the destruction of the First Temple of Jerusalem. History's claim is more modest. It points to a few Hebrew inscriptions on tombstones, found in the Roman town of Volubilis, to the west of modern Fez, which constitute evidence of Jewish presence in the country in Roman times. That the indigenous Berber population was exposed to Judaizing influences is shown by an old tradition, first recorded by Procopius in the sixth century, to the effect that the Berbers had originally come from Palestine after their King Thalut (a distortion of the Hebrew *Shaul*, Saul) killed Jalut (i.e. Goliath). Other Berber traditions, reported by Ibn Khaldun, the great North African Arab historian of the fourteenth century, had it that the Jews made many converts among the Botr, one of the two major Berber moieties. Persecutions in Spain by the Visigoths brought many Jews to Morocco between 581 and 693. In the late seventh century, when the Muslim Arabs conquered the Maghreb, or 'West', as they termed the whole of North-West Africa, they found in the country numerous Jewish Berber tribes; the leader of one such tribe, the semi-legendary seeress-queen Dahia al-Kahina, succeeded in blocking the Arab advance for several years. Arab victory meant the victory of Islam, and by the early eighth century the Jews were reduced to a small minority in the midst of either Muslim Arab or Muslim Berber majorities. It can be assumed that the Jewish tribes and communities, which survived in the mountains of Morocco and the oases of the desert down to the twentieth century, were the remnants of the old Berber Jewish tribes. In any case, they spoke Berber, looked like Berbers, and were Berbers in everything except their religion.

The dependence of Morocco on the Baghdad caliphate ended in 788 when Idris I seized power. Under his successor, Idris II (791–828), the Jews were allowed to settle in his new capital, Fez. This inaugurated the most brilliant period in the history of Moroccan Jewry which continued under the Almoravids (1051–1147). The great names of Moroccan Jewry in this period include those of Dunash ibn Labrat (c. 920–c. 990) and Judah ben David Hayyuj (c. 940–c. 1010), the two greatest early Hebrew philologists, and R. Yitzhaq Alfasi (1013–1103), the first post-Talmudic codifier of Jewish law, all three of whom were born or lived in Fez; and several physicians and rabbinic scholars mostly of Spanish origin. The great Maimonides (1135–1204) himself, although a native of Spain, lived for a number of years in Fez which in his day was an important centre of Jewish learning.

During the inimical Almohad rule (1146–1267) persecutions of the Jews were frequent. The compulsory wearing of the Jewish badge was introduced. Many Jews left for Spain and the lands of the east.

In the late fourteenth century began the decline of the Muslim west, and with it the further degradation of the Maghrebi Jewry, both materially and spiritually. In 1438 the Jews of Fez were confined to a special quarter, the first Moroccan *mellah*.

Nevertheless, many of the Jews exiled from Spain in 1391 and in 1492 and from Portugal in 1496 sought refuge in Morocco. They settled in the cities of the coastal area where, however, they were not spared tragic vicissitudes. In addition, diseases, famines, and conflagrations decimated the ranks of natives and newcomers alike.

The initial negative attitude displayed by the native Jews, called *toshavim* (residents), to the newcomers, termed *m'gorashim* (exiles), precluded intermingling. The former continued to speak Arabic, the latter, Castilian Spanish. The ranks of the Sephardim were augmented by the arrival of Marranos, Iberian crypto-Jews, who in Morocco were able to return openly to Judaism.

When, in the early sixteenth century, the Portuguese occupied some regions on the Atlantic coast of Morocco, the Sephardi Jews who had settled in several parts only a few decades earlier, became the intermediaries between them and the Arab rulers of Morocco. They served as ministers of the Moroccan Muslim courts and as ambassadors to the Portuguese and other Christian kings. Once the Sephardim thus established themselves as the Jewish elite of Morocco, the *toshavim* began to assimilate to them in several northern cities, such as Tetuan and Tangier. This, in turn, brought about the development of a Jewish colloquial, which consisted of a mixture of Spanish, Hebrew, and Arabic.

Very different was the situation in the hinterland where the Jews spoke Arabic in Arab-dominated areas, and Berber among the Berber majority. Among the latter, the position of the Jews as *dhimmis*, tolerated, protected people, was in

above Jewish beggars in the *mellah* in Marrakesh.

right Two elderly men in the *mellah* at Fez.

A Jewish coppersmith, Marrakesh, 1949.

general better than in the government-controlled parts of the country. There were many Jews who carried weapons – a sign of free men – and did not pay the *jizya*, the special head-tax imposed on the Jews as payment for being tolerated.

In the seventeenth century Moroccan Jewry was shaken by the news of the appearance of Shabbatai Zevi, the pseudo-Messiah, in Turkey. Their Messianic enthusiasm could not be checked despite the efforts of the leading Sephardi Moroccan rabbis. Even after the Shabbataian debacle (1666), the Messianic expectation continued undiminished, nourished by Kabbalistic studies to which most of the learned Moroccan Jews devoted themselves.

The second half of the eighteenth century saw the beginnings of treaty relations between Morocco and the West. Isaac Pinto and Isaac Cordoza Nuñez, two Sephardi Jews, were largely responsible for the 1787 treaty between Morocco and the United States which provided American payment to Morocco in return for the protection of US ships in the Mediterranean. Sultan Mulay Muhammad (1757–90) entrusted all his diplomatic contacts with Western countries to Jewish statesmen. His son, Mulay al-Yazid, to whom some wealthy Jewish merchants had refused a loan prior to his succession, wrought bloody vengeance among all the Moroccan Jews, and hanged dozens of their leaders by their feet until they died. Hundreds of Jews were massacred, and the devastation of Moroccan Jewry was near total. His successor, Mulay Sulayman (1792–1822), although not prone to violence, ruthlessly oppressed the Jews, confining them to *mellahs* in all the major cities. In addition, the Jews suffered as much as the Muslims from the epidemics which claimed 65,000 victims in Fez alone in 1799, and which struck again in 1818.

The European intervention in Morocco in the nineteenth century was a mixed blessing for the Jews. On the one hand, the European powers granted consular protection to an increasing number of Jews whose services they needed. On the other, the populace blamed the Jews for any unpopular actions of the European powers, and frequently attacked them. The intervention of Sir Moses Montefiore

A *beignet* (dumpling)
pedlar, Marrakesh, *c.* 1950.

(1784–1885) with Mulay Muhammed brought some temporary relief. Outbreaks of hostility continued to alternate with outbreaks of epidemics. A plague in 1900 claimed more than 3,000 Jewish victims in the *mellah* of Fez alone. The overcrowding in all the *mellahs* became indescribable.

The establishment of the French protectorate over Morocco in 1912 triggered a pogrom in Fez in which more than 100 Jews were killed. However, once the French took control, the Jews began to enjoy greater security. In general, the forty-four years of the French Protectorate in Morocco (1912–56) was a period of tranquillity and gradual advancement for the Jews, although punctuated by occasional local outbursts of Muslim mob violence against them.

Many of the Jews in the coastal cities received a French-oriented education, mostly in the schools of the *Alliance Israélite Universelle*, the first of which were established in Morocco in the early 1860s. Gradually, a new Jewish middle class came into being, comprised of many professionals and officials. The work of the *Alliance* led to rapid Westernization, and, in some sectors of the Jewish population, frequently to a discarding of Jewish tradition.

In 1939, when the total number of the Jewish school-age population (six to fourteen years old) was about 56,000, the forty-five *Alliance* schools in Morocco had 15,761 pupils. Schools were also run by *Otzar haTora* and *Em haBanim*, and, from 1950, by the Lubavicher Hasidim. In addition, the traditional *kuttab*, the equivalent of the East European *heder*, in which children were taught only to read Hebrew and to understand, memorize and translate by rote the Bible and the prayer book, also continued to function in both villages and cities. The number of Jewish university students and professionals was very low; in 1964 the combined number of Jewish physicians, dentists, pharmacists and lawyers was 169. (However, this low figure was still about ten times higher proportionately than the corresponding number in the country as a whole.)

Little outside influence reached the southern cities and the hinterland, where

Jews continued to live in Arab or Berber villages. Their number until the end of World War II can be only very roughly estimated at one-third to two-fifths of all the Jews of Morocco. They continued to speak their age-old languages, Judeo-Arabic and Judeo-Berber, and were poorly and sporadically educated in their old-fashioned *kuttabs*.

As for their occupational structure, they eked out a living in handicraft, retail trade, and service occupations. The city of Meknes in 1900 can serve as a typical example. Of about 1,000 gainfully employed Jews, 150 were lace and button makers, 136 tailors, 102 druggists and hardware-mongers, 81 shoemakers, 62 dressmakers, 59 cobblers, 55 public criers, 52 tinsmiths, 48 goldsmiths, 25 money changers and lenders, 24 ritual slaughterers and clerks of the rabbinical courts, 22 flour merchants, 18 rabbis and teachers, 15 each gardeners and waxmakers, 14 each carpenters and hairdressers, 7 each scribes, silk thread retailers and grocers, 6 each wool carders, furnace operators, and muleteers, 5 each dyers and cotton goods retailers, 4 each bellows makers, and gold and silver stirrup inlayers, 3 each bookbinders, clockmakers, and scabbard makers, and 2 each masons, snuff makers, kiln operators, suppliers, stokers, and waggoners.[1]

The general attitude of the Muslim majority to the Jews was one of contempt, which the Jew had to tolerate submissively. This was one of the reasons why interaction between Jews and Muslims was minimal. It was a sad fact that, until the early twentieth century, the Jews of Morocco could feel safe only behind the gates of their *mellahs* within which they had to remain from sunset to sunrise.

All that has been said so far can still convey no idea of the specific quality of the life led by Moroccan Jews. For the poverty and oppression from which they suffered, the absence of amenities which we would deem basic prerequisites of a normal life, the limited education of the menfolk and the almost general illiteracy of the women, the narrow horizon which rarely extended beyond the *mellah* or the village – all this did not mean that the life of the Moroccan Jews was on the whole poor and miserable or that the general tone of their existence was one of unhappiness and despondency. Quite to the contrary: the average Moroccan Jewish man and woman felt that their day-to-day life was colourful, exciting, and enjoyable. The one factor chiefly responsible for this positive note was the prevalence of folk custom and belief which literally filled their days and made them rich in content, variety, and attraction. The few words which can be said

here on this aspect of Moroccan Jewish life cannot begin to do justice to this important subject.

To begin with oral folklore, hundreds of folk tales were known, and frequently told, in the Judeo-Arabic colloquial, by the older people, more often by women than by men, for the edification and entertainment of the younger generation, whose members in turn memorized them and became their future transmitters. In addition, they recited *qasidas* (in Arabic *qsida*, plural *qsa'id*), that is, poems or *chansons*, some of them quite long, and always with a difficult rhyme structure. Whenever the folk poets were inspired by a significant event, they composed new *qsa'id*, for instance, describing the cruelties of Hitler, deploring the emancipation of women, extolling the State of Israel as a place of security for the Jews, etc. While the *qasida* itself is an old pre-Islamic Arab poetic heritage, these modern Jewish *qsa'id* were the manifestation of a live poetic spirit among the Moroccan Jews.[2] Another very popular form of oral folklore was the proverb, of which thousands were in circulation and which encapsulated philosophical attitudes to the exigencies of life and the experience of age-old folk wisdom.

opposite: top left A Jewish wedding in 1910. The bridegroom is wearing the traditional *talis* or prayer shawl.

opposite: top right The Abulafia family in Mogador in 1920. They were one of the most prominent and wealthy families in Morocco.

above Moroccan Jewish women preparing tea.

above The consecration of the new synagogue in the Ville Nouvelle, Fez, 1958.

above right A Bar Mitzvah boy, about to be initiated into the Jewish religious community. As part of the ceremony he must read a portion of the Law.

Moroccan Jewish folk art found its expression in the making of gold and silver ornamental jewellery which was an almost exclusively Jewish speciality; in embroidery, leather work, and the tailoring of very decorative and ornate clothes, especially for women. Rich jewels and colourful clothes were the pride and joy of the Moroccan Jewish women whose beauty attracted the eye of many a foreign visitor. As an illustration, a single quotation will have to suffice, taken from an Italian traveller who visited Morocco in the 1880s:

It seems to me that there is no exaggeration in the reports of the beauty of the Jewesses of Morocco, which has a character of its own unknown in other countries. It is an opulent beauty, with large black eyes, broad low forehead, full red lips, and statuesque form – a theatrical beauty that looks well from a distance, and produces applause rather than sighs in the beholder. The Hebrew women of Tangiers do not wear in public their rich national costume; they are dressed almost like Europeans, but in such glaring colours – blue, carmine, sulphur yellow, and grass green – that they look like women wrapped in the flags of all nations. On the Saturdays, when they are in all their glory, the Jewish quarter presents a marked contrast to the austere solitude of the other streets. . . .

A company of Hebrew women have been here. . . . They were the wives, daughters, and relations of two rich merchants; beautiful women, with brilliant black eyes, fair skins, scarlet lips, and very small hands. The two mothers, already old, had not a single white hair, and the fire of youth still burned in their eyes. Their dress was splendid and picturesque – a handkerchief of gorgeous colours bound about the forehead; a jacket of red cloth, trimmed with heavy gold braid; a sort of waistcoat all of gold embroidery; a short, narrow petticoat of green cloth, also bordered with gold; and a sash of red or blue silk around the waist. They looked like so many Asiatic princesses.[3]

Folk custom and belief were so ubiquitous that they dominated the life of the people. Many were associated with religious observances; others, even though contrary to religious doctrine, were just as strictly observed and subscribed to. The belief in *baraka* was as prevalent among the Jews as among the Muslims. Some rabbis were visited daily by many believers who came to obtain their blessing, to consult them about every possible plan or problem, and to leave behind a proper contribution. The Sabbath and the New Moon and all the annual holidays had

A group of rabbis at Canaas.

their complement of customs, as had the great stations of the human life cycle, birth, menarche, marriage, and death. Illness, which struck only too often in the unhygienic and often overcrowded living conditions, was in general attributed to the evil eye or to *jinns* (Arabic pl. *jnun*), and the popular prophylactic measures resorted to were innumerable. The one device or design used most widely among both Jews and Muslims was the *khamsa* (five), a flat brass or silver plate cut out in the shape of a hand and engraved with decorative patterns, which was considered the best means of averting the evil eye. Silver amulets in this shape or in the form of a ball with five conspicuous knobs and studded with pieces of coloured glass, were made mostly by Jewish craftsmen but used by Jews and Muslims alike. The lamps used in Jewish homes or in the synagogues were often suspended from a large, decorated brass hand. The Jewish silversmiths also made charms in the shape of a crescent. The Star of David (*Magen David*), called by the Arabs 'the six-pointed seal of Solomon', was also much sought after as an amulet by both Muslims and Jews. Some Jews knew how to write a special amulet called *tsebrid* which was believed to make its wearer bullet proof.

The belief in *jinns* was equally widespread among Jews and Muslims. Both believed that the tribes of the *jnun* duplicated those of the humans, so that there were Jewish, Muslim, Christian, and pagan *jnun*, and that the Muslim *jnun* were white, green, and yellow, while the Jewish and Christian *jnun* were black. The Muslim *jnun* attacked people on Fridays, the Jewish on Saturdays.[4]

The worship of deceased saints was widespread. In addition to Jewish saints venerated by Jews, and Muslim saints venerated by Muslims, there were saints worshipped by adherents of both religions. A student of Moroccan folk religion, L. Voinot, found thirty-one saints venerated by both Muslims and Jews, thirteen cases of Muslim saints worshipped by Jews, and fifty cases of Jewish saints invoked by Muslims. The typical form of saint worship was the pilgrimage: an individual or a group would pay an annual visit (the so-called *ziyara*) to the *hawsh* (sanctuary) of the saint, which in most cases was nothing more than a small whitewashed building sheltering the saint's actual or reputed tomb. Such sanctuaries were scattered all over the Moroccan countryside.[5]

Until the independence of Morocco many Jews lived in small towns and

A rabbi teaching the Bible to a
class of young children
in Casablanca, *c.* 1940s.

villages. In the southern third of the country, comprising the provinces of Marrakesh, Agadir, and Tiznit, where the Muslim population was largely Berber, there were no fewer than one hundred and seventy *mellahs* as late as 1951, located in the Atlas Mountains, in the oases of the pre-Sahara region, and in the five cities. Some of the *mellahs* were so small as to barely deserve this name. For example, Houm Hauch in the Tazenakht district had in 1949 one Jewish house inhabited by a family of eight. *Mellahs* with ten to twenty houses and fifty to a hundred souls were common. Between 1920 and 1950, thirty-two of these small *mellahs* had disappeared due to internal migration to the larger centres. But even the latter became reduced in size as a result of emigration or migration to the largest cities. Thus, the Casablanca Jewish community increased by 15,000 from 1940 to 1950, to 75,000, or 34 per cent of all the Jews of Morocco.

The typical Moroccan *mellah* suffered from over-crowded living conditions. As an example we can refer to Marrakesh, the most important city in the south of Morocco which, according to the 1951 census, had 220,000 inhabitants, including some 17,000 Jews.[6] In 1949, the density per hectare (1,000 square metres, or 2·471 acres) was 35 inhabitants in the European quarter, 450 in the *medina* (the old Muslim quarter) and 1,300 in the *mellah*, the Jewish quarter, which averages out at the incredible density of 1·3 Jewish souls per square metre. The disproportion between the economically active Jews in Marrakesh and the total Jewish population also points to the great poverty of the majority: this proportion was one to ten. Each *mellah* was inhabited by many Jews who had moved there from the villages and became fishermen, day-labourers, porters, water-carriers (among them women), or remained unemployed and were mendicants. Nor were prostitutes absent from the *mellah*, among them Muslim women whose clients felt safer visiting them in the *mellah* than in a Muslim quarter.

Most of the children in the Marrakesh *mellah* attended school, almost all of them schools of the *Alliance*. In 1948, 1,851 Jewish boys and girls aged six to twelve attended school, 300 were employed, and 600 were without any occupation.

In 1949, about one half of the economically active Jewish population of Marrakesh belonged to one of forty-nine guilds, each headed by its own *amin* (chief). These professional organizations included those of wholesalers, merchants of coal, necklaces, scrap iron, legumes, dry legumes, horse hair, fish, and poultry; manufacturers of trays, threads, slippers; shoemakers, harness makers, carders, mattress makers, tinsmiths, carpenters, makers of roof gutters and watchmakers. Among the silversmiths the workshops owners and employees each had their separate organization, as had the European tailors, native tailors, haberdashers. The dressmakers were all women with a woman *amina* at their head. There were also guilds of hairdressers, bakers, butchers, European grocers, native grocers, used-clothes dealers, sewing-machine repair men, pastry cooks, stationers, druggists, herbalists, waiters, electricians, and knife grinders. The water carriers who, mostly clad in rags, carried a huge earthenware jar full of water on their shoulders, had their own guild, and so had the waggoners, taxi drivers, agents, brokers, and even agriculturists, cyclists and musicians. The members of each guild submitted the names of three candidates to the Pasha of the city and to the Chief of Municipal Services, who designated one of them as the *amin*. The *amin* safeguarded the interests of the guild, and apportioned among its members the taxes and the charitable contributions for the poor.

In addition, there were numerous occupations whose practitioners did not form guilds and had no chief. Among these were the rabbis (there were in Marrakesh 120 rabbis, or one for every 150 Jews), ritual slaughterers, porters, donkey drivers, chauffeurs, distillers, public criers, and cooks (for marriage festivities).

As for the women, work by them outside the home was frowned upon, so that no more than 400 women, or 10 per cent of their age group – mostly widows and divorced women – were engaged in gainful occupations, However, the trend for young girls to work after finishing school and until they got married, was noticeable in the 1940s.

above Jews from Asni in the Atlas mountains on a pilgrimage to the tomb of the Saint of Ouirgane Anzar.

right A folk-custom: sprinkling water in the streets at the festival of Shavuot, in the Atlas Mountains.

Social status with all its appurtenant honours and obligations was the function of either intellectual excellence or riches. Of the former, we have already spoken, albeit briefly; of the latter all that has to be said is that the few rich Jews, found in every sizeable community, were its leaders. A sign of the changing times was that in the past the well-to-do Jews tried to hide their affluence, while by the 1940s they paraded it openly. The big homes of the rich would invariably house three generations, each exhibiting its particular cultural orientation from traditionalism to modernism.

Characteristic of the *mellahs*, as they have existed for many generations, was the absence of a middle class. Surrounding the few well-to-do was the great majority of the poor, including the 80 or 90 per cent who were totally destitute. Poverty also meant lack of interest in communal affairs, or, perhaps, it would be more correct to say, it robbed the Jews of the *mellah* of the ability to take an interest in such affairs. In 1951, when elections were held for the committee of the Jewish community in Marrakesh, of the 17,000 Jews only 448 had the right to vote,[7] and of them only 153 exercised their right. About the same time, among the 75,000

Jews of Casablanca there were only 145 voters! In Marrakesh, in 1950, the Jewish community gave financial support to 2,000 indigents, or 12 per cent of the total number of Jews; in Taroudannt this proportion reached 40 per cent, or 400 out of a total of 1,000 Jews.

Poverty and overcrowding resulted in a general physical underdevelopment. The average Moroccan Jewish man was 163 centimetres tall and weighed 57 kilos; the woman – 149 centimetres and 52 kilos. Endemic diseases (especially the 'three T's': trachoma, tuberculosis, and *teigne* (i.e. scurvy), were prevalent.[8] We have no statistics of life expectancy, but the Jewish mortality rates were much higher than those of the Muslims.

Yet despite their poverty and poor health, despite the discrimination against them and the occasional attacks to which they were exposed, the Jews of Marrakesh – as those of all other Moroccan communities – were sustained by their religious traditions, their strong beliefs and colourful practices, their veneration of the dead saints and reliance on living rabbis, their absorption in the minutiae of

ritual, the feeling of moral security in the *mellah*, in the Jewish milieu, the home, the extended family, the rhythmical interruption of everyday life by the Sabbath, the New Moon, the annual holy days, the pilgrimages to saints' tombs, and the family feasts of the individual life cycle. To all this was added the inevitable tension between the generations, the conservative, tradition-bound, religiously observant older people, and the freer, better-educated, dissatisfied, forward-looking younger men and women, impatient to throw off what they perceived as the yoke of the old customs and the restrictions of the old morality. The turbulence created by these tensions was intensified by the increasing desire in the younger generation to leave the *mellah*, and to go to the biggest cities of the country, or to emigrate to Israel, to France, or some other western country. Thus, the inner ferment inexorably pushed the *mellahs*, and especially those of the south, toward a rapid self-liquidation and a transplantation of its most vital young element into other worlds.

The above brief comments on the history and life of the Jews in Morocco cannot, of course, give more than a fleeting glimpse of what the Moroccan Jewish

left The Street of the Jews in Tetuán.

community was like with its many bright and dark spots and intermediate shadings. But neither word nor picture can recapture the vibrancy of existence, the colourful varieties of family life, the specific flavour of the personalities, the relations between men and women, the smells and the sounds, the filth, stench, poverty and squalour, the clamour and the tensions, of the slums, the opulence and luxury of the few who were rich with their perfumed, bejewelled, silk- and velvet-clad women, the sweaty and dusty drudgery of manual labour and the shrewd business activities and commercial manipulations, the Sabbath joy and relaxation, the holiday bustle and elation, the serene faith in God and the superstitious belief in *jinns* and magic, and the many other aspects of being, feeling, and willing, of trusting and fearing, whose sum total made up Moroccan Jewish life and comprised the unique Moroccan variety of a Jewish world that is no more.

above Women mourners in the Jewish cemetery in Tetuán.

Algeria

The Chief Rabbi (centre) in the synagogue in Ghardaia, Algeria.

The history of the Jews in Algeria, the eastern neighbour of Morocco, parallels that of the Moroccan Jews in many respects. In both countries legend seeks the origin of the Jewish community in the times of the First Temple of Jerusalem. In both, historical data such as epitaphs show Jewish presence from the first few centuries of the common era when the territory was under Roman rule. However, since the names in most of the Algerian Jewish tomb inscriptions are Latin, which is not the case in Morocco, one must assume that these early Algerian Jews came from Italy.

The number of Jews in Algeria had increased under the Vandals. Justinian (sixth century) singled them out in his discriminatory edict together with Arians and heathens. The persecutions by the Visigoths in Spain in the seventh century brought a wave of Jewish refugees from that country. At that time, Berber tribes which, according to Ibn Khaldun, had adopted Judaism, were numerous both in Morocco and in Algeria. As in Morocco, so in Algeria the Jews, jointly with the Berbers, opposed the Muslim Arab invaders, and the Arab victory in both countries spelled the end of Judaism as a major religious factor. Those who remained true to their Jewish faith became in both countries *dhimmis*, clients, or subject, protected people, who had to pay the *jizya* (head tax) in order to be tolerated by their Muslim overlords.

In the eleventh to thirteenth centuries the north of the territory which today comprises Algeria was ruled by the Almoravids and the Almohades. Subsequently, local autonomous kingdoms and tribal groupings emerged, several of which were Berber, such as the kingdoms of Ashir, Tahert (Tiaret), and Qalʿat Hammad, in each of which there were Jewish communities.

The first Sephardi Jews appeared in Algeria as ambassadors appointed by the Christian kings of Spain. This enabled the Sephardi Jews to become acquainted with the Jewish condition in Algeria, which in that period was relatively favourable. Consequently, in 1391, when the Jews were expelled from the Spanish mainland and the Balearic Islands, many of them settled in the Algerian coastal cities of Wahran (Oran), Mostaganem, Tenes, Cherchel, Algiers, and Bougie, and also penetrated into the interior.

In contrast to the attitude they encountered on the part of the native Moroccan Jews, the Sephardi newcomers were at first well received by the established Jewish population of Algeria. Before long, the talented and energetic Sephardim became leaders of commercial activities in the country. The Sudanese gold route was known as the 'Jewish road', and its end station, the city of Tlemcen in north-west Algeria, which was also the gate to the Mediterranean, became an important centre of Jewish trade.

As the number of the Sephardi newcomers increased, the native Jews began to be apprehensive about maintaining their own positions. Tensions developed between the two Jewish elements, and conflicts surfaced as the older community resisted the attempts of the newcomers to dominate community life. It took several generations for these difficulties to disappear. Gradually the Sephardim gave up their Ladino colloquial, adopted the local Judeo-Arabic, and the two communities merged into one.

Before that happened, however, the Sephardi Jews had organized intercontinental trade, exporting gold from Touat and ostrich feathers from the Mzab, as well as rugs, cloaks, wool, pelts and cereals, and importing European products in exchange. Wealthy Jews owned estates, slaves, and livestock. As descendants of immigrants (called also here, as in Morocco, *mʿgorashim* or exiles), they were exempt from the onerous head tax. For several generations, until their final merger with the native Jewish majority, the Sephardim lived in separate quarters, had their own synagogues and cemeteries, and wore a different garb. The distinction in clothing earned the newcomers the name *baʿale hakappus* or *kabbusiyyim*, i.e., 'wearers of berets', while the native Jews were called *baʿale hamitznefet*, or 'turban wearers'. By the end of the seventeenth century all these distinctions had disappeared, and the Sephardim had assimilated in every respect, including language, to the native Jews. Their place as a distinct and elite group was subsequently taken by the *Gorneyim* or *Grana*, whose name was derived from that of the Italian city of Leghorn (Livorno). These were originally Spanish and Portuguese Jews who, upon their expulsion from the Iberian Peninsula, found refuge in Livorno, became Italianized, and arrived in Algeria (and Tunisia) as wealthy merchants with international connections. They settled in the coastal cities of Algeria, and especially in Algiers, in the seventeenth century. Most of them were to return to Italy soon after the French conquest of Algeria.

The Sephardi immigration of 1391 re-invigorated not only the economic, but

also the moral, religious, and organizational life of Algerian Jewry. Numerous Algerian cities became important centres of Jewish learning, and several of them became the seats of outstanding rabbinical authorities. On the other hand, the Spanish exile of 1492 did not result in any considerable additional Sephardi immigration to Algeria, with the exception of the city of Tlemcen, which by that time was the most important commercial centre of the country.

The Spanish exile had other serious repercussions for Algeria. Anti-Jewish agitation started, and a few years later the powerful Jewish communities of Tlemcen in the north and Touat in the south were destroyed by fanatical mobs. The Spaniards themselves occupied the coastal cities of Oran and Bougie in 1509, proceeded to pillage Jewish property and sell Jews as slaves. Some time later, however, influential Jewish leaders succeeded in convincing the Spaniards that their interests were better served by allowing the Jewish communities to continue.

Under Turkish domination, from 1519 on, Algerian Jewry enjoyed a period of relative tranquility and security, although the indignities appertaining to their *dhimmi* status continued. The whims of the local pashas and *deys* were unappealable law, and Jewish life and property were defenceless against them. Still, conditions in the cities controlled by the Spaniards were much worse. In 1563 1,500 Jews were killed or enslaved by the Spaniards in Tlemcen, and in 1669 the Jews were expelled by them from Oran. In the villages occupied by the Spaniards and exposed to fighting between the Muslims and the Christians they suffered from both sides.

The deep south, the borders of the Sahara and the oases, were as a rule beyond the reach of either Turks or Spaniards, and the native Jews (there was no Sephardi settlement) fared better than their brethren in the north. While the sovereign *deys*

who governed the provinces treated the Jews roughly and exploited them through taxation, they made exceptions in the case of the few wealthy and influential Jews who, from the seventeenth century on, were mostly *Gorneyim*, and whom they used as emissaries to European powers. Still, even these privileged Jews were not safe from the violence of the Janissaries. In 1792, when the Spaniards were forced to evacuate Oran, the Jews were re-invited to the city and their community was re-established. In 1805, following the assassination of the *dey's* Jewish chief aide, occurred the only massacre of Jews to take place in Algiers.

For several centuries prior to the French conquest of Algeria the Jewish communities enjoyed self-government. They were headed by a *Shaykh al-Yahud* or *Z'qan ha Y'hudim* (Elder of the Jews), also called *Muqaddam* (foreman), who was appointed by the Muslim authorities. He in turn named the officers called *G'dole haQahal* (the great ones of the community) or *Ziqne haQahal* (Elders of the community). Only the Sephardim were, for some time, able to choose their own officers, called *Ne'emanim* (trustees). The communities themselves chose and paid their *Bet Din* (law court) consisting of three rabbis. The sentences of the *Bet Din* were carried out by the *Muqaddam*, who had the police and a prison at his disposal. Conservatism and rigid adherence to the local custom *(Minhag)* left the rabbis no choice but to approve of local practices; the penalties including fines, floggings, and, in extreme cases, excommunication. An unpopular and onerous task of the head and the council was the apportioning and collecting of the taxes imposed on the Jews by the government. The expenses of the *Qahal* were defrayed from taxes levied on meat, matzoth, etc. Donations for the poor were collected mainly at New Year, Yom Kippur, Hanukka and Purim.

After the French conquest in 1830 Jewish communal self-government was soon abolished. Jurisdiction over the Jews passed to French courts. The *Muqaddam* was replaced by a Jewish deputy mayor. The loss of community autonomy displeased many Jews so much that they preferred to emigrate. *Gorneyim* returned to Leghorn, members of the middle class, tradesmen, and craftsmen went to Morocco and Tunisia. However, a reverse migration also took place: attracted by the French presence, Moroccan and Tunisian Jews moved to Algeria. Internal migration, from the villages of the south to the coastal cities, also set in.

The French proceeded to reorganize the structure of the Jewish communities along centralized French lines. Jewish consistories, similar to those of France, were set up in the main cities. Chief rabbis were brought from France, paid by the government, and charged with the task of working for the emancipation, that is, Frenchification, of their congregants. Before long, there was a powerful movement toward assimilation in the northern cities, and as in Europe, so in Algeria many Jews left Judaism.

On the other hand, these measures also brought about an upsurge of interest in modern Jewish culture. Hebrew printing shops were established in Algiers and Oran. New Talmud Tora schools were opened. The *Alliance Israélite Universelle* began its French-Jewish educational work. A Jewish intelligentsia emerged, endeavouring to combine Jewish tradition with French culture. Jews began to enter the liberal professions and became physicians, lawyers, engineers, university professors, army officers, magistrates.

In these Jewish *evolué* circles, the clamour for French naturalization increased. In 1865 individual Jews were granted the right to opt for French citizenship, and in 1870 the Crémieux Decree gave French citizenship collectively to all the 35,000 Algerian Jews, except for those of the Territories of the South who were not *evolué*. Therewith Judaism officially ceased to exist in Algeria as a nationality, but it remained as a religion recognized by the state.

As was typical of modern Muslim North Africa everywhere, major political events were usually followed by anti-Semitic outbursts. From 1881 to 1900 Jews were attacked in one city after the other, the incidents taking on new violence after the Dreyfus affair of 1894.

Little of these events touched the Jews of the southern Saharan territories of Algeria. Here the Jews, living in towns and villages of the remote oases in the midst of either an Arab or a Berber Muslim majority, had their well-defined niches in the economic structure, and had achieved a well-functioning social and occupational adjustment. Their conditions and their way of life did not change until the traumatic events of the mid-twentieth century which motivated them to emigrate to Israel or to France. A typical settlement was that of Ghardaia, the main town of the large Mzab oasis, some 300 miles south of the Mediterranean coast. In the early 1950s there were 1,642 Jews in Ghardaia, all of whom were gone by the end of 1962. The economically-active male population, although resident in Ghardaia, where the Jews had their special quarters, would actually sojourn in the town only during Passover and the High Holy Days in the autumn. At other times, the men would go to work in the neighbouring oases, or in the north, following thereby the custom and mode of life of all Mzabites. They were merchants, who, until the late nineteenth century, controlled the trans-Saharan trade of the Mzab, and jewellers, leather- and woodworkers, butchers, tinsmiths, blacksmiths, and makers of cards for the combing of wool. They would practice their trade wherever they were sure of finding the most customers. Down to the very end of their presence in the oasis, metal- and woodworking were almost entirely in the hands of Jews. The Jews also engaged in those occupations which were forbidden to Muslims or considered by them as degrading, such as money lending, the collection of fees and taxes in the market-place, and the sale of alcoholic beverages. In the past, there used to be a few Jewish pastoral nomadic groups, but the last of these became sedentary in the late nineteenth century.

Physically the Jews of Ghardaia looked very much like the eastern Berbers, except that they had very long and narrow heads, and dark brown eyes which had a reddish tinge when seen in a strong light. The preferred marriage among them, as among the Jews and Muslims all over the Middle East, was between children of brothers. An anthropologist who studied the Jews of the Sahara in the late 1950s remarked that despite this intense inbreeding neither mental nor physical defects were more frequent among them than in the population of the United States. He also made the puzzling observation that well-to-do Jews in the Mzab often took Arab married women as mistresses, but that the offspring of these unions were usually absorbed by the Arab community for they were generally thought to be the children of their mothers' husbands.[9]

Until the arrival of the French the Jews were forbidden to own land, and to live in any town of the Mzab other than Ghardaia. They had to wear a distinctive garb consisting of a black turban and black outer garments. More recently, they chose to wear different but equally distinctive clothes, consisting of a soft fez of red felt worn far back on the head like a skull cap, and a *gandoura*, a loose cloak made of a large rectangular piece of white cotton.

There were in the past Jewish groups much farther south than Ghardaia. As deep in the Sahara as Touat (700 miles due south from Algiers), they had a sizeable community from the early fourteenth to the sixteenth century, and were in control of trade. In Timimoun, halfway between Touat and the Moroccan border, and in Gourara further south, a Jewish remnant was found as late as the 1950s. They were called *muhajirin*, that is, 'refugees' or 'emigrants'.[10]

Most of what has been said above about the popular culture of the Moroccan Jews holds good for their Algerian brethren. However, in Algeria the contrast between the tradition-bound Jews of the hinterland and the Frenchified Jewish middle class in the northern cities was greater than in Morocco.

In the last few decades prior to the independence of Algeria there was a deterioration in the condition of the Jews. Hitler's rise to power caused great rejoicing among the local Jew-haters; the swastika became their much-displayed symbol, and their campaigns resulted in a bloody pogrom in Constantine in 1934. A new crisis erupted in 1936 when Léon Blum, a Jew, became premier of France. After the French defeat by the Germans (1940), the Crémieux Decree was abrogated, and the racial laws of Vichy were applied by the Algerian administration with great severity. It took all the determination of the Algerian Jewish leaders to save their community from total destruction. Algerian Jews organized and headed the resistance which succeeded in 1942 in neutralizing the capital while the Allied forces landed in the country. Despite all this, the victorious French leaders who were in control of Algeria continued the anti-Semitic policy of Vichy, set up a detention camp for the Jews, and promulgated many inhuman legal measures against them. It required the vigorous protests of the French Committee of National Liberation in London and of international Jewish organizations, and finally the personal intervention of President Roosevelt, to have the rights of Algerian Jews restored, late in 1943. Finally, in 1947, the Organic Law of Algeria proclaimed that all persons of French nationality in Algeria without distinction as to origin, race, language or religion, had equal rights.

The establishment of Israel in 1948 had no repercussions in Algeria. The assimilation of the Jews to French civilization continued, but, although most Algerian Jews felt thoroughly French, sharp distinctions between them and the French *colons* remained in force. The Algerian struggle for national independence, which began in 1960, spelled the end of Algerian Jewry. Anti-Jewish riots broke out, and on Christmas Eve the Great Synagogue in Algiers was ravaged. The terror and counter-terror of 1961 and 1962 had catastrophic consequences for the Jews whose quarters were mostly located between those of the Arabs and the French, and who thus suffered attacks from both sides. Jewish emigration increased, and by July 1962, when Algeria gained independence, 70,000 Jews had left for France and 5,000 for Israel. Thereafter, the Jewish exodus continued to accelerate, and by 1969 fewer than 1,000 Jews remained in Algeria which only twenty years earlier had a large Jewish contingent of 130,000.

Libya

Musci Fellah, a wealthy Jewish landowner of Tripoli, in the 1930s. He was murdered during the November 1945 pogrom in Tripoli.

Modern Libya comprises three provinces: Tripolitania in the west, Cyrenaica in the east, and Fezzan in the south. The earliest testimony to the presence of Jews in Libya pertains to Cyrenaica, where Ptolemy I Soter (d. 282 BCE) settled Jews in Pentapolis, the five Greek cities of which the most important was Cyrene. These originally military settlements rapidly developed into civilian towns in which an important factor was the well-educated Jewish population. One of the earliest Jewish historians was Jason of Cyrene, who emigrated to Palestine in the days of the Hasmonean uprising (166 BCE). Regrettably, his five-volume history of the Maccabees is lost, but an abridgement of it survives in the apocryphal Second Book of the Maccabees. In the late first century BCE Strabo, the Greek historian, wrote that the Jews constituted one of the four population elements in Cyrenaica.

As their co-religionists in Egypt to the east, so the Jews of Cyrenaica could not escape the influence of Hellenism, as indicated by the appearance of Jewish names among the graduates of the city gymnasia in Cyrene and Ptolemais. However, the Jews of the rural communities, and they were the majority, were less exposed to Greco-Roman influence. Each of the Jewish rebellions ended in defeat, and resulted in the expulsion of the surviving Jews from the coastal cities to the south, to the borders of the desert, where some of their descendants continued to live down to the 1940s.

There is little information on the Jews of Libya from the Arab conquest (642) to the Spanish invasion of Tripolitania (1510), although scattered references show that during these nine centuries Jews lived in many parts of the country.

In 1510, when the Spaniards invaded Tripoli, 800 Jewish families fled partly to Tajura, a coastal village to the east of Tripoli, and partly to Jebel Gharyan, some fifty miles to the south from the coast (see below p. 125). In 1551 the Turks conquered Tripoli, expelled the Spaniards, and established their rule which was to last until 1911. About the same time R. Shim'on Lavi, an exile from Spain who was on his way from Fez to Palestine, decided to remain in Tripoli and teach the Jews the elements of their religion. According to the traditions of the Tripolitanian Jews, the work of R. Lavi (who remained with them until his death in 1580) laid the foundations of the Tripoli Jewish community, its institutions and customs. In 1588 or 1589 there was a religious-inspired Arab uprising against the Turks in Tripolitania, in the course of which thousands of Jews were forced to convert to Islam. Many others who served in the Turkish army were killed before the rebellion was put down.

In the seventeenth century the Jewish community of Tripoli was reinforced by the arrival of *Gorneyim*, Jewish immigrants from Italy. One of them was Abraham Michael Cardozo (1627–1698/1700), a Jew of Spanish Marrano background, who lived for several years in Venice and Leghorn, then in Egypt, and who was a staunch believer in Shabbatai Zevi even after the conversion of the psuedo-Messiah to Islam, and effectively spread Shabbataian beliefs in Tripoli and other parts of North Africa. In fact, a Judeo-Arabic poem, composed by Tripoli women and containing a prayer for 'the coming of the Messiah and his disciple Nathan [of Gaza]', was still recited in the second half of the nineteenth century.

In the eighteenth century, trading activity between Livorno (Leghorn) and Tripoli increased, due to the initiative of several Jewish traders. From Tripoli the imported goods were sent on to the oases of Fezzan and farther south, as far as Bornu in southern Nigeria. However, periodic famines and epidemics, which plagued Tripolitania as much as they did other areas in the Middle East, caused impoverishment and steep increases in the prices of basic commodities. The trans-Saharan trade of Tripoli declined in the late nineteenth century, when new trade routes were opened, seaports were established along the coasts of Africa, and the Anglo-Egyptian Sudan became an effective competitor.

Most of the Libyan Jews earned their livelihood as artisans (they were the only blacksmiths who produced agricultural implements) down to the very end of their existence in the country. According to an Israeli census of Libyan Jewish immigrants who arrived in 1948–51, 47 per cent were artisans, 15·4 per cent merchants, 7·5 per cent clerks and administrators, 7·1 per cent construction and transport workers, 6·1 per cent farmers, 3 per cent professionals (including rabbis and teachers), and 13·9 per cent worked in personal services or were unskilled labourers. One can assume that the occupational structure of Libyan Jews prior to their emigration did not differ substantially from this picture.

Internally, the heads of the Jewish community of Tripoli kept a strict rein on its members. The well-to-do had to pay a tax, called *gabella*, on all imported goods. This tax was at first 2 per mil and from the mid-eighteenth century 3 per mil, of the value of all merchandise, based on the *'fattura'*. The income of the community was used to support the children in school, to pay the *dayyanim* (religious judges), the teachers, the Yeshiva students, and the ten *batlanim*, men who had no occupation but studied Tora all day long. Payment of the taxes had to be rendered under pain of excommunication. In the nineteenth century new taxes were added such as a tax on dyeing silk. A tax was paid also on meat – a luxury item in all Middle Eastern countries. An important source of community income was the

right A Jewish cabinet-maker in his home displaying his work, *c.* 1900.

various functions performed at services in the synagogues, which would be auctioned off to the highest bidder, as was customary in all tradition-abiding Jewish communities.

The native rabbis of Tripoli were more attracted to the study of the Kabbala than to that of the Halakha, and left behind a number of Kabbalistic works. Some of them also wrote religious poetry in Hebrew or in Arabic, often dealing with the persecutions suffered by the Libyan Jews. These literary activities continued into the present century. The chief rabbis were appointed by royal *firman* from Istanbul. The secular head of the community was the *Qa'id* (chief) who represented the Jews *vis-à-vis* the governmental authorities.

From the end of the nineteenth century Italian efforts to gain a foothold in Libya became apparent. In 1876 an Italian Jew was sent to Tripoli to establish the first Italian school, in which thousands of Jewish boys and girls (Jewish pupils were the majority) were to receive their education. The *Alliance Israélite Universelle* started its educational work in 1890. In 1911 Italy officially took possession of Libya, and proceeded to conquer the hinterland and to suppress rebellions. While the position of the Jews under Italian rule did not improve as much as they had hoped, they had no reason to complain until 1942, when the Fascist anti-Jewish laws were introduced. During this period the chief rabbis of Tripoli all came from Italy. When Libya became a theatre of war, the Jews suffered more than the Muslims; men of eighteen to forty-two years of age were sent to labour camps near the front, and when, after a brief period of occupation, the British army had to withdraw from Cyrenaica, the Italians exiled the Jews to the south, to a concentration camp. Conditions in this camp were so bad that within fourteen months 562 people, or one-quarter of all the detainees, died of hunger and typhus. The survivors, liberated by the British in January 1943, returned to their homes.

After the war the Jews set about rebuilding their private and community lives, but by the end of 1945 the indifferent attitude of the British army enabled Arab mobs to run wild in several cities and to kill and wound many Jews, loot their property, and set fire to their synagogues. These events gave the impetus to the Jews to set up a self-defence organization (initiated by an emissary from the *Yishuv*) which in 1948 successfully repulsed another Arab attack on the Jewish quarter of Tripoli.

Libya is unique in the Jewish Diaspora in that some of its Jews in the hinterland, in Gharyan and, farther south, in Tigrinna, were cave-dwellers. Although these Jews differed little in their way of life from their Berber Muslim neighbours, and although they were largely cut off from contact with the Jews of the coastal cities, they remained faithful to the religion of their fathers, and preserved many old Jewish traditions. Entire villages were built into caves, consisting of dwellings, houses and storage rooms, connected by passage-ways cut into the soft red loam hills, with open courtyards in front of them.

A traveller who visited Gharyan in 1818–20 mentions that the cave dwellings of the Jews were clean, and that they were dug into the mountain slopes in a manner superior to that of the Arabs.

According to a report by Nahum Slouschz, who visited Libya in 1906, there were at that time about 1,000 Jews in Kafr al-ʿAbbas, and 300 in the village of Tigrinna, the two cave-villages still inhabited by Jews. Some time prior to his visit, the number of Jewish cave-dwellers had been much larger, but most of them had moved to the city of Tripoli. From the description of Slouschz it appears that the cave-village he visited was a well-functioning Jewish community, with underground synagogues, with *kuttabs* (Tora schools) attached to them, with rabbis and ritual slaughterers. All the men could read Hebrew. Most of them were craftsmen, gold- and silversmiths, or blacksmiths, or else itinerant pedlars who plied their trade all over the desert. The women and children worked in the vineyards and small fields they had nearby. In the village of Gharyan the *hakham* also functioned as a healer who took care of the sick of his village, and wrote verses in Hebrew and Arabic. In 1950–1 the remaining Jewish cave-dwellers joined the other Jews of Libya and emigrated to Israel.

Within three years of the establishment of Israel (1948–51) thirty thousand Jews emigrated from Libya, leaving only 8,000 in the country. After the Six-Day War of 1967, which triggered renewed anti-Jewish riots in Libya, almost all of the remaining Jews emigrated. When Colonel Qaddafi gained control (September 1969), the 400–500 Jews who were still in the country were placed in a camp in Tripoli, but within a year they were allowed to emigrate. At the end of 1970 no more than seventy Jews were left in Libya, and in 1976 only forty.

left Pupils of Rosh Pinah, a school for Jewish children established by local Tripoli Jews in 1933.

right The interior of the synagogue at Homs, 1912.

Egypt

The Zionist 'Committee of Delegates' visiting Egyptian Jews in 1918. In the centre, with bald head, Chaim Weizmann.

Egypt, the easternmost of the five Arab countries which line the southern coast of the Mediterranean, differs essentially from the other four. In Morocco, Algeria, Tunisia, and Libya, the seashore is the place of the greatest concentration of the population, the cultural centre in relation to which the hinterland is backward and provincial. Not only the major cities, but also the agricultural lands in each of them, stretch in a relatively narrow strip along the Mediterranean, and, in Morocco, along the Atlantic coastline. The more one moves away from the sea, to the south, the more one is surrounded by the merciless desert in which settled life is possible only in the few oases which dot the barren expanse of stone and sand like fertile green islands.

In Egypt the sea is far less important than the Nile. Although there is one great city on the seashore, Alexandria, and several minor towns along both the Mediterranean and Red Sea, the overwhelming majority of the Egyptians live, and have lived for six millennia, on the banks of the Nile or in the huge triangle of its delta.

Egypt occupies a special place in Jewish history. It was the first country to receive 'Jewish' refugees; it was to Egypt that the patriarch Jacob and his family of seventy souls fled from famine which drove them out of the Land of Canaan. It was the country in which the few dozen children and grandchildren of Jacob-Israel multiplied and became a people of twelve large tribes. It was also the first country to exploit, oppress, and enslave the Children of Israel, practise genocide upon them, and refuse them permission to emigrate – all prototypical events which were to occur again and again in the course of the long history of the Jews. Egypt was

The Jewish Sanua family in
Cairo, 1923.

the first country in which the House of Israel was seized by the desire to return to the promised land of its fathers, and from which miraculous circumstances enabled it to escape. It was on Egypt's borders, in the Sinai, that the Children of Israel received the Law which was to become the basis of their existence and the badge of their separate identity in the world of nations for all times.

When, seven centuries later, the First Temple of Jerusalem was destroyed by the Babylonians, it was again Egypt to which a band of Judean refugees fled, taking with them a reluctant Jeremiah, prophet of Jerusalem's doom. Several decades prior to their arrival Jewish civilians and mercenaries had settled on the island of Elephantine in the upper Nile, opposite modern Aswan, where the Jewish soldiers constituted a frontier garrison. They built themselves a temple which survived until 411 BCE. The religion of the Elephantine Jews was a variant of the popular Jewish religion, practised by the people in Judah until its destruction by the Babylonians in 586 BCE. In Jerusalem they worshipped, alongside Yahweh, Asherah, and in Elephantine, next to Yahu (i.e., Yahweh), two female deities, Ashambethel and Anathbethel.

From that time on, from 586 BCE to be exact, there was never again a period in which Jews would not have lived in the ancient land of the Pharaohs, which is the more remarkable since Egypt is the only country in the world to which the Children of Israel are explicitly forbidden to return by a Biblical commandment (Deut. 17:16; cf. Hosea 11:5).

Egypt itself changed hands many times in the course of its long history: after many Pharaonic dynasties, it was ruled by the Greek Ptolemies, who were followed by Romans, Byzantines, Arabs, Mamelukes, Turks, French, British, and finally by its own autochthonous independent Egyptian Arab rulers. Its language and culture also changed: Egyptian was replaced by Greek, and Greek by Arabic, while its dominant religion, after Egyptian and Greek polytheism, became first Christian, and then, from the seventh century on, Muslim. Yet throughout all these transformations, Egyptian Jewry remained true to itself and its heritage, its Jewish religion and traditions, its Hebrew ritual language, its Jewish ethnicity, its love of the land of Israel.

The greatest challenge Judaism faced in Egypt was that of Hellenism. After being conquered by Alexander the Great (332 BCE), Egypt, and especially the great city of Alexandria where many Jews settled, became the centre of Greek culture, philosophy, literature, science. The Jews, too, became Hellenized, and participated intensively in all the Greek cultural activities of Alexandria except science. They spoke Greek, translated the Bible into Greek, wrote Greek plays, histories, poetical and philosophical works, served as commanders of the army and the police, and were as much part of the life of the country as were, in later ages, the Jews of Spain, Germany, or America, of theirs. But they remained true to their religion, and built themselves great synagogues and even a temple in Leontopolis (Lower Egypt, in 161 BCE). Moreover, in their literary, epic, dramatic, philosophical and historiographic works their central purpose was to demonstrate, uphold, and argue the excellence of the Jewish people. Their primary concern with Jewry and Judaism seems to be the reason for the total abstention of Jews from the many fields of science—mathematics, geometry, geography, astronomy, medical studies, philology, etc.—in which Greek Alexandrians were the leaders of their age. It would seem that these fields did not attract the Jews because they felt that by engaging in them they could not have furthered the over-riding purpose to which they were committed: the advancement of the Jewish cause.

In the first century BCE Egypt came under Roman rule, and the situation of the Jews worsened. The Jews, like the Egyptians, were reduced to the lowest class of people and had to pay a poll tax; anti-Semitic literature began to proliferate. A number of pogroms took place. Jewish attempts at retaliation or rebellion (e.g., in 66 and 115–17 CE) were crushed. The number of the Jews diminished rapidly. By the second century CE, Christianity, centred in Alexandria, turned sharply against the Jews, and it was not until about 300 CE that Jewish life could rally again.

Little is known of the Jews of Egypt from the Arab conquest (640) to the end of the tenth century, although there are indications that Jews were not only active in commerce but had achieved high standards of scholarship and culture, as shown, for example, by the appearance of a genius of the stature of Saadya Gaon who was born in 882 in Fayyum (south of present-day Cairo). The Fatimid conquest of Egypt (969) initiated a period of prosperity and intense intellectual activity, which continued until the end of the Ayyubid rule (1250). The generally liberal attitude of the Fatimid caliphs – with the exception of the fanatic al-Hakim (996–1020), founder of the Druze sect – enabled the Jewish community to flourish. Although small in number (in the twelfth century it was estimated at 12,000 to 20,000), Jews were well-to-do merchants, engaged in various trades, served the caliphs as court physicians and were courtiers and administrators of provinces. The scholars among them produced a rich literature, and maintained an academy in Fostat, whose heads were referred to as *Geonim* and whose authority was recognized as far away as Aden in South Arabia. The secular head of the autonomous Jewish community had the title *nagid* (roughly 'prince'), or, in Arabic, *ra'is al-Yahud* (head of the Jews), a position held until 1370 by descendants of Maimonides.

In 1301 the Mameluke rulers issued decrees directed against the non-Muslim population. Among them was the edict which provided that the Jews had to wear yellow turbans, the Christians blue turbans, and the Samaritans red ones. Half a century later attacks occurred against the non-Muslims, and monopolies were introduced which proved ruinous to the Jews. Under the Cherkess Mamelukes, from the late fourteenth century, the oppression increased; there was a general depopulation, and the Jewish communities, too, diminished. At the end of the fifteenth century there were no more than 500 to 650 Jewish families in Cairo, 25 to 50 in Alexandria, 30 to 50 in Bilbeis, as well as 150 Karaite and 50 Samaritan families in Cairo. This was the low point in the history of Egyptian Jewry.

In 1492 Jews expelled from Spain began to arrive, and to establish their separate communities. Among them were outstanding scholars whose presence had a beneficial effect on the cultural level of the Egyptian Jewry. A few years later occurred the conquest of Egypt by the Ottoman Turks who were at first tolerant toward the non-Muslim minorities, and entrusted the financial administration of the country and the tax collection to Jewish agents and administrators. From about 1560 the Jewish finance minister (titled *chelebi* or 'gentleman') was recognized as the leader of the Jewish community. However, to be that high in the service of a Turkish governor was a very risky thing, and many of the Jewish ministers in the seventeenth century ended up by being executed.

Since Jewish immigrants from North-West Africa also settled in Egypt, the Jews of Cairo and Alexandria were divided into three communities: the *Musta'rabim* (Arabized, i.e., native Jews), Sephardim (immigrants from Spain), and *Moghrabim* (immigrants from the Maghrib, North-West Africa). As in other Middle Eastern countries where there were Jews of different extraction, here, too, there were occasional disputes between these communities.

The rapid increase of the Jewish population of Egypt in the wake of the Sephardi immigration is indicated by the number of synagogues: in the seventeenth century there were in Cairo thirty-one, and in the eighteenth century thirty-six synagogues. Egyptian Jews were in the forefront of trans-Mediterranean trade with the coastal cities of both the Ottoman Empire and the Christian powers.

In the seventeenth and eighteenth centuries the Turkish pashas who governed Egypt became increasingly rapacious and tyrannical, which spelled much suffering for the Jews in general and for their wealthy upper class, employed in the service of the government, in particular. Shabbatai Zevi, the pseudo-Messiah, visited Egypt twice, and received an enthusiastic welcome from the Jews and their wealthy head, Raphael ben Joseph Hin, who held the position of *chelebi* at the time, was a Kabbalist, an ascetic, and a flagellant, and ended up by being executed in 1669.

The Jews established a great number of clubs and youth associations in Cairo:

right A group at the barrage.

opposite: above left Members of the Judeo-Espanol Club on board a boat on the Nile.

opposite: above right A group from the Camping Club fishing.

The movement toward independence from Turkey, which began with the revolt of ʿAli Bey, governor of Cairo, in 1768, brought great hardships on the Jews. ʿAli Bey tried to extend his rule over Palestine, Syria, and Arabia, and thus to reconstitute the old Ayyubid empire. In order to finance the expenses of his campaigns, he imposed a huge tax on the Egyptian Jews.

Napoleon's conquest of Egypt (1798) stirred up the country as a whole and brought new confusion into the life of the Jews. On the one hand, Napoleon issued a manifesto in which he promised the Jews their return to their ancient homeland; on the other, he imposed a heavy levy on the Jews, and ordered the razing of a synagogue in Alexandria.

Although the French occupation of Egypt was short-lived – the French army withdrew from the country in 1801 – its impact was great enough to trigger Egypt's modernization and Westernization.

The reforms brought a large influx of Europeans, among them many Jews. While about the middle of the century there were an estimated 6,000 to 7,000 Jews in Egypt, the 1897 census counted 25,000 Jews, half of them foreigners who enjoyed a privileged status. The so-called capitulations exempted them from taxation, and from the jurisdiction of the state courts, and placed them under the protection of their consuls. The Jews began to play an important role in the economic and cultural development of Egypt, and to participate in the incipient Egyptian nationalist movement, in the newly founded newspapers, and in the new Arabic-Egyptian literature. An early figure in this Arabic cultural upsurge was Yaʿqub Sanuʿ (or Sanua) (1839–1912) and Egyptian Jewish author who wrote and produced satirical plays in colloquial Arabic and published Arabic newspapers until he was expelled from Egypt in 1878.

The British conquest of Egypt (1881) brought further improvements, and the Jews became a leading element in the country. Their economic status improved, their education advanced, their cultural level rose, and in every respect they were, and felt, superior to the average native Egyptian. The relations between the Muslims and Jews were normal, and, although there were several blood libels (in 1844, 1881, and again in 1901–2) and disturbances, these were considered but minor and ephemeral incidents. The well-to-do Jews moved into new suburbs and built themselves luxurious villas. New synagogues were built, rabbis of renown were invited from Jerusalem to serve as chief rabbis of Cairo, and from Italy to serve in the same capacity in Alexandria.

An *Oneg Shabbat* ('Sabbath Pleasure') gathering attended by
Jewish soldiers in Cairo during World War II.

Modern Jewish schools were established as early as 1840, and by the end of the century a very high percentage of the Egyptian Jews (almost all of whom lived in the two main cities) enjoyed the benefits of modern education. The Zionist movement found an echo among them, and in the late nineteenth century Zionist organizations were created. Jewish newspapers began to appear from 1880 on in Arabic, Ladino, and French. In the early decades of the twentieth century Jews were found among members of parliament, senators, and ministers of state. The 1917 census showed that there were about 60,000 Jews in Egypt, approximately half of them in Cairo, and that 58 per cent of the Jews were foreigners.

Thus, in the early twentieth century, irrespective of their extraction and origin, the Jews of Egypt were a largely European, or Europeanized, urban population which had its niche in the Egyptian economy and state structure, but which was, and felt itself, a foreign element as far as its culture, language, interests, and tenor of life were concerned. The majority attended foreign schools and were more at home in French, Italian, or English culture and language than in Arabic. They had their own sports, youth, literary, and philanthropic organizations, their B'nai B'rith lodges, and *landsmannschaft*-type associations of Sephardi, Corfu, and Italian Jews.

After the end of the British rule in Egypt (1922) this peaceful situation continued for a number of years. Even when, after the August 1929 bloody Arab riots in Palestine, the mufti of Jerusalem, Hajj Amin al-Husayni, made an attempt to establish anti-Zionist and anti-Jewish centres in Egypt, he could make no headway against the opposition of King Fuad.

However, in 1937 the privileges enjoyed by foreigners were abrogated, and in 1938 anti-Jewish agitation began. In 1939 attempts were made to bomb three synagogues in Cairo. During World War II, when Egypt was an important centre of the British war effort, the situation was quiescent. But on 2 November 1945, on the anniversary of the Balfour Declaration, members of the Egyptian youth organization and of the Muslim Brotherhood attacked the Jewish quarters in Cairo, set fire to a synagogue, and demolished a Jewish hospital and old peoples' home, and other Jewish institutions. Thereafter, any significant political event in connection with the Jews of Palestine served as an occasion for mob attacks on the Jews of Egypt.

The Egyptian Jews tended to be less traditional in their religious observances than other Jews in North Africa. Here the Sanua family celebrate:

left The marriage of André and Vicky Sanua.

right The *B'rit* (circumcision) of the son of Max and Clementine Sanua.

Mob action was paralleled by governmental moves. In 1947 the so-called 'Company Law' was enacted which required that most company directors be Egyptian nationals. Since only 15 per cent of the Jews were Egyptian nationals at the time (20 per cent were foreign nationals, and the rest, about two-thirds of the total, were stateless), this decree was a blow to the Jewish economic position. This law was followed by several others (e.g., prohibiting non-Egyptian nationals from working as doctors, brokers, etc.) whose effect was dire for the Jews. In 1948 numerous acts of mob violence against the Jews occurred, including bombings, killings and looting. The Jews were forced to make huge contributions to the Egyptian army, many Jews were put in detention camps, and Chief Rabbi Hayyim Nahum was induced to proclaim that it was the duty of Egyptian Jews to defend Egypt against Zionism.

Before concluding the tragic story of the liquidation of the ancient Jewish community in Egypt, let us cast a glance at the position of the Egyptian Jews just before the deterioration set in.

In 1947, when the number of Jews in Egypt reached its high point in modern times (65,639 according to the decennial census), no less than 96 per cent of them resided in Cairo and Alexandria. While urbanism is a general Jewish characteristic in every country, nowhere did the urban concentration of the Jews even approximate the extent it manifested in Egypt. While this was an indication of the largely foreign identity of the Egyptian Jewish community, it also meant that practically all the Jews in Egypt enjoyed the advantages offered by the economic, health, educational, and cultural institutions which were available only in the two main cities. In contrast to the Jews in the other North African countries, the Jews of Egypt were, in their occupational structure, more similar to a Jewish community in a European than in a Muslim city. In 1947, 59·1 per cent of all gainfully employed Jews were engaged in commerce, 21·1 per cent in industry and crafts, 10·4 per cent in general administration and public services, 6·3 per cent in personal services, 2·4 per cent in communications, and 0·6 per cent in mining, agriculture and fishing. Also, there were great differences between the Jews of Egypt and those of the other North African countries with respect to the proportion of the breadwinners to the dependents. In Egypt each breadwinner had only 2·1 dependents, which low figure was never even approximated by the Jews in other North African countries. Another feature similar to Europe was the relatively high percentage of Egyptian Jewish women employed in commerce, industry, building, clerical work, medicine, etc.

These occupational attainments of the Egyptian Jews were the outcome of education and schooling, which were more widespread among them than among the other North African Jewish communities. By 1947, of all Jewish males aged five and over, 89·7 per cent were literate, and of all Jewish females 75·9 per cent. Primary education was general; 10·7 per cent of all Jewish men aged sixteen and over had completed at least secondary school, and 4·0 per cent of those aged twenty or over were graduates of colleges or universities. Among the women the corresponding percentages were 3·2 and 0·6 respectively. It should be mentioned here that Arabic, taught as a foreign language, was part of the curriculum of the foreign schools, in which the language of tuition was French, Italian, or English. The Jews shared with the other foreigners, as well as with the thin layer of upper-class Westernized Muslim and Coptic Egyptians, an attitude of contempt for Arabic, which contributed to their feeling of being foreigners.

The foregoing observations would lead one to expect that the religious attitude of the Egyptian Jews would be less tradition-bound than that of their brethren in other North African countries. And this, indeed, was the case. As far back as the late nineteenth century some young Egyptian Jews threw off the yoke of the *mitzvot* (the religious commandments), influenced, it would appear, by the many European Jews who had settled in Egypt. By the middle of the twentieth century, many of the Egyptian Jewish youth were largely ignorant of their religion and lax in their observances. Even the Sabbath rest was not observed by many, whether

unauté Israélite
Aschkenazi

left The instructors of the Ashkenazi school in Cairo, 1921.

below A Junior High School outing to the pyramids at Sakhara in 1935.

they worked for non-Jewish employers, or had their own stores, workshops, or other businesses.

It should also be mentioned here that Egypt was the home of one of the largest concentrations of Karaites, the descendants of those Jews who, in the eighth century, split from the main body of Judaism (called Rabbanites in contradistinction to them). The Karaites consider the Bible the sole source of their law and creed, and reject the Talmud and all other rabbinical developments of Judaism. It was estimated that in 1932 there were 10,000 Karaites in Russia (mainly in the Crimea), and their number in Egypt in 1947 was estimated at 4,500. Subsequently almost all of the Egyptian Karaites, and most of the other Karaites outside Russia, emigrated to Israel where their number in 1970 was about 7,000.

The beginning of the end of the House of Israel in Egypt dates from 1954 when, with the assumption of power by Gamal Abd-al-Nasser, anti-Semitism became a cornerstone of Egyptian government policy. In the same year, arrests of Jews became frequent, and two Jews were hanged for spying for Israel. Anti-Jewish publications were issued, including an Arabic translation of the notorious forgery, the *Protocols of the Elders of Zion*. Emigration to Israel was all but halted.

After the Sinai Campaign of 1956 these measures became more severe. Hundreds of Jews, among them the wealthiest and most respected members of the community, were arrested and their properties confiscated. A policy of mass expulsion was instituted, so that from November 1956 to September 1957 more than 21,000 Jews had all their possessions confiscated and were forced to leave. Within the next two years another 15,000 Jews left, so that by 1960 only 8,500 remained. Thereafter, the new Egyptian exodus continued apace, and after the Six-Day War of 1967 only 800 were left, many of them languishing in prison. In 1980 it was estimated that no more than 300 were left of the House of Israel in Egypt which looked back upon a history of thirty-two centuries.

Part Five
The Near East
Under the Yoke of Ishmael

The *mori* (rabbi) in a synagogue in Yemen.

Syria-Lebanon

A Jewish tinker cutting metal.

Syria is the only country outside the Biblical land of Israel (which included present-day Jordan) which at one time in its history was under Hebrew rule. King David conquered Damascus in the tenth century BCE, and when, after David's death, it regained its independence, King Jeroboam of Israel recaptured it. Thereafter connections between Syria and Israel continued and in the fifth century BCE, the history of Jews in Syria began.

The report of the Jewish historian Josephus Flavius (c. 38–100 CE) that the Persian king Xerxes ordered Ezra to appoint judges for the Jews in Syria and Phoenicia indicates the presence in those countries of Jewish communities in the fifth century BCE. During the Second Jewish Commonwealth the most important Syrian Jewish community was that of Antioch near the north-eastern corner of the Mediterranean, whose members enjoyed rights of citizenship equal to those of the Greeks. Because the territory of Syria was contiguous to that of Palestine, the sages of the Mishna in the second century CE equated Syria in certain halakhic respects with the Land of Israel.

Byzantine rule was not favourable to the Jews, but after the Arab conquest of the country (seventh century) their situation improved. When the inhabitants of the coastal town of Tripoli (today in nothern Lebanon) fled, the Arabs placed a Jewish garrison in the city to protect it against the Byzantines. However, since under Arab rule the numerically most important *dhimmis* were the Christians, the Jews played a lesser role in Syria than they did in North Africa. Still, they had their full share of hardships caused by the invasions of the Karmatians from Bahrein and the repeated incursions of the Byzantines. Many Jews concentrated on occupations in which the Muslims were not allowed, or reluctant, to engage.

The famous tenth-century Arab geographer, al-Maqdisi, mentions that in Syria 'most of the bankers, dyers, and tanners were Jews'.

At the beginning of Fatimid rule over Syria (969) Jews occupied some of the highest positions in the country. The vizier of the Caliph al'Aziz, Ya'qub ibn Killis (930–91), a converted Jew, appointed another Jew, Manasseh ben Abraham al-Qazzaz, governor of Damascus (990–6). The sons of Qazzaz, too, held high government posts and also filled the position of *nagid* (prince, head) of the Damascus Jewish community.

The twelfth-century Jewish traveller, Benjamin of Tudela, reports that many of the Jews in Syrian towns were dyers. Other sources state that many of the Jews in the coastal city of Tyre were engaged in glass making and in international commerce. Another Jewish traveller, the Hebrew poet Y'huda al-Harizi, who visited Syria in the early thirteenth century, adds that many Jews in Damascus and Aleppo were physicians and government officials. The Mameluke rulers of Syria (1260–1516), although they often issued anti-Jewish decrees, needed and therefore retained the services of Jewish officials. In 1400 Tamerlane devastated Aleppo, Homs, and Damascus, and wrought havoc equally among Muslims, Jews, and Christians. This catastrophe contributed greatly to the impoverishment of the Syrian Jews, whose number in the fifteenth century was about seven thousand.

In 1516 Syria was conquered by the Turks and, about the same time, Sephardi Jews expelled from Spain began to arrive. Before long, the Sephardim assumed the leadership of Syrian Jewry, while assimilating to the native Jews culturally and linguistically, and adopting their Judeo-Arabic dialect. Despite the instability and arbitrariness of the Turkish rule the Jews prospered in international trade, and developed, in addition to their two major concentrations in Aleppo and Damascus, numerous smaller communities all over the country, including the southern coastal area which after World War I was to become the Republic of Lebanon. Economic rise was accompanied by scholarly-religious activities, especially in the fields of the Kabbala and homiletics.

In the eighteenth century, a class of wealthy Jewish bankers emerged in Damascus, served the local government in leading positions, and managed to acquire an influence which reached as far as Istanbul. In 1832, Ibrahim Pasha, the son of Muhammad 'Ali of Egypt, conquered Syria, and abolished the discriminatory laws against the *dhimmis*. Soon thereafter (in 1840) followed the notorious Damascus blood libel, in which Italian Capuchins accused the Jews of having killed a member of their order, and which necessitated the intervention of leading European Jews, including Moses Montefiore and Adolphe Crémieux, before the Jews were vindicated and those of them imprisoned set free. For several years thereafter, the Syrian Christians gave vent to their anti-Jewish feelings in various other unfounded accusations. However, during the remaining decades of Ottoman rule in Syria, no cases of official discrimination against the Jews occurred, except for one single decree which, in 1910, forbade non-Ottoman Jews in Syria and Palestine to register land and real estate they had acquired, so as to prevent Zionist 'expansion'. In this period, Jews served as civil servants, and had their representatives on municipal and district councils. At the same time, the economic condition of the Jews of Damascus was adversely affected by the increase of imports from Europe, and by the cessation of trade with Persia across the Syrian desert due to the opening of the Suez Canal. Many Jews from Damascus moved to Beirut, or emigrated to the Americas. During the same period there was a sizeable emigration of Aleppan Jews to Palestine.

The Chief Rabbi with his
Khawas and secretary in Aleppo.

The four centuries of Turkish rule over Syria and Lebanon made no linguistic impact on the Jews. They continued to speak Arabic, and remained largely Arabized in names, customs and behaviour as well.

During the quarter of a century of French mandatory rule which followed World War I, the position of the Jews remained, in general, satisfactory. French education made headway, especially among the Jews of the coastal area (Aleppo, Beirut), and some Jews volunteered for the French army. Less satisfactory was the relationship between the Jews and the other natives. In 1925 a Druze attack took place on the Jewish quarter in Damascus. In addition, blood libels, most of them spread by Christians, were occasionally levelled against the Jews, and several incidents were staged by Muslims. In the late 1930s, anti-Zionist agitation started, and attacks on Jews by young Arabs, incited by emissaries of the mufti of Jerusalem, became both more frequent and more violent – harbingers of more serious events to follow within a few years.

Economically, there were conspicuous differences between the communities of Aleppo and Damascus. Until the seventeenth century Aleppo in the north of Syria was a major trading station between Europe and the Far East; thereafter, it lost importance, and the number of well-to-do Jews who had had a share in that trade declined. This process, which continued into the twentieth century, brought about a new wave of Jewish emigration, while those who remained behind became impoverished, so that by 1942 no less than 40 to 65 per cent of the Jews required assistance. The very few Jews left in the city in the 1970s lived in great distress, and were, in effect, held captive by the Syrian government.

Damascus has been for centuries a great centre of traditional Arab crafts, in which the Jews had an active share. Most of them were goldsmiths, cobblers, matmakers, etc. Many were pedlars who made the rounds of the villages with their wares. A few were rich international merchants, who, as late as the nineteenth century, had splendid and luxurious houses with marble halls and large pools, which, from the outside, were surrounded by mud walls and had simple doors, so as not to let passers-by suspect the riches that lay behind them – a precaution taken by wealthy Muslims too.

On the eve of World War I, many Jews of Damascus were still gold- and silversmiths, and worked in weaving, dyeing, spinning and wood, but their share in foreign trade and in the Damascus *suq* (bazaar) was negligible. In 1926, when there were 6,635 Jews in Damascus, each breadwinner had on average two dependents – a surprisingly low figure! One third of the earners were artisans, 17 per cent clerks, 14 per cent pedlars, 9 per cent merchants, gold- and silversmiths, 4 per cent maids and servants, and 1 per cent rabbis, with the remaining 23 per cent engaged mostly in services. Many of the Jews were employed as workers in small workshops owned by Muslims or Christians.

In Beirut, in the nineteenth century when it was the most important port-city on the East Mediterranean coast, most of the Jews were engaged in commerce, and travellers reported that the majority were well-to-do, with only a scattering of poor among them. They enjoyed full economic freedom, and their position remained favourable until the Six-Day War of 1967, in whose wake most of them left the city.

The institutions of the Jewish community of Damascus were financed partly by the taxes imposed by its own assessment committee and collected under threat of excommunication. There was also a tax *(gabella)* on the ritual slaughtering of animals. From 1882 on there functioned in the community several Jewish charitable societies which provided the poor with medical care, bread, and alms.

The assimilatory effects of education in missionary schools were counterbalanced by the proximity of the *Yishuv* (the Jewish population of Palestine). Beginning with the expulsion of Jewish leaders from Palestine by the Turks in World War I, Palestinian Jewish educators, as well as social and political leaders, came to Damascus and worked among the Damascan Jews. They founded and headed schools, organized Zionist groups (such as the HeHalutz, Maccabi, Maccabi ha Tza'ir), and implanted the idea of 'aliya (immigration into Palestine) into the mind of the young Jewish generation.

Traditional Jewish education in Syria and Lebanon was represented by old-fashioned *kuttabs*, Hebrew schools in which, as elsewhere, the emphasis was on reading the Bible. In the late nineteenth century there were several Yeshivot in Aleppo, one in Damascus, and a Talmud Tora school in Beirut. In 1875, a Beirut *hakham*, Zaki Kohen, founded a private school called *Tiferet Yisrael*, in which children of rich Jews of Beirut, Damascus, Aleppo, Jaffa, Izmir, and Istanbul, were taught Hebrew, Arabic, Turkish, French, and German. It functioned until 1904. In the early twentieth century the traditional schools declined, and their place was taken by the *Alliance* schools, the first of which was opened in Damascus in 1864, in the face of opposition from rabbis and *heder* (traditional Tora school) teachers.

In 1945, when Syria achieved independence, the government closed all the foreign schools, including those of the *Alliance*, whereupon a new school, named *Talmud Tora Ben Maimon*, was opened. Two years later, when the *Alliance* was permitted to resume its work under the name *al-Ittihad al-Isra'ili*, or Jewish Unity, this Talmud Tora closed down. In 1939, about 2,000 Jewish children attended the *Alliance* schools in Syria, and about 1,000 in Beirut, accounting for almost half of all the Jewish school-age population. In the mid-1940s the *Alliance* opened a co-educational secondary school in Beirut.

In contrast to the Jews of Egypt and Turkey, those of Syria and Lebanon were generally religiously conservative and observant. Despite the fact that many of them had attended Christian schools, even after the *Alliance* had established its institutions, conversions to Christianity were extremely rare, although a few cases occurred in Beirut. Conversions to Islam, which was the religion of the less-educated and poorer half of the Lebanese population, did not occur either in Lebanon or in Syria where it was the dominant religion.

The life of Jewish women in Syria and Lebanon was less restricted than that of the Muslim women, and similar to that of the Christian women. All women observed the rules of segregation of the sexes, but in Aleppo and Beirut they went about unveiled like the Christian women, while in Damascus they wore the veil and the robe when outdoors, as did both the Christian and the Muslim women.

Two political developments, the achievement of independence by Syria in 1945 and the establishment of Israel in 1948, hastened the end of the Syrian Jewish community. As happened in several other Arab countries, stirrings of independence led to mob violence against the Jews. In 1944 and 1945 several attacks took place on the Jewish quarter of Damascus. They intensified in 1947 when, in the course of large-scale rioting, much of the Jewish quarter of Aleppo was ruined. In 1948 dozens of synagogues were destroyed in Damascus and Aleppo; dozens of Jews were murdered; Jewish girls were abducted and raped. In 1949, after the Syrian army was defeated by Israel, the mob took its revenge on the Jews of Damascus, threw bombs at the Jewish quarter, and killed and wounded dozens of Jews.

After the independence of Syria there began the promulgation of anti-Jewish governmental measures. The Syrian Jews were refused passports. Many were detained and tortured. In 1950 an *Alliance* school in Beirut was demolished by a bomb. Muslim organizations extorted money from Jews. Jews trying to flee Syria were arrested, and their property confiscated.

Despite such obstacles, most Syrian Jews succeeded in leaving the country. The census of 1943 showed 30,000 Jews in Syria. After Syrian independence, illegal Jewish mass emigration to Palestine began. After 1947 most of the emigrants went to Lebanon and Turkey, and from there on to Europe and Israel. In the mid 1950s the number of Jews remaining in Syria was estimated at between 3,000 and 5,000, and no further change in this number seems to have taken place until the present.

In Lebanon, the 1944 census found 5,666 Jews. Immigration of Syrian Jews added to their number, so that in 1958 it was estimated at 9,000. Thereafter, emigration reduced this number to 5,000 in 1967, 1,000 in 1972, and 400 in 1976.

A rabbi from Aleppo.

Iraq

A Jewish wedding in Baghdad in 1935.

Territorially, Iraq is the heir of the area called Mesopotamia, in and around which were located the ancient empires of Sumer, Assyria, and Babylonia. It is also the place of the oldest Jewish Diaspora and the one with the longest continuous history, from 721 BCE to 1949 CE, a time-span of 2,670 years.

The first exiles from the Kingdom of Israel were taken to what was then Assyria by King Tiglath-Pileser III in 734–2 BCE. A few years later (721 BCE) came the destruction of Israel by Shalmaneser, king of Assyria, and the settlement of the 'ten tribes' of Israel in the northern part of Mesopotamia. Exiles from Judah were added in 597 BCE and again in 586 BCE, when Nebuchadnezzar, king of Babylon, took Jerusalem, destroyed the First Temple, and exiled to Mesopotamia King Zedekiah, the nobles, and a part of the population of Judah. Although in 539 BCE, only forty-seven years after the Exile, Cyrus, king of Persia, conquered Babylonia and allowed the Jews to return to their country, most Jews chose to remain in Mesopotamia and continued to build their community there.

During and after the Jewish-Roman war of 66–70 CE, which ended with the destruction of the Second Temple of Jerusalem, many Jews fled to Babylonia, and before long Babylonian Jewry achieved a cultural, scholarly, and religious development which first rivalled, and from the third century CE surpassed, that of Palestine. In fact, the intellectual achievements of Babylonian Jews were so overwhelming that for almost a thousand years they enjoyed a cultural hegemony over the whole Jewish people. After the compilation of the Mishna in Palestine in about 200 CE, and until the end of the Gaonic period (1038), the most important religio-legal works, destined to become the basic building blocks of the Jewish cultural edifice for all times, were produced in Babylonia. Out of its academies came the Babylonian Talmud (completed *c*. 500) which, next to the Bible, is the most important religious source book of Judaism. For more than five centuries thereafter the Geonim, heads of the Talmudic academies in the Babylonian towns of Sura and Pumbeditha, were the supreme religious authorities in Judaism. They also produced a profusion of religious, legal, ethical, philosophical, linguistic, midrashic, historical, and poetic works. The greatest of them was Saadya Gaon (892–942), an outstanding philosopher and the first translator of the Bible into Arabic.

The conquest of Babylonia by the Arabs in the seventh century did not greatly affect the internal life of the Jews. Their secular head continued to be the *Resh Gelutha* (lit. 'Head of the Exile'), or exilarch, a scion of the House of David and a prince not only of his own people but of the country as well. The exilarchs governed Babylonian Jewry for more than twelve centuries, from 140 CE until their office was abolished by Tamerlane in 1401. During much of this long period they were recognized by other Diasporas as well.

Because of the unsettled political conditions and troubles from the fourteenth century to the Turkish conquest of Iraq in 1534, many of the Jews of Baghdad fled and sought refuge in the mountains of Kurdistan, thus replenishing the old Jewish communities there. The Turkish rule, as in other parts of the Ottoman Empire, was, on the whole, liberal toward the Jews, although the latter's position depended largely on the whim of the pashas whose average tenure as governors of Baghdad lasted only two years in the seventeenth century and again in the nineteenth and twentieth centuries. Until the early eighteenth century, a leader of the Jewish community, always a descendant of the House of David, would be appointed as *sarraf bashi* (chief treasurer) of the local government and *Nasi* (duke) of the Jews. When the Jewish duke rode out on his white horse, criers would run before him shouting, 'Give honour to the son of David!' and he was popularly referred to as 'King of the Jews'. The office of Nasi was abolished only in 1849 when the *Hakham Bashi*, or chief rabbi, became the head of the Jewish community.

As long as Iraq, Syria, and Lebanon were parts of the Ottoman Empire, all laws pertaining to the Jews which were promulgated by the Sublime Porte in Istanbul covered also the Jews of those countries. One of the most important of these laws was the one which abolished the *jizya*, the old head-tax, made the Jews citizens with equal rights, and introduced a collective levy in payment for the exemption of the Jews from military service. In 1909, this levy was also abolished, and the Jews of the Ottoman Empire were required to serve in the Turkish army like other citizens.

In 1876, Jews were represented in the first Iraqi parliament, and began to be appointed to law courts, and municipal and district councils. Their increasing sense of security prompted many Baghdad Jews to move out of the old Jewish quarters and to settle in mixed neighbourhoods. Also, a movement from Baghdad

Rabbinical scholars and rabbis in Baghdad, 1910.

to cities and villages formerly not inhabited by Jews commenced.

The relatively safe position the Baghdad Jews enjoyed can be seen from the fact that until 1914 there was only one single mob attack on them. This took place in 1908, when the Jews openly showed their joy at the seizure of power by the Young Turks, an attitude resented by a Muslim group, who fell upon the Jews of the city; Muslim notables, however, put an end to the tumult.

During World War I, many Jews were recruited into the Turkish army, while others were subjected to extortion and torture to finance the local garrisons. No wonder that the entry of the British army into Baghdad in 1917 was greeted with great rejoicing by the Jews.

The Anglo-Iraqi treaty of 1922 assured the Jews equal rights, freedom of conscience and worship, and the right to maintain their own Hebrew schools. Jews served in the Iraqi parliament, and as civil servants and judges. Throughout the mandatory period their security was not impinged upon, and the only restrictions placed on them were limitations on Zionist activities, limitations which became more stringent after the 1929 disturbances in Palestine.

This was a period of economic, social, and educational advancement for the Iraqi Jews, as well as a time of their Arabization. The share of the Jews in Iraq's growing economy can be shown by a few figures. In 1932 it was estimated that of the country's 1,000 importers 800 were Jews, as were 400 of the 500 exporters, 2,500 of the 3,000 merchants, 40 of the 50 money changers, 170 of the 200 real estate agents, and so on.

Iraq became independent of Britain in 1932, and instantly political ferment began: in seven years (1932–9) there were five military revolts. The position of the Jews deteriorated. Gradually, anti-Jewish measures were introduced, the number of Jews admitted to state secondary education was limited, the teaching of Hebrew in the Jewish schools was prohibited, and obstacles were put in the way of those wishing to emigrate to Palestine.

In 1936, after the outbreak of the Arab riots in Palestine, attacks against Jews took place in which several Jews were killed. Bombs were thrown into Jewish clubs and a Baghdad synagogue, and the president of the Jewish community, Rabbi Sasson Kadoori, was persuaded to sign a declaration to the effect that the Jews had no interest in Palestine. These incidents, which continued through 1937 and 1938, were instigated or carried out by Palestinians and Syrians. Outside the capital, in Mosul, Kirkuk, Arbil, and Amara, as well as in Basra in the south, only demonstrations and lootings, but no murders, took place.

When Rashid ʿAli al-Kaylani seized the government (1941), the influence of Hajj Amin al-Husayni, the notorious mufti of Jerusalem, was strongly felt, and beatings and arrests of Jews were frequent occurrences. Upon the approach of the British – these were the days of World War II – Rashid ʿAli fled Baghdad, and the Jews, unwisely but understandably, again gave unrestrained expression to their joy. The Arabs, including members of the army and the police, rioted, and within a few days, before they were checked by Kurdish soldiers, they killed some 170 to 180 Jews. This large-scale pogrom was a terrible shock for the Jews of Iraq who had never imagined that such a calamity could befall them. However, gradually they recovered and devoted themselves to mending the torn fabric of their lives.

Culturally, the Iraqi Jews were more assimilated to their Arab neighbours than any other Jewish community in the Middle East. In contrast to the Jews of North Africa or Lebanon, and even Syria, all of them spoke Arabic in the street as well as at home. Of course, their language was Judeo-Arabic which differed from that of the Muslim Arabs in pronunciation, syntax, and also vocabulary, containing as it did many Hebrew, and to a smaller extent also Persian, Turkish, French and English words. Especially in the large Jewish community of Baghdad, and, more particularly, among the Jewish women, limited contact with the Muslims meant that many did not speak the colloquial of the latter correctly.

There were noticeable differences between the Iraqi Jews and Arabs in attire, although these diminished after World War I. Before that Jewish men wore the red fez, while the Arab men wore a turban wound around their head. Since both wore the long robe (except for the few rich notables who wore a kind of gown called *zibun*), the headdress was the only, but at the same time most visible, distinguishing mark between Jews and Arabs. After World War I most Jews took to wearing the *sidara* or *faysaliyya*, a dark or black cap forming a crest at the top, from front to back, which, among the Arabs, was worn only by the rich and the intellectuals. At the same time, more and more Jews began to wear European clothes, while among the Arabs this Western fashion made only slow headway. In recent years, however, both Arabs and Jews wore European suits, and many of the young men of both groups went bareheaded. As for the Jewish women, until World War II they wore the long street robe when going out, and veiled their faces in the manner of the Muslim women. After the war, most Jewish (and Christian) women discarded both robe and veil, while most Muslim women retained them.

A notable manifestation of Jewish assimilation, either to the Arab environment or to the Western culture introduced by the British after World War I, was the adoption of either Arabic names (such as the popular royal names of Ghazi, Faysal) or else European names (such as Albert, Richard, Maurice).

However, nothing is as sensitive an index of the attitude of one ethnic group to another as the behaviour of the children. As long as a child could easily be recognized as Jewish, which was mostly the case down to most recent times, the Arab children would insult, slap, or beat them, and frequently steal their hats, books, or whatever they happened to have in their pockets. Since the Jewish children were always few while the Arab children were many, any attempt at resistance or self-defence was futile and only caused more trouble for the Jewish children. Thus the Jewish child grew up in fear of the Arabs.

This feeling remained with the Jews throughout their lives, nurtured and intensified by subsequent experiences. The characteristic Arab excitability and periodic outbursts of temper found ready outlet in attacks against Jews, in which pupils of secondary schools (of whom there were many in Baghdad) took a leading part. While the mob regarded the Jews as fair game, the Muslim notables considered it their duty to protect the Jews, and especially so in the provincial towns where the number of Jews was small.

More than one half of the Iraqi Arabs were Shiʿites (the rest, as well as the Kurdish minority, were Sunnis), and the Shiʿites in general have been more intolerant of the Jews (and of other religious groups) than the Sunnis. They considered the Jews impure, and in some Shiʿite Iraqi cities (such as Amara and Samarra) signs reading 'For Muslims only' or 'Entrance forbidden to Jews' could be seen on cafés or bath-houses.

The football team of a boys'
Alliance school in Baghdad,
1931.

The pupils and teachers of a
Baghdad Jewish girls' school in
1900.

All in all, the position of the Jews in Iraq was such that, despite their readiness to assimilate to the Arabs, they could never feel an integral part of the country. Although the Jews had lived in Mesopotamia for almost 2,700 years, and had become an Arabic-speaking group soon after its conquest by the Arabs in the seventh century, the humiliations of their *dhimmi* status and the increasingly inimical attitude of the populace in modern times made it impossible for them to become 'Iraqis of the Jewish faith' which would have been the counterpart of the feelings and convictions that developed among the Jews in the West after their Emancipation.

No satisfactory statistics are available from Iraq and hence we know neither the exact number of Iraqi Jews nor their occupational structure. The 1947 census, considered unreliable, gave the number of Jews as 118,000, as against which it is known that in 1948–51 about 123,500 Iraqi Jews emigrated to Israel, and several more thousands to other countries, while around 6,000 Jews remained in Iraq. That is to say, the total number of Iraqi Jews must have been about close to 140,000.

As for their occupations, the Israeli statistics of Iraqi Jewish immigrants contain the only reliable data. They show that of the Jewish breadwinners who arrived in Israel in 1950 and 1951, 32 per cent were engaged (prior to leaving Iraq) in crafts and industry, 27·5 per cent in commerce, 15·8 per cent in administrative and clerical jobs, 6 per cent in professional and technical work, 4·3 per cent in personal services, 3·3 per cent in agriculture (almost all of them in Kurdistan), 2·4 per cent in transport, 1·5 per cent in building, and the remaining 7·2 per cent were unskilled labourers. Each Iraqi-Jewish earner supported three dependents, which, in view of their high birth rate, is a rather low figure.

Although, as we have seen, from Talmudic times until the thirteenth century Iraq was the main centre, or, in the later part of this period, a main centre, of Jewish learning, from the thirteenth to the nineteenth century there were no Yeshivot, but only *heders*, elementary Hebrew schools, in Iraq. The first Yeshiva in modern times was founded in Baghdad in 1840, and in 1864 the *Alliance* opened its

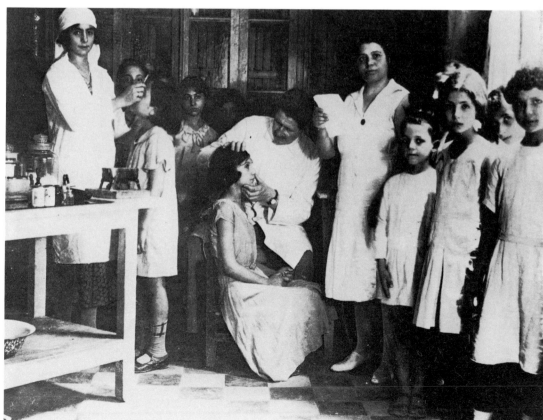

A doctor's check-up at a school in Baghdad, *c.* 1930.

first school. From that time on, a small number of Jewish children and youths, all concentrated in Baghdad, received modern education.

In the traditional *heder*, attended by most Jewish boys from their fourth year, all children, often fifty or more, irrespective of age, sat in one room in the teacher's house, or in one group in his courtyard, and were taught to read the Bible in the traditional cantillation. At a later stage, they were taught to translate what they read, to write the Hebrew alphabet, to do some arithmetic, and to write commercial letters in Arabic but with Hebrew characters, Most of the children attended the *heder* only for a few years. Corporal punishment was freely meted out by the teacher, caning the palms or soles of the child. The few girls who attended the *heder* for a year or two sat together with the boys. In the two Talmud Tora schools, which were opened in Baghdad in 1832 and in 1907, the pupils (only boys) were taught the same subjects, but the children were divided into four classes according to their knowledge. While the *heder* was a private business of the teacher, the Talmud Tora schools were directed by a public committee. The introduction of secular subjects into the Talmud Tora curriculum was opposed, so that only in 1935 was there one modern Talmud Tora school, in which both religious and secular subjects were taught, opened in Baghdad.

A network of modern schools, for boys and for girls, was set up by the *Alliance* in the late nineteenth century, when the Jewish communities themselves also founded modern elementary schools, as well as a few secondary schools. From 1922 on more girls than boys attended the *Alliance* schools.

These efforts greatly improved the educational level of Iraqi Jews after World War I, as shown by the Israeli census of 1961. The data in that census showed that among Iraqi-born Jews aged sixty and over, 72·2 per cent were illiterate (48·7 per cent of the men and 93·2 per cent of the women). While it was assumed that most of the illiterate men were from Iraqi Kurdistan, the extremely high percentage of illiteracy among the women indicated that, as late as until World War I, only a minute proportion (6·8 per cent) of all Iraqi Jewish women were taught how to read and write. Subsequently the situation rapidly improved, so that among the young people aged fifteen to twenty-nine (in 1961), who had reached school age from 1937 on, only 17·3 per cent of the males and 43·9 per cent of the females were illiterate. In 1949–50 some 12,000 Jewish children attended the six classes of all elementary schools, a figure which can be estimated as amounting to about 60 per cent of all Jewish children of the six- to twelve-year age group. In the secondary schools (five years, ages thirteen to eighteen), 3,500 Jewish pupils were enrolled, and in higher education there were some 500 Jewish students. The number of Jews who graduated from Iraqi institutions of higher learning (law, medicine, pharmacy, engineering, teacher training, economics) increased from year to year, but their total for the fifty years of 1901–50 reached only 1,000, which averages out at twenty annually.

In the second half of the nineteenth century a few Iraqi Jews contributed articles to Hebrew papers published in various countries, and in Baghdad itself they published a Hebrew newspaper from 1863 to 1871, and another Hebrew paper, as well as seven Arabic papers, between 1909 and 1948. After World War I, several Arabic newspapers were founded by Jewish journalists, and a number of Jewish poets and writers wrote and published their works in Arabic, with a style and content indistinguishable from the writings of the contemporary Arab authors.

In the present century, the traditional religious conservatism of Iraqi Jews began to wane, and the young generation, the product of modern schools, became lax in its religious observance. Religious duties fulfilled were in most cases confined to fasting on Yom Kippur, maintaining a kosher kitchen at home, closing Jewish-owned businesses on the Sabbath, circumcision, and being married and buried according to the Jewish ritual. As for conversions to Islam, they were extremely few (which was the case also in other Muslim countries), and there were no mixed marriages.

The status of the Jewish woman in Iraq (as in all Muslim countries) was greatly influenced by, although it was better than, the status of her Muslim sisters. The view expressed in the Koran, according to which women are inferior to men, has left its stamp on Muslim society down to modern times. The birth of a girl, while no longer considered a misfortune as in Koranic times, has remained among both Muslims and Jews an undesirable event, greeted with words of comfort such as 'May boys follow her!' A man who had only daughters was called derisively *abu banat* (father of daughters).

This traditional attitude found its expression also in the conviction that girls needed no schooling, that all the things they had to know could be taught to them by their mothers, aunts or older sisters, and that the main aim of educating her was to bring her up a virgin, hidden from the sight of all men except her father and brothers, and to marry her off as soon as possible. Marriages were, wherever feasible, arranged between a girl and her father's brother's son, the typical *ibn ʿamm-bint ʿamm* match, which was considered preferable or even obligatory in the entire Middle East. As late as until World War I, all over the Middle East, girls were married well before the onset of puberty; the boys were, ideally, only a little older. All this held good for the Iraqi Jewish girls to the same extent as for her Muslim Arab sisters.

After marriage the young couple usually lived in the house of the groom's father where a room would be assigned to them. Thus residence was patrilocal, the family an extended family, and the continuation of old traditions was ensured. After World War I young couples began to live alone. At the same time the old general Middle Eastern custom of the women serving the meals to the men and then having their own meals alone in the kitchen was gradually abandoned. Still, the well-to-do women very rarely set foot outside of the house, and never alone.

The widespread old Jewish custom of divorcing a wife who bore no male heir to her husband within ten years of marriage was not observed in Iraq. Instead, the husband would marry a second wife – polygamy was legal according to both Jewish and Iraqi (Muslim) law. Nevertheless, such plural marriages were rare. Divorce was even rarer. Of the 27,042 Iraqi Jewish women who immigrated to Israel in 1950–1, only 226, or 0·8 per cent were divorced. The number of women who were gainfully employed was very small: only 7·6 per cent of the total Jewish working population consisted of women, and of all women aged fifteen and over, only 6·5 per cent had worked. Sixty per cent of them were seamstresses (whose work could be done at home), 20 per cent worked in personal service, or as midwives, nurses, pharmacists, doctors, clerks, or commercial employees. While their number was insignificant, it still testifies to the changes which had taken place in the position of the Iraqi Jewish women in the twentieth century.

The vote at the United Nations for the partition of Palestine and the establishment of a Jewish state (29 November 1947) triggered vehement anti-Jewish and anti-Israel demonstrations. These intensified in the course of 1948. The government chimed in, many Jews were arrested on trumped-up charges, and one of them was publicly hanged. These anti-Jewish measures were parallelled by others aimed at the Jews' economic activities. Emigration of Jews was prohibited. Nevertheless thousands of Jews managed to get across the border into Iran. When, in 1950, a new law permitted Jewish emigration, all Jews were ready to leave the country, and within one year (June 1950 to June 1951) some 110,000 emigrated to Israel, although they had to leave all their possessions behind. All in all, some 125,000 Jews left Iraq, with only 6,000 remaining by 1952, 3,000 in 1967, and no more than 350 by 1972. Thus came to an end one of the oldest continuous settlements of Jews in the world, after twenty-seven centuries of uninterrupted existence.

Kurdistan

A child from the Jewish village of Sandur in Kurdistan.

Kurdistan is a rugged mountainous region of about 70,000 square miles, divided politically between Turkey, Iraq, and Iran. Its approximate boundaries are: in the west, the Tigris River and a line running west of Lake Van up north to the Aras River; in the north, the Aras River and the Armenian SSR; in the east, Lake Urmia and the Zarineh River; and in the south, the thirty-fifth parallel. Although Kurdish tribes and villages can be found outside this area as well, within it the Kurds are the majority population, and have been ever since ancient Assyrian times.

The Kurds are a Sunni Muslim people speaking three dialects of Kurdish (an Iranian language). Their total number has been estimated at 3,000,000 in 1948, at 6,000,000 in subsequent years, and as high as 12,000,000 in 1980. They are a people possessed of a fierce ethnic consciousness whose consuming ambition in recent decades has been to obtain independence, or at least autonomy. They have a long-standing reputation for physical prowess and courage, an inclination to violence, a flaring temper, a valuation of freedom above all, and overriding tribal loyalties. These qualities have frequently prompted them to rebellions against one or other of the countries which have exercised political control over them. The cruelty with which these attempts at independence were put down has become legendary.

Among the Kurds have lived, ever since antiquity, two non-Muslim minorities: Assyrians or Nestorian Christians, and Jews, who, in the course of time, were to no small extent influenced by the Kurdish national character. However, neither the Nestorians nor the Kurdish Jews adopted the language of the Kurds; they spoke Aramaic, albeit in greatly differing dialects. The Jews of Mosul spoke Arabic, and hence some scholars do not consider them Kurdish Jews.

According to the traditions of the Kurdish Jews, they were the descendants of the ten tribes, exiled from the Kingdom of Israel by the Assyrians in the eighth century BCE.

The earliest reliable information about the Jews of Kurdistan comes from two Jewish travellers, Benjamin of Tudela and Petahia of Regensburg who visited and described the Jews of Kurdistan in the twelfth century. According to them there were 25,000 Jews in the town of Amadiya, 6,000 to 7,000 in Mosul, 4,000 in Jeziret al'Omar, 1,000 in Nesibin, and others in more than a hundred small localities. In the same century the Kurdish Jews were seized by two Messianic movements, that of Menahem b. Solomon ibn Ruhi (or Dugi), and that of David Alroy. In later times, and especially from the sixteenth century on when the Turks and the Persians contended for the Kurdish area, all the inhabitants of the region suffered greatly, and the number of Jews widely fluctuated within short periods.

From 1832 to 1847 there were numerous Kurdish uprisings against the Turkish rule, and whenever the Kurds were defeated the conquerors let their vengeance be felt by Muslims, Jews and Christians alike. The Turks also managed to incite one local population against the other, and often the Kurds and the Nestorians fought each other with a cruelty that exceeded that of the Turks. That the Jews were not wiped out in this inter-community warfare was due to the fact that they had no political power, no country-wide organization, no territorial ambition. Thus they represented no threat to the contending powers or parties, and neither the Turks nor the Kurds felt it worth their while to attack them at a time when they needed all their strength to fight each other.

In the mid-nineteenth century the Jewish traveller known as Benjamin II visited Kurdistan and estimated the number of Jews in their major settlements at 1,710 families (or about 10,000 persons), not counting the villages.

In the late nineteenth century, cases of attacks on Jews in the Kurdish towns of the area were not unusual. At the time of the 1941 pogrom in Baghdad (see above, p. 144–45), and again in 1942, demonstrations were staged in the main Kurdish cities, in the course of which several Jews were injured. In general, however, the Kurds – themselves a minority with serious grievances against the Arab government of Baghdad – were sympathetic to the Jews.

To be sympathetic to the Jews, of course, did not mean a recognition of their equality. The idea that a Jew could be the equal of a Kurd never entered the latter's mind. But the Jew was a very useful chattel to own, and therefore it was in the interest of the Kurdish *aghas*, tribal or village chieftains, to protect him. For the Jew, the protection of the *agha* was a vital matter in the specific Kurdish situation which was one of the crassest examples of might makes right. Central authority was totally unknown; every tribe, and often every village, was an independent little centre of power, in which a weak individual or group was fair game for anybody stronger. By being protected by a powerful *agha*, the Jews enjoyed

left Slaughtering a lamb.

top The rough shelters of a typical Jewish village in Kurdistan.

above Weaving was one of the many essential crafts of the Kurdish Jewish village women.

relative safety from attack; or, if attacked nevertheless, would be avenged by the *agha* who could not tolerate his property being damaged with impunity. Being clients of their *agha*, the Kurdish Jews suffered much less than did the other Iraqi Jews who lived among Arabs.

Nor did the Christian (Nestorian) neighbours of the Jews in Kurdistan ever accuse them of ritual murder, although such libels were several times floated by Christians against Jews in other parts of Iraq, in Syria, and elsewhere.

The power the *agha* had over his Jews was greater than that of a feudal lord over his serfs. The *agha* literally owned his Jews, could extract from them whatever taxes and forced labour he wanted, got one-third of the bride-price paid by a Jewish bridegroom to the father of his bride, or, if he was very powerful as well as very greedy, even the entire bride-price. A Jewish pedlar could make the rounds of only those villages which belonged to his *agha*; if he wanted to go outside the *agha*'s territory he had first to obtain his permission. If an *agha* needed money he could literally sell one of his Jews to another *agha*, or to somebody else.

Of the Jews who lived in Iraqi Kurdistan in the 1940s, 80 per cent were urban and 20 per cent rural. Most of the urban Jews were either merchants or craftsmen. Of the merchants, there were a very few wholesalers; the others sold dry goods, groceries, and spices; many were shopkeepers or pedlars who made the rounds of the villages with their bundles. Among the Jewish craftsmen were weavers, dyers, tailors (most of the tailoring was done by women), carpenters, tanners, cobblers, gold- and silversmiths. There were also many Jewish donkey drivers and ferry-men who transported timber down the rivers to Mosul. In addition, many were labourers who, after their arrival in Israel, became porters.

A Jewish child In Sandur.

The Jewish peasants lived mostly in mixed villages in which they constituted a minority; but there were also villages inhabited only or mostly by Jews. They grew wheat, barley, rice, sesame, lentils, tobacco, or had orchards, vineyards, as well as cattle. In addition to taking care of their own fields and animals, the Jews had to provide unpaid group-labour to the *agha* and the rich landowners in the village. Because of periodic drought many of the Jewish peasants had to migrate to other places (which they could do only by sneaking off without the knowledge of their *agha*), or they went to Baghdad to eke out a living there.

Even in recent years the marriage age for Kurdish Jewish girls was very young, twelve to fourteen years. The menarche of their daughter was considered the last warning for the parents to marry her off. A nubile girl who remained unmarried in the house of her parents was believed to bring misfortune upon her whole family.

In contrast to the custom among the Arabic-speaking Jews farther south in Iraq, in Kurdistan the bridegroom had to pay a bride-price, *neqda*, to the father of his bride. This was in accordance with the prevalent Arab custom. In the villages, the bride-price was looked upon as a payment due to the father for bringing up the girl. Unless he had a rich father (which very few had), the young Kurdish Jew had to work in order to collect money for the *neqda*. When the bride-price started to rise, the rabbis of Amadiyya decreed a limit on it, which, however, was not able to stem further increases. The insistence on the bride's virginity was as strong in Kurdistan as in other parts of the Middle East, and, immediately upon the deflowering of the bride the blood-stained sheet was triumphantly exhibited. Were a girl found not to be a virgin, she would be put to death by her own father or brothers – a cruel custom found also in other parts of the traditional Middle East.

After marriage the woman became a servant of her husband and his mother, and, in addition, she had to work to augment the meagre earnings of the family. On the other hand, she had more freedom than the Jewish woman of Baghdad. On joyful festive occasions she could even dance with men. Although among the Jews of Kurdistan polygamy was more frequent than among the Arabic-speaking Jews of Iraq, it was still a rare occurrence, with not more than 5 per cent of the married men having more than one wife.

Education among the Kurdish Jews was less widespread than among the other

Iraqi Jews. The Kurdish Jews lived scattered in many villages and small towns, where there were no state schools, and the Jewish community was too small and too poor to maintain schools of its own. The few Jewish schools which did exist lacked printed books, and the children were taught to read from hand-written texts. Most of them attended school only for one or two years, and left before they learned to write or to translate the Bible, or even before they could read fluently. In the major Kurdish Jewish communities of Mosul, Zakho and Amadiyya, and some others, where most of the Jewish boys attended school, there were also Talmud Tora schools which existed until 1950. In Arbil (Irbil), north of Kirkuk, there was even a Yeshiva which supplied religious personnel, rabbis, cantors, beadles, etc., to the Kurdish Jewish communities. However, studies were conducted only in the evening and on Sabbaths; the rest of the time the students worked to earn a livelihood. In the villages, if a man could afford it, he would send his son to the town for a period of study.

Early in the present century the *Alliance* established schools for boys in Mosul and Kirkuk. Still, in general, only a small percentage of the children of Kurdish Jews attended school. Girls were sent to a school only in the rarest of cases. Consequently, down to 1950, illiteracy remained widespread among Kurdish Jews.

In the schools of the Kurdish Jews the teaching methods and the subject matter taught did not differ substantially from those we are already familiar with from the other Middle Eastern countries. Where the Kurdish Jewish school differed from the others was in the degree and cruelty of physical punishment meted out to the children. When the father first brought his child, aged about four, to the school, he would say to the teacher, 'His flesh for you, his bones for me,' meaning that he agreed that the teacher should beat the child as much as he wanted to, as long as he hurt only his flesh and did not break a bone in his body. But the children were subjected to more severe abuse than simple beating. The very meagre equipment of the school included two wooden planks, each with two semi-circular notches at their edge, which would be clamped over the ankles of the child to be punished, and held up high by two children, while the teacher would apply his cane to the culprit's soles. Yet another punishment which was nothing short of torture, was to sling a rope over a beam of the ceiling, and string the child up by his feet, head down. Then the teacher

above left These children may have never had the opportunity to go to school as the village was too poor and too small to maintain one.

above A young boy trimming a stick.

would let the other children put a small heap of dung beneath the head of the child receiving the punishment and set fire to it so that the acrid smoke would rise into the face of the poor victim who in the meantime was ordered to recite the weekly portion of the Tora.

These customary methods of punishment are important for our understanding of the Kurdish Jewish character. They undoubtedly are a reflection of the cruelty, brutality, and savagery which characterized life in Kurdistan in general. Their effect on the character of the Jews was to make them the hardest, fiercest, and most ruthless, but also the bravest, most audacious, and most fearless of all the Jewish tribes whose remnants were ingathered in Israel. These character traits, developed to the fullest by the child-rearing techniques and subsequently by the relationship of the Kurds to the Jews, had their corresponding physical complement: the Kurdish Jews, both men and women, were a physically well-developed race, of medium stature, with heavy bones, strong and muscular, with great capacity for work and effort.

The women shared the rough and tough nature of the men. Were this not the case they could not have endured the treatment meted out to them by their husbands. What the boy took in beatings in his childhood from the teacher and the father, the woman suffered after her marriage: there was among the men a tendency to be harsh to their wives, to beat and abuse them, often so severely that they became bed-ridden. Since to dominate one's wife was considered proper behaviour – a proverb even stated that 'He whose wife is subservient will live long' – the husband did not hesitate to beat his wife even in public, so as to demonstrate his mastery over her.

In these circumstances it was not surprising that some women became unfaithful to their husbands. If a woman was caught in adultery, she was either killed by her husband, or, if he was more law-abiding, he would immediately divorce her, whereupon they would cut off her hair, seat her backwards on a donkey, make her hold on to the donkey's tail as a bridle, and let her ride in the streets while the children would beat her and pour sour milk over her.

In Kurdistan, as in all Middle Eastern Jewish communities, while the wife could not divorce her husband, he could easily get rid of her even against her will. An unusual feature in comparison with other Jewish communities, but in keeping with the Kurdish Jewish character, was the reaction of the mother to being cut off from contact with her children who, in case of divorce, would remain with their father. It is said that the mother easily separated from her children, and that after divorce no contact at all was maintained between her and them. In general, a divorced woman remarried quickly. An unmarried woman was an almost unknown phenomenon among the Jews of Kurdistan.

The religious life of the Jews of Kurdistan consisted of the same two elements which comprised belief and observance in all Middle Eastern Jewish communities. On the one hand, there were the prescribed daily, Sabbath, and holiday prayers, the services in the synagogue, the observance of the festive rituals at home, and, of course, the basic and uncompromising belief in the one God and in his selection of Israel as his people. On the other, and in unnoticed contradiction to the above, there were the beliefs in the evil eye and in demons, and the innumerable occasions on which amulets had to be resorted to against them. There were the other magic prophylactic measures to be taken, and the pilgrimages to be made to the tombs of saints. As in other Jewish communities, but even more so, the participation of women in religious life was severely limited. Girls were not sent to school, did not know how to read, knew only a very few prayers which they had learnt by heart, and rarely went to the synagogue (in most Kurdish synagogues there was no women's section).

Two Jewish women. Most Kurdish Jewish girls married between the ages of twelve and fourteen.

It is remarkable that despite their generally rudimentary Jewish education, and the absence of any general education, the Kurdish Jews produced an extensive literature of religious and secular poems, partly in Hebrew, but mostly in their neo-Aramaic colloquial, and mostly transmitted orally. They also had a rich

far left One of the older members of the village community.

left Carrying a Tora scroll.

musical tradition of their own, influenced by, but different from, the songs of their Kurdish neighbours.

As for the total number of the Kurdish Jews prior to their mass exodus to Israel, only estimates exist. Statistics are available only for Iraqi Kurdistan, according to which they numbered 14,835 in 1920; 14,603 in 1932; and 19,767 in 1947, living in 146 localities. In the 1920s 1,900 Kurdish Jews made their *aliya, followed in 1936 by another 2,500. Immigrants from one township had such a strong feeling of separateness from the others (a typical Kurdish trait) that each group established a separate community in Jerusalem. The same period saw, in Kurdistan itself, the beginning of the village-to-town movement with which we are familiar from other Middle Eastern Jewish communities, and which resulted in the evacuation of many small localities. After the establishment of Israel, in 1950–1, almost all the Kurdish Jews (19,000 from Iraq; 8,000 from Iran and about 3,000 from Turkey) were ingathered in the ancient homeland from which their ancestors were exiled almost twenty-seven centuries earlier.

Yemen

A Jewish timber market in Yemen, 1928.

Yemen lies in the fertile south-western corner of the Arabian Peninsula, which the Romans designated by the name of *Arabia Felix*, or Happy Arabia, in contradistinction to the more northern arid stretches of the peninsula referred to as *Arabia Deserta*. Legends current among the Yemenite Jews had it that their ancestors arrived in Yemen after the destruction of the First Temple of Jerusalem (in 586 BCE), and that when Ezra returned from Babylonia to the land of Israel he sent letters to all Jewish communities, among them to the Yemenite Jews, asking them to join their Babylonian brethren in rebuilding their ancestral land. Being prophetically gifted, the Yemenite Jews foresaw that the Second Temple of Jerusalem would also be destroyed and Israel would again be exiled. Therefore they preferred to stay in the happy land of Yemen. Thereupon Ezra cursed them that they should always live in dire poverty.

While this legend is a fine example of the mythical justification of an existing situation, as well as of the tendency of ethno-history to 'telescope' events separated by centuries and compress them into a single continuous sequence, there are no historical data as to the presence of Jews in Yemen at that early date. History knows of Jews in Yemen, or in any part of Arabia for that matter, only some five centuries later. In 25 BCE, when a Roman expeditionary force under Aelius Gallus was sent to southern Arabia, King Herod supplied Jewish auxilliary troops to go along. It is quite possible that these Jewish soldiers, or rather those of them who survived the Roman defeat near Najran (today located just north of the

Yemen-Saudi border), remained in the country. If so, they were the first Jewish settlers in the Yemen area.

In the course of the next two centuries, numerous Jews must have lived in southern Arabia, as attested by epitaphs of several Jews from Himyar (a designation applied loosely to all of what is today Yemen and South Yemen) found in the catacombs of Beth Shearim, east of Haifa, Israel, which served as a central burial place in the first and second centuries CE also for Jews of Syria and Mesopotamia. It appears that the Himyarite king Ab Karib Asad (r. 385–420) converted to Judaism, and that in his time, as well as in the next two centuries, there was a strong movement of conversion to Judaism in South Arabia. That they maintained connections with Palestine becomes evident not only from Beth Shearim but also from the fact that the last Jewish king of Himyar, Yusuf Dhu Nuwas (r. 517?–525) had contact with the Jewish sages of Tiberias.

From the first century CE on, epitaphs attest also to the presence of Jews in settlements along the coastal region of north-western Arabia, and from the fourth, also in Yathrib (later Medina) and Mecca. In the generation before Muhammad (570–632) the Jewish community was large and influential in the Hijaz. The names and Arabic works of several Jewish poets are known from this age and place, and, according to Arab historians, many Jewish tribes had lived there for generations.

The influence of Jewish law and lore on Muhammad is too well known to require more than passing mention, but it should be pointed out that in his time some of the most powerful tribes in and around Yathrib were Jewish. However, the victory of Islam meant that most of the Jews who lived in the coastal region, from Transjordan in the north to Yemen in the south, chose or were forced to convert to the creed of Muhammad. Those who managed to remain faithful to Judaism were condemned to lead the life of *dhimmis*, already familiar to us from other countries conquered by Islam. Scattered evidence indicates that, in addition to their main concentrations in Yemen, Jewish communities survived down to the present century also in central Arabia, as well as along the western and southern coastal regions of the peninsula.

From about 900 to 1960 Yemen was ruled by the Shi'ite Zaydi dynasty. Shi'ism is traditionally more intolerant than Sunni Islam, and consequently, the life of the Jews in Yemen was more difficult than in Sunni countries. While the Christian population disappeared from Yemen long ago, the Jews succeeded, as they did in other Muslim countries, in adjusting to the conditions under which the Zaydi Yemenites grudgingly tolerated them. Internal autonomy was the form of existence for the *dhimmis* in all Muslim lands, and in Yemen, too, the Jews for several generations had their own chiefs, variously titled *aluf* (elect), *wakil* (representative), or *nagid* (prince). They were also able to maintain religious contact and trade relations with the Jews of Egypt, North Africa, and Persia.

In the twelfth century, many Yemenite Jews were forced to convert to Islam. Among the reactions to these persecutions was the appearance of a self-styled pseudo-Messiah, and the readiness, nay eagerness, of the Jews to believe in him. Their *nagid*, Ya'qov ben N'tanel al-Fayyumi, turned for guidance to Maimonides, whose extant reply, the well known *Iggeret Teman* (Epistle to Yemen, c. 1172), contains valuable information on the Yemenite Jewish condition.

In the centuries that followed, the fate of the Jews in Yemen was characterized by the same periodic ups and downs which marked their history in other Arab countries, except that the downturns were more frequent and steeper than in the Sunni lands. Even in periods when they were not actively and acutely persecuted,

right The market in San'a, the capital of Yemen.

both the rulers and the Muslim populace saw to it that the old Koranic rule which provided that the Jews and other 'people of the Book' must be 'brought low' (Koran 9:29) should be strictly observed. The details of how they made sure that the Jews were kept in their place assigned to them by the Arabian prophet varied somewhat from one period to another, but their essence and intent remained constant: the Jews must be humiliated, humbled, oppressed, brought low and kept there.

Yemen was exceptional among Arab countries not only in that Shi'ism was its dominant religion, but also because its society was structured within a rather rigid class system. The population was divided into several ranking groups according to descent and occupation. The Jews, considered serfs, were at the very bottom of the social ladder, and could exist only by acquiring, not unlike the Kurdish Jews, Muslim patrons who, in exchange for a levy, would protect their life and property. The rigid class system of the Muslim environment left its mark on the internal social structure of the Jews as well. The Jews of the capital, San'a, considered themselves the elite of Yemenite Jewry and looked down upon the Jews of other towns, and especially of the villages, as low-class people, descendants of converts to Judaism, with whom they refused to intermarry.

Conversions to Judaism were, of course, possible only in the *jahiliyya*, the days of ignorance, as the Muslims refer to the period prior to the appearance of Muhammad. Had a Muslim converted to Judaism, his punishment would have been death. On the other hand, although both Muhammad and the Caliph Omar had instructed the Muslims to allow the Jews to live in the House of Islam, Islamic religious fervour was such, especially in Shi'ite countries, that forcing the Jews to convert to the religion of Muhammad seemed the proper thing to do. Pressure on the Jews to convert to Islam was implicitly present at all times. Periodically, if a Jew refused to convert, he was imprisoned and tortured. Occasionally, the Jews were subjected to wilful maltreatment: they were forced to go bareheaded, their synagogues were destroyed, they were prohibited from praying publicly, and were given the choice between conversion and expulsion. In 1678 the Jews were expelled from San'a; many died while searching for a place where they would be

Lighting the Hanuka candles. Hanuka celebrates the purification and rededication of the Temple in Jerusalem by the Maccabees after the expulsion of the Syrians.

permitted to stay. When, three years later, the survivors were allowed back to San'a, they were not permitted to return to their houses, but were given a place outside the city walls to set up a new quarter for themselves.

The early nineteenth century was a time of great hardship for the Yemenite Jews. Again, as many times in the past, famines decimated their ranks, internecine wars claimed many more victims, and those who survived had to put up with new indignities. In 1806 a decree was issued imposing upon the Jews the task of removing the animal carcasses from the streets of San'a and to clean its latrines. The Jewish community made payment available to a few poor Jews who undertook to fulfil this onerous duty. This decree remained in force until the Jewish evacuation of Yemen in 1948–9.

From 1872, when the Ottoman army occupied San'a, the position of the Jews improved somewhat. They were permitted to construct a new quarter, allowed to build a synagogue, and exempted for a while from the duty of collecting animal carcasses. On the other hand, the Turks did not abolish the poll-tax, forced the Jews to grind flour for their army, and, in general, the Turkish soldiery treated them no better than did the local Arab population. These circumstances seem to have intensified the desire to emigrate to Palestine, which was translated into action when the rumour reached Yemen that Rothschild – whom the Jews believed to be something like a king of the Jews – had bought large tracts of land in Jerusalem and was giving it away free to Yemenite Jews. The first group of one hundred Jewish families set out from Yemen for Jerusalem in 1891, and, after Sinbad-like adventures on land and sea, arrived in Palestine in the summer of that year, several months in advance of the first 'aliya from East Europe.

In 1905, after the Imam Yahya succeeded in dislodging the Turks from San'a, he issued a decree which reminded the Jews that the old rules, abolished or not enforced by the Turks, were again to be unfailingly obeyed. They included the duty of paying the *jizya* and other taxes, and the prohibition of building houses higher than those of Muslims, disturbing Muslims in their path, encroaching upon the occupations of Muslims, cursing any prophet, irritating Muslims in their beliefs, riding on a donkey outside the city except if sitting sideways (within the city they were forbidden to ride any animal, and nowhere were they allowed to ride horses or camels), pointing to a Muslim's nakedness, displaying the Tora outside the synagogues, raising their voices while reading, and blowing the shofar loudly. The decree also established a Jewish law court of four (whose members were admonished not to change anything in their law), reaffirmed the right of Jews to come before Muslim judges, and appointed a chief to head the Jewish community.

This decree, which remained in force until their emigration to Israel, was by no means a complete catalogue of the humiliations which were the fate of the Yemenite Jews. The restrictions imposed upon them also included the prohibition of testifying against a Muslim, wearing stockings and new, fine, or bright clothes, and engaging in money transactions. They also had to rise in deference whenever a Muslim passed them in the street, and to step down into the gutter lest their touch defile him. They were, quite literally, the untouchables of Yemen. In 1921, the Imam issued a new decree which provided that Jewish children younger than thirteen, whose father died, were to be taken from their homes (even if their mother was alive) and brought up as Muslims. In the capital and the other towns these rules were enforced mercilessly; however, in the villages, especially in the south and the east, where only one or two Jewish families lived in a locality, the relations between them and their Muslim neighbours were better. In one or two villages the Jews could even wear in their belt the large J-shaped dagger which was the hallmark of every free Yemenite Arab man, and which was strictly prohibited to them in all the other places.

How, one is inclined to ask, could people live in such conditions for many centuries? The answer, I believe, is to be sought in two factors. One was that the Yemenite Jews had learned the art of accepting insults with self-effacement,

suffering cruelty with patient endurance, reacting to humiliation with humility. The Yemenite Jews themselves recognized that humility and timidness were basic features in their character.

Joseph Qafih, a Yemenite Jewish author who was born, brought up, and lived in San'a before emigrating to Palestine in 1943 with his wife and children, observed that, in addition to the Hebrew and Aramaic words which the Yemenite Jews mixed into their Arabic speech, they differed greatly from the Muslims in that 'the manner of speaking of the Jew had a certain blandness and evasiveness which was not the case with the Muslim. Of a Jew who spoke arrogantly they said, "He talks like a Gentile".' In order to survive in a basically inimical and contemptuous social environment, they had to learn to bear silently, and without any outward reaction, the jeers of the Muslims, their abuse, and their vilification. In the course of many centuries of such environmental conditioning, the Yemenite Jews had no choice but to become humble, modest, undemanding and peaceable, and, yes, bland and evasive.

The other factor was their deeply-ingrained religiosity, comprising an unshakeable belief in God, in the supreme value of the *mitzvot*, the commandments, and the supreme Jewish duty of observing them.

Not that the religious faith of the Yemenite Jews was of a particularly pure monotheistic character; in fact, they were greatly addicted to many magic beliefs and practices. One of the tasks of the Yemenite *mori* – their term for rabbi – was to dispense magical remedies, write or otherwise prepare amulets, and thus to minister to the psychological needs of a people who had to have supernatural comfort to be able to endure a life of poverty, hardship, and humiliation. But still, their faith in God who in His mercy enabled the *mori* to alleviate suffering, was unwavering, and the conviction that only they, the Jews, knew how to serve God as He wanted to be served, endowed them with a sense of inner superiority towards their Muslim neighbours, a feeling which secretly compensated them for all the sufferings caused them by the same inferior, but more numerous and more powerful, neighbours.

While most Yemenite Muslims were illiterate, there were very few Jewish men in Yemen who could not read Hebrew. Since without reading the Bible and the prayer book a Jew could not fulfil the basic commandments of his religion, he had to know how to read. The knowledge of writing was not a religious requirement, and hence there were many who could read but not write. As for the women, they could fulfil all the religious duties required of them without being able either to read or to write, and consequently all Yemenite Jewish women were illiterate.

In a village where only a few Jewish families lived, the fathers would teach their sons the rudiments of reading. In the urban communities, the boys were sent to school at the age of three and a half. The school, called *Little Kanis* (i.e., little synagogue), was in most cases nothing more than an unfurnished room, in which the children would sit on the floor, in a circle, around one or two books placed on top of a wooden box or a stool, pressing against one another for lack of space, and would learn to read the Hebrew text whether looking at it from front, right, left, or upside down. In these small, overcrowded and airless rooms the children, occasionally divided into age-groups, would spend the whole day, from early in the morning until after sundown, with two brief intermissions so as to enable them to go back home for breakfast and lunch. After the evening prayer, the older children would remain for further study. The only indispensable teaching aids were the teacher's rod and whip, to which he would give free play whenever a child became guilty of inattention or betrayed ignorance. To the age of six or seven they learned to read the Tora and prayers. Then they studied the Aramaic translation of the Pentateuch and of the Haftora (the weekly portion from the Prophets). From nine to twelve years, those who still continued to study, read Sa'adya Gaon's Arabic translation of the Tora in Hebrew characters, and sometimes the *Yad haHazaqa*, the halakhic code of Maimonides.

Since the general view was that only merchants needed to know how to write,

A Yemenite Jewish family. The women and girls wear the *gargush*, their traditional head-dress.

Music and dance were most important to the Yemenite Jewish way of life.

little time was spent on practising writing. Those children who did master writing were given some religious text to copy: the Passover Hagada, the prayer book, a book of poems. Since the emphasis was on fluency in reading, in many cases neither the children nor the adults understood what they read. Because to learn to read was considered a religious duty, parents who did not send their sons to school were ostracized. Occasionally, young boys would be sent to a remote village to serve as teachers. Only in a few better schools were the children taught a little arithmetic.

While the Hebrew education of the boys was in the hands of the teacher, each father taught his son the trade which he himself had learned from his father. A daughter, when she was five or six years old, began to receive practical instruction in housework; a little later, in sewing and embroidery; then came the religious prescriptions she had to know in connection with cooking. By the age of ten a girl had acquired all she had to know to manage her household, and was ready to become engaged. At the age of twelve, she would be married off. The average age of a boy at marriage was sixteen to nineteen.

The discipline enforced by beating, and the fear of the father, produced quiet, obedient, and ultimately self-controlled children. This factor, added to the terror infused into both Jewish children and adults by the Arab environment, were probably the major influences which formed the Yemenite Jewish character.

Apart from a short-lived attempt to set up a somewhat better-organized school, initiated by a group of Jews known as *Dor De'a* (Generation of Knowledge; the name was commonly abridged in pronunciation as *Darda'*), no modern Jewish school was ever established in Yemen. Nor were Jewish children permitted to attend Muslim state schools.

All in all, the religious knowledge of the Yemenite Jews was limited, and even in San'a there were only a few learned Jews, among them several Kabbalists and mystics. On the other hand, religious conservatism was general, and even in the young generation there was none of that turning away from observances which we found in other Middle Eastern Jewish communities.

Despite their depressed economic, social, and cultural conditions, the literary output of the Yemenite Jew was most impressive. They wrote, either in Hebrew or in Arabic, commentaries to the Bible and the Mishna, Masoretic studies, glosses on the Code of Maimonides, philosophical treatises, responsa, fine Hebrew poetry, and even travelogues and histories. Most important are their Kabbalistic and Midrashic works, some of the latter based on older sources which subsequently disappeared.

Music added much colour to the life of the Jews in Yemen. In addition to the traditional cantillation of the Bible, the men found pleasure in chanting the prayers in the synagogue, in strongly rhythmical and fortissimo group singing, performed with great enthusiasm and expenditure of vocal energy. Outside the synagogue, in the home, on holidays and at festivities, the men would sing Hebrew and Arabic religious songs, often dance as well, occasionally with the participation of women who would accompany the men's songs by interjecting their high-pitched vibrant ululations, the traditional expression of female rejoicing all over the Middle East. The women's own domain comprised secular songs, in Arabic, which they would sing while performing their daily chores or embroidering, or while attending weddings where they would gather in quarters apart from the men. Dancing, which was engaged in on festive occasions, would be done separately by men and women. In contrast to the lively, graceful, leaping, exuberant and accelerating style of the men's dances, those of the women were characterized by quiet dignity and restraint, and by slow and strictly limited movements. Drums, copper trays and, more recently, empty tin cans, were employed for rhythmic accompaniment; no other musical instruments were used.

To the very end, the Jews were easily distinguished from the Muslims by their clothing. On weekdays, and especially when going out of the house, both the men and the women wore black. The men covered their heads with a black cap, tied around with black kerchief criss-crossed by white pin-stripes. In the street, the men wore over one shoulder, serape-like, a tallit, the ritual prayer-shawl with the prescribed four fringes. The tallit was either all black, or white-and-brown striped. One end of it was often used for carrying fruit or other food which the men (and not the women) would buy in the market, on their way home from the morning prayers in the synagogue.

The women tied around their heads a white kerchief, over which they always, whether outdoors or in the house, wore the hood-like *gargush* (spelled *qarqush*), made of two oblong pieces of material, sewn together at the top and the back, coming down to the shoulders on both sides of the face, and pulled together under the chin by a loop and button. The *gargush* worn on weekdays, Sabbaths, and holidays was black, decorated with some embroidery along the opening which framed the face. For a wedding the bride wore an extremely ornate apparel. The fully caparisoned bride in her fantastically lavish attire, in which she could move only with difficulty, looked like a gold-encrusted living statue.

The position of the Jewish woman in any country is the ultimate gauge by which to measure the extent of the influence exerted by the non-Jewish environment on Jewish life. In Yemen, while a certain separation between the sexes was customary among the Jews, it never reached the stage of complete segregation observed by the urban Muslims. The Jewish women were not veiled; they could, and frequently did, visit each other; on Sabbath and holiday afternoons they would stroll along the streets of the Jewish quarter, or sit around in the open. At home, in contrast to the Muslim custom, husband and wife would take their meals together, which was expressive of the higher status in the family enjoyed by the Jewish woman compared to her Muslim sister.

When the great stations of the human life cycle were reached, when a child was born, a marriage took place, or a person died, the women had their full share in

A young jeweller from San'a with traditional sidelocks.

the proceedings, even though mostly they assembled separately from the menfolk. While excluded from formal schooling, the girl-child nevertheless acquired from her mother not only the practical skills of a housewife, including the delicate art of embroidery, but also a considerable store of oral tradition – legends, stories, songs, proverbs – in the Judeo-Arabic colloquial.

The magical element in the religion of the Yemenite Jews, referred to above, was more in evidence in the beliefs and practices of the women, which was probably a correlate of their exclusion from the official and communal aspects of religion centring on the synagogue. Nevertheless, the Yemenite Jewish woman had a measured, controlled – one would almost be inclined to say Apollonian – personality, which expressed itself classically in her dance style, and which enabled her to create a serene home atmosphere for her menfolk and produce a young generation free, even in the upheavals of adjustment to Israeli life, of the stigma of juvenile delinquency.

While there were a very few rich Jews in San'a, almost all Yemenite Jews were poor, and the majority was destitute. Most of them, about 46·1 per cent of all the gainfully employed, were craftsmen, 30·2 per cent worked in commerce, 15 per cent worked in agriculture (an exceptionally high proportion, exceeded in the whole Middle East only among the Jews of Kurdistan), 4·1 per cent in building and transport, 3 per cent in professional and technical occupations (mostly rabbis and other religious functionaries), and 0·7 per cent in administrative and clerical jobs. Of all immigrants to Israel from Yemen and Aden in 1948–50, a little over 11 per cent had been gainfully employed; this means that there were about nine dependents per earner, which is an unusually high proportion.

In addition to working as gold- and silversmiths, which was a Jewish monopoly, Yemenite Jews engaged in dozens of other occupations which served the needs of the general population. There were among them millers, slaughterers,

A Jewish woman: the Yemenite
Jewish women were unveiled
and enjoyed a higher status in
the family than their Muslim
counterparts.

distillers, snuff makers; spinners, weavers, cotton workers, cushion sewers,
tailors; shoemakers, and cobblers, furriers, tanners, flayers, saddle makers,
leather workers; building labourers, stone cutters, house painters, carpenters,
cabinet makers, wicker workers, sieve makers; potters, millstone chamferers,
charcoal burners, pulver makers, soap makers; barbers, cuppers, porters, donkey
drivers, manure collectors, cleaners of courtyards; clothes merchants, shopkeepers, pedlars; copyists, bookbinders. Most of these occupations were
transmitted from father to son.

It was estimated that in 1947 about 3,000 Jews lived in the capital, Sanʿa,
another 2,000 in the four cities of Radaʾ, Dhamar, ʿAmran, and Shaybam. The rest
were dispersed in many villages – in 134 according to Israeli immigration statistics,
or, according to one authority on Yemenite Jews, in as many as 1,000 localities.

Due to poor sanitary conditions and their great poverty, most of the Yemenite
Jews were physically underdeveloped; they were slight, lean, and small of
stature. The number of surviving children per married couple was small, 1·7 to 1·8
on the average. On the other hand, the adult life span, too, was low, so that among
the immigrants who came from Yemen and Aden to Israel in 1948–52 two-thirds
were under thirty years of age, and only 11 per cent over fifty.

Since no census has ever been taken in Yemen, we have only the vaguest idea as
to the number of the Yemenite Jews prior to their mass arrival in Israel in 1949–50.
Previously, their number was variously estimated from 15,000 to 50,000. From
1910 to 1948 about 19,000 Jews from Yemen (and Aden) had emigrated to
Palestine, and in 1949–50, Operation Magic Carpet brought 44,000 Jews born in
Yemen and 3,000 born in Aden, to Israel. Within a few years, the 4,000 who had
remained behind also transferred to Israel, so that by 1967 it was estimated that no
more than two to three hundred Jews were left in the entire Arabian peninsula.

Part Six

India
Jews Black and White

The interior of a 'White Jews' synagogue in India.

Young Black Jewish children study the Hebrew inscription on a tomb in a Jewish cemetery.

The caste system, of which the classical land is India, has left its mark on the Jews of the sub-continent no less than on its other inhabitants. While mutual demarcations, separating disparate Jewish communities dwelling in the same locality, are known from other countries as well – as discussed for example in the chapters on the Balkans and North Africa – in none of them were these separatisms as pronounced or as numerous as in India, nor did they approximate to the caste-like character assumed by the Indian White, Brown, and Black Jews, Baghdadi Jews, Cochin Jews, and Bene Israel.

As in many other countries, so in India, legends current among the Jews claim that their origin goes back to remote antiquity. In fact, the Bene Israel, the largest and oldest of the Indian Jewish communities, maintain that their ancestors arrived on the west coast of India shortly after the Northern Kingdom of Israel seceded from Rehoboam, the son of King Solomon, who retained control only over the Southern Kingdom of Judah. Their very name, they say, testifies to their descent:

they are called Bene Israel, i.e., 'Children of Israel', because they are the offspring of the ten tribes of Israel. Those among them who know the Bible well, point to the story of King Solomon's fleet which once every three years visited an unnamed country and brought back gold, silver, ivory, apes, and peacocks (1 Kings 10:22) – all Indian products. Hence the route to India must have been well known, and those 'Children of Israel' who after Solomon's death wished to go there had no difficulty in doing so.

Others hold that the ancestral migration from Israel to India took place, not at the beginning, but at the end, of the history of the Northern Kingdom. When the Assyrians conquered Israel (in 721 BCE), some of the Children of Israel, they say, managed to escape and sought refuge in India. Still others place the event in the days preceding the Maccabean uprising, when Antiochus Epiphanes (175–164 BCE) subjected the Jews of Palestine to severe persecutions; or in the period of the destruction of the Second Temple of Jerusalem by the Romans (70 CE). All versions have in common the arrival by ship from the west, the storm which wrecked the ship off the Konkan coast, and the drowning of almost all voyagers except for seven couples who were cast ashore and settled in the first village they reached, Nawgaon, some twenty-six miles south of present-day Bombay, where they became the ancestors of the Bene Israel. Because of their complete isolation from other Jews they forgot much of their Hebrew language and Jewish religion, and adopted the language (Marathi), the customs, garb, and names of their Hindu neighbours. But they clung tenaciously to the rudiments of Judaism, observing circumcision, dietary laws, the Sabbath and some festivals, and never forgot the *Sh'ma'* prayer. Because they earned their livelihood by producing oil, their neighbours called them Shanwar Telis, i.e., 'Sabbath-keeping oilmen'. Since oil-pressing was considered a very humble occupation, the Teli caste, to which the Bene Israel were assigned, was a low one: the touch of one of its members polluted the person and also the possessions of members of higher castes.

At some time in the course of their history, the Bene Israel themselves became divided into two castes, the *Gora*, or White, and the *Kala*, or Black. The Gora were believed to be the pure descendants of the seven couples who landed on the Konkan coast; the Kala – offspring of unions between Bene Israel men and non-Bene Israel women. This traditional distinction was not borne out by the skin colour of the two Bene Israel castes. There were Gora who were darker than most Kala. This, of course, could not go unnoticed by the Gora, but they explained that the darkening of the skin colour of some of them was due, not to inter-marriage, but to the poverty and the great heat of India which affected the fair complexion of their ancestors. The inter-relationship between the Gora and the Kala resembled that of the Indian castes. The Gora, believed to be superior, imposed certain restrictions on social intercourse between them and the Kala. Only in recent years, and especially among those Bene Israel who moved to Israel, did these old restrictions begin to break down, and inter-marriages between the two groups have become, if not common, at least not unheard of.

While their myth of origin goes back to antiquity, the culture-hero of the Bene Israel lived, according to their tradition, in the Middle Ages. He was David Rahabi who the Bene Israel believe to have been the brother of Maimonides. If so, he lived, and arrived in India, in the late twelfth century. Actually, this legendary Rahabi seems to be none other than David Rahabi (d. 1726), who came from Aleppo in Syria, to Cochin in 1664, and whose figure was apparently conflated with that of his son Ezekiel (1694–1771), diplomat in the service of the Dutch East India

Company from 1726 to 1771. It was Ezekiel Rahabi who, in the course of his travels, became acquainted with, and interested in, the Bene Israel of the Konkan. He became convinced that the Bene Israel were true Jews, and, appalled by their ignorance of Judaism, he decided to stay with them. He taught them Hebrew and prayers, and familiarized them with the developments in Jewish religion that had taken place after their arrival in India. He also selected the three most proficient of his pupils, young men from the Jhiratkar, Shapurkar, and Rajpurkar families, to serve as teachers and preachers, with the title *kaji*, evidently a corruption of the Arabic *kadi*, religious judge. By that time the Bene Israel were dispersed over dozens of villages, and thus the kajis had to travel from place to place, to settle disputes, and to attend important ceremonies such as circumcisions and weddings. The office of the kaji became hereditary, although it had to be confirmed by the local rulers. By the second half of the nineteenth century the authority of the kajis had dwindled due to their ignorance in both religious and secular matters. By the twentieth, it was a mere title which members of the kaji families used much as if it were a family name.

above Reading a prayer book in a quiet corner of a Jewish home.

above right A Jewish couple in Jew Town Road.

right Celebrating a Jewish festival.

In the mid-eighteenth century the Bene Israel began to leave their villages and to settle in Bombay, attracted by employment opportunities in the growing city as skilled labourers and clerks, and by the possibility of serving in the regiments of the East India Company. Their first synagogue in Bombay was erected in 1796. By 1833, about 2,000 Bene Israel, or one-third of their total number, lived in Bombay. There, they received instruction in Judaism from Cochin Jews (see below) who served them as teachers and preachers, and were materially helped by a few wealthy Baghdadi Jews (such as the Sassoons) who had come to Bombay in the early nineteenth century, and who established a school for them. Also the American Mission opened a Hebrew school in Alibag, in the Konkan, as did other missions. A Marathi translation of the Bible, prepared by missionaries, appeared in instalments from 1819 on, and Dr John Wilson of the Scottish Presbyterian Mission published a Hebrew grammar in Marathi. Though these missionary efforts resulted in only very few conversions to Christianity, they did spread the knowledge of the Bible and the Hebrew language among the Bene Israel in general. The Bene Israel also learned English from the missionaries, which in turn enabled them to read Jewish publications from England and America.

The Baghdadi Jews, who arrived in India beginning in the early nineteenth century, played a role *vis-à-vis* the native Jewish communities not unlike that of the Sephardi Jews or the Grana in North Africa. They were well educated in Jewish lore and strictly religious. They were also wealthy, and pioneered different industries, providing employment for many thousands of people. They had a community consciousness, subsidized religious, educational and charitable institutions, built public libraries and museums, and shared the privileges of the Europeans in India. And they kept themselves strictly apart and aloof from the native Jews. Entering into an environment in which caste, often manifested in skin colour, ruled supreme, it was almost inevitable that the Baghdadi Jews should find it imperative to erect a barrier between themselves and their dark-skinned co-religionists who occupied a low-caste position in India. They argued that there was a vital difference between them and the Bene Israel, because 'pure Jewish blood does not flow in their veins'. This position manifested itself in acts that were more insulting than injurious: thus the Baghdadis did not count the Bene Israel as part of the *minyan*, the quorum of ten adult male Jews required for public worship; they did not call them up to the reading of the Tora; tried to exclude them from the use of beds reserved for Jews in the biggest hospital in Bombay, and from membership in the single synagogue in Rangoon; and practiced other such segregationist policies.

The resentment on the part of the Bene Israel was considerable, but not as intense as it would have been in a society not built on the caste system. They complained, fulminated, protested, but it never came to organized action on their part, nor to open conflict.

The nineteenth century was a time of changes for the Bene Israel. Several new synagogues were built in Bombay. Education became widespread. Many served in the British 'native' regiments, or found employment as civil servants in government, the railways, the postal and customs services, or worked as shopkeepers, artisans, carpenters, masons; some of them were agriculturists. The most important development, however, was the intensification of contacts between the Bene Israel and other Jewish communities. This was greatly facilitated by the concentration of the majority of the Bene Israel in Bombay. Before the end of the nineteenth century, Bombay had become a veritable, small-scale 'ingathering of exiles'. In addition to the Baghdadi Jews, there were Jews from Cochin, Yemen, Afghanistan, Bukhara, and Persia. (A few decades later the rise of Nazism in Europe was to bring a number of German, Polish, Rumanian, and other European Jews.) As a result of this cosmopolitan character of the Bombay Jewish community, the Bene Israel became aware of the international quality of Jewry, and reached out, not only to the other Jews in Bombay, but also to Jewish communities and organizations in other parts of the world. In 1897 they were invited to attend the First Zionist Congress in Basle, Switzerland, but they declined on religious grounds, as did many other religious Jewish bodies at the time, and it was not until 1919 that the first Bene Israel Zionist Association was founded in Bombay.

Following India's independence (1947) and the official abolition of the caste system, the distinctions between the Baghdadis and the Bene Israel diminished. While under the British Raj white skin was a guarantee of privileged position, now, with the Indians having become the rulers in their own country, a pale complexion stamped its owner as a foreigner and an unwanted alien. Whereupon, as Louis Rabinowitz put it, 'the formerly privileged class has hastened with almost indecent haste to welcome the Bene Israel as brothers and co-religionists'.[1] Despite this post-independence rapprochement, marriages between Baghdadi Jews and Bene Israel have remained very rare. When they do occur, they are the outcome of falling in love, which itself is something new among the Jews of India, the traditional mode of marriage having been, and remaining, by arrangement between the parents of usually very young boys and girls.

Three Indian Jewish women, one holding a prayer book, dressed in highly ornate and decorative clothes.

Following independence, it became fashionable all over India to frown upon caste distinctions, at least in theory, and, with the general trend towards modernism and the greater opportunities for boys and girls to meet, love marriages increased and, inevitably, so did marriages between Gora and Kala Bene Israel.

As for the occupational structure, and social, business, and professional relations, the Bene Israel presented the typical picture of a community in the course of assimilation. However, there were certain features in respect of which the Bene Israel differed from most other Jewish communities. For one thing, very few of them were merchants. For another, some 10 per cent of the earners were carpenters and 'he is a carpenter' was a derogatory remark; the majority of the breadwinners, however, were clerks in government and private offices and many Bene Israel as well as outsiders referred to their group as a 'clerk caste'. Some (according to the estimate of one of them as many as 10 per cent) were doctors, lawyers, engineers, and other academically and professionally trained people. The Bene Israel doctors and lawyers were among those with the highest reputation in the country, but the Bene Israel themselves preferred to use the services of non-Bene Israel professionals, which is at variance with the typical Jewish behaviour elsewhere. Similarly, although there was a Bene Israel Co-operative Banking Society (estb. 1918), many Bene Israel preferred to borrow from other sources. Those among the Bene Israel who were employers, owners or managers, rarely employed co-members, and Bene Israel businessmen were little patronized by their co-members. The majority of Bene Israel children attended non-Bene Israel schools. The few wealthy Bene Israel tended to isolate themselves from their community, or at least reduce contact with it to a minimum.[2]

In Bombay, where some 75 per cent of all Bene Israel were concentrated in recent decades, they were organized in three religious unions. The first, the Union of Orthodox Jewish Congregations in India, was linked to the organization of the same name in America. The second, the United Synagogue of India, was affiliated with the Conservative World Council of Synagogues. In belief and practice there were no differences between the two. All four Bene Israel synagogues and three prayer halls, consisting of one or two rooms rented for purposes of worship, were located in the poor areas of Bombay where most Bene Israel lived. (Of the two Baghdadi synagogues, one was located in a poor Jewish neighbourhood, the other in a prosperous and more fashionable district.)

The third organization, the Jewish Religious Union, had affinity with the Liberal Jewish movement in England. Its membership consisted mainly of Bene Israel in prestigious occupations, and was restricted to a small section of the community. Moreover, some of its members belonged also to one of the Orthodox or Conservative synagogues. The style of services in the Liberal prayer-hall differed but little from that of the synagogues belonging to the other two unions, so that the differences between the Liberal union and the two others boiled down to the quality of the membership: those in the former were better educated, had more prestigious occupations, higher incomes, more influence, broader intellectual interests, and, in general, a more established social status, than those who belonged to the Conservative and Orthodox unions.

One of the most interesting aspects of the religious life of the Bene Israel was their attitude to Hindu religion. The Bene Israel (and the other Jews of India) were the only Jewish community in modern times (if we disregard the handful of Chinese Jews) to live in a polytheistic environment. Ever since Biblical times, nothing has been so abhorrent to Jewish religious leaders and their followers as polytheism, in which they saw nothing but sheer idolatry, the fountainhead of immorality and inhumanity, the source of all vice and sin. Remarkably, but, in the circumstances, understandably, no traces of this ancient, ingrained Jewish anti-heathen attitude could be found among the Bene Israel. The insidious influence of the Hindu environment over the centuries produced in the Bene Israel what can be called an appreciative understanding, nay, positive attitude, towards Hinduism, its beliefs and values. Another factor in the development of this positive attitude

The lavishly decorated ark and Tora scrolls of a synagogue.

to Hinduism seems to have been the absence of hostilities, persecution and oppression and the multiple caste system which allotted to the Jews their special niche within which they could live in peace. In this socio-cultural environment, the religion upon which such a social relationship was based had to appear in the eyes of the Bene Israel as having redeeming values, as being possessed of features not incompatible with their own faith. Thus, in the Bene Israel view, the polytheistic character of Hinduism could be disregarded, or at least relegated into the background, and its moralistic features, its teachings of kindness, of non-violence, of the sanctity of all life, whether human or animal, emphasized, appreciated, and upheld.

Before leaving the Bene Israel and the Baghdadi Jews, a word about their numbers. In 1837 the Bene Israel numbered 5,255; in 1881 – 7,000; in 1941 – 14,805; in 1947 – 17,500. After the independence of Israel, emigration caused their number to decrease; by 1961 only 15,000, and by 1968 only 13,000 of them had remained in India, and their number continued to decline. Israeli statistics showed that by 1969 over 12,000 Bene Israel had emigrated to Israel, settling mainly in the Negev.

As for the Baghdadi Jews, their statistics show a similar curve. In 1837 they numbered 657, in 1941 – 5,675 (the increase was largely due to immigration), and in 1947 – 6,500. By 1968 emigration had reduced their numbers to 1,500.

While the numbers of the Bene Israel and the Baghdadi Jews only diminished after India's and Israel's independence, another, smaller, indigenous Indian Jewish community, that of the Cochin Jews, disappeared altogether from India as a result of their transplantation to Israel. Today Cochin is a city of some 45,000 in the state of Kerala, on the west, Malabar, coast of India, near the southern tip of the peninsula, at a distance of some 650 miles from Bombay. In 1502 Vasco da Gama established a trading post in Cochin making it the earliest place of European settlement in India. St Francis Xavier began his missionary work in Cochin in 1530, and the Dutch captured the town in 1663. In 1795 it was occupied by the British.

The myths of origin of the Cochin Jews resemble those of the Bene Israel just discussed. They too tell of the arrival of an ancestral group from the Land of Israel, either in the days of King Solomon, or at the time of the Assyrian exile of Israel, or the Babylonian exile of Judah. Historians are even more divided in their opinions as to the arrival of Jews in Cochin: some hold that it took place in the second century CE, others put it as late as the eleventh century.

The earliest and the most important historical document, carefully preserved to this day and cherished by the Cochin Jews, are the copper tablets, which contain an engraved text, variously dated from 974 to 1020, in the ancient Tamil language. They state that the Hindu ruler of Malabar, Bhaskara Ravi Varma, has granted to a certain Isuppu Irappan, i.e., Joseph Rabban, the village of Anjuvannam (in the immediate vicinity of Cochin) as a hereditary estate, together with proprietary rights, the tolls on elephants and other mounts, the revenues from the village, tax exemption, and such insignia of high rank as a lamp, a cloth to walk on, a palanquin, a parasol, a drum, a trumpet, a gateway, a canopy, an arch, and a garland.

The next reference to Cochin Jews comes from the famous Spanish Jewish traveller, Benjamin of Tudela. He reports about 1170 that there were a hundred Black Jews (according to a variant reading 'several thousand') on the Malabar coast, who, he says, 'are good men, observers of the Law, possess the Tora of Moses, the Prophets, and have some little knowledge of the Talmud and the Halakha'.[3]

A Hebrew tombstone inscription dated 1269 found on the island of Chennamangalam, slabs of synagogue inscriptions, and scattered references, by Arab and Christian travellers and geographers (including Qazwini, Marco Polo, and Ibn Battuta) in the twelfth to the fourteenth centuries, to Jews on the Malabar coast testify to their presence in this general area. A Polish Jew, Yusuf Adil, was an official of the Muslim ruler of Goa, and became known under the name of

Gaspar da Gama, after Vasco da Gama captured him (in 1498) and compelled him to embrace Christianity. His wife, a Cochin Jewess, bought for the Cochin community many Jewish books which had been confiscated from the Jews of Portugal. In 1524 the Jewish settlement of Cranganore (north of Cochin), which was so impressive that it gave rise to the notion that the Jews had an independent kingdom in that place, was destroyed by the Portuguese, and many of the refugees settled in nearby Cochin. They were joined by Jews and Marranos from Spain and Portugal, and later by some from Aleppo, Holland, and Germany. The rajah of Cochin welcomed the Jewish immigrants, allotted them land near his own palace, granted them religious and cultural autonomy, and appointed one of them to the office of *mudaliar*, hereditary chief, invested with privileges, prerogatives, and jurisdiction in internal matters. It was only thanks to the continued protection of the rajahs that the Jews of Cochin were able to survive the period of Portuguese rule (1502–1663). The mudaliars became close advisors and trusted agents of the rajahs, assisting them in diplomatic and financial matters. The Cochin Jews in general helped the rajahs in their frequent armed struggles with neighbouring potentates, and earned the reputation of strong and courageous fighters. Around 1600, they numbered 900 households, or about 4,000 souls.

In the course of the Portuguese-Dutch struggle for Cochin (1662–3), the Portuguese plundered and massacred the Jews, burning their synagogues and homes. The victory of the Dutch ushered in an era of prosperity, cultural autonomy, and religious freedom for the Cochin Jews. Contacts with the Jews of Holland were established. The remote and exotic Jewish community in Cochin aroused the interest of the Dutch Jews, and in 1686 they dispatched a delegation headed by Moses Pereira de Paiva to learn about its history and way of life, and sent with the delegation a most precious gift – Hebrew books. De Paiva's comprehensive report, *Noticias dos Judeos de Cochim* (Amsterdam, 1687), is to this day one of the most valuable sources on the Cochin Jews in the seventeenth century. His interest was focused in particular on the White Jews, although he deals also with the Black Jews whom he terms 'Malabar Jews', and whom he regards as Jews only by religion but not by race. According to de Paiva, the White Jews had come to Cochin from Cranganore, Castile, Algiers, Jerusalem, Safed, Damascus, Aleppo, Baghdad, Persia, and even Germany. He mentions 25 households of White Jews, as against 465 of Malabar Jews.

While there is little doubt as to the Middle Eastern (and partly also European) origin of the Cochin White Jews, the origin of the Black Jews remains a matter for conjecture. Since in the twelfth century Benjamin of Tudela calls the Jews of the Malabar coast 'Black Jews', one must assume that for some time prior to his day intermingling between Jewish immigrants and local 'black' people had taken place resulting in a Jewish community with a skin-colour like that of the Indian population of Malabar. The conversion of native slaves and servants to Judaism must have been an added factor in this process. Such interbreeding inevitably takes place whenever an immigrant element – usually consisting mostly or exclusively of males – settles in a new country. What is more remarkable is that the later Jewish immigrants, those who arrived in the fifteenth and sixteenth centuries, managed to preserve their separate identity. The strong barriers put up by the Indian caste-system against contact between disparate ethnic groups may have facilitated this self-isolation of the White Jews.

In the seventeenth and eighteenth centuries the White Jewish community of Cochin became augmented by immigration of a number of Jews from the West who attained leading positions in the community and the country, and whose descendants remained the dominant element in Cochin for several generations. The first such newcomer was David Rahabi whom we have met before, and whose son Ezekiel purchased land for the Black Jews near Cranganore, built a synagogue, imported Hebrew books, and became the historian of his community. Ezekiel's son, David Rahabi (d. 1790), wrote several Hebrew works, including one which contains a comparison of the Jewish and Muslim calendars. He and his brother Elias also translated parts of the Bible and the prayer book into the vernacular, Malayalam. A later scion of the same family was Naphtali Eliahu Rahabi (Raby or Roby, 1863–1951), author of several Hebrew books on the history of the Cochin Jews and his own family.

The White Jews of Cochin boasted of quite a number of Hebrew poets, scholars, translators, scribes, and copyists. Some of them pioneered the introduction of Hebrew printing into India. Among other works, they printed in Bombay, in the early nineteenth century, Hebrew liturgical texts for their own community, as well as for the Bene Israel. In Cochin itself a Hebrew and Malayalam press was established in 1877 on the initiative of a teacher, Joseph Daniel Kohen. (Among the Black Jews of Cochin there were no Kohanim.) Interest in matters Jewish and in the Land of Israel was augmented, from the eighteenth century on, by emissaries from the Land of Israel, and when news of the Zionist movement reached Cochin, N. E. Roby (Rahabi) wrote to Theodor Herzl (on 15 October 1901) offering the financial support of the leading Jews in Cochin and elsewhere.[4]

A third Jewish 'caste' in Cochin, not mentioned hitherto, was the one called *Meshuararim*, whose name is a slightly corrupted form of the Hebrew term *m'shuhrarim*, meaning 'liberated ones'. The Meshuararim were the descendants of White and Black Jewish men and their slave concubines and of the emancipated slaves of either White or Black Jews. Accordingly, they fell into two sub-groups: those of the White Jews and those of the Black.

As for the demographic development of the Jews of Cochin, we have some data to draw on. In 1781 the Dutch governor, Adrian Moens, wrote a memorandum in which he reported that the 'Jewish nation' in Cochin inhabited six localities: the Jewish quarter (subsequently called 'Jewtown') near the 'palace of the king of Cochin' (i.e., the Paradesi synagogue) – 150 families; Angicaymal (now Ernakulam) – more than 100 houses and two synagogues; Parur – nearly 100 houses and one synagogue; Chenotta (Chennamangalam) – 50 families and one synagogue; the island of Territur – ten families and one synagogue; Muttam (Madatankil) – 12 families and one synagogue; or a total of 422 families (or ca. 2,000 souls) with seven synagogues. In 1837 there were 1,039 Jews in Cochin – a 50 per cent decline within 56 years. In 1931, about a century later, their number had again increased to 1,600 Black Jews, 144 White Jews, and 30 Meshuararim, a total of 1,774. They still had their seven synagogues, including the Paradesi of the White Jews. In 1941 the number of Cochin Jews was 2,000, and in 1948, just before their emigration to Israel started, they numbered 2,500, including 100 White Jews.[5]

By 1968 all the Black Jews had emigrated to Israel. About 100 White Jews remained, because they were unwilling to leave without their assets which Indian government regulations did not allow them to take out of the country. In the same year the number of Cochin Jews in Israel was 4,000.

To sum up the demographic ups and downs of the Jews of India in the nineteenth and twentieth centuries, in 1837 there were 6,951 Jews in the sub-continent; in 1941 – 22,480; in 1947 – 26,500; and in 1968 – 14,600. Of the various elements which made up these totals, there was one, that of the Black Jews of Cochin, which in its entirety was transplanted to Israel. According to Israeli statistics, in 1968 about 23,000 Jews from India lived in Israel. Another 2,000 lived in England. The sum total of these three figures is 39,500, which would represent an increase of about 50 per cent in two decades. If these figures are correct, they show that the Indian Jews had one of the highest rates of natural increase in the period in question, with the lion's share going to the Bene Israel.

A studio portrait of a Bar Mitzvah boy in Calcutta.

Notes

Introduction
1. CE–Common Era (AD).
2. BCE–Before Common Era (BC).

Chapter One
1. Cf. R. Moses Isserles, *Responsa* no. 73.
2. Heinrich Graetz, *History of the Jews* (Philadelphia 1894, reprint 1956), vol. 4, pp. 639–40.
3. For the Talmudic sources of this belief and practice, cf. R. Patai, *Man and Temple in Ancient Jewish Myth and Ritual*, 2nd ed. (New York 1967) pp. 172ff.
4. Patai, *Tents of Jacob: The Diaspora Yesterday and Today* (Englewood Cliffs, New Jersey 1971), pp. 296–301.

Chapter Three
1. Joseph Nehama, *Histoire des Israélites de Salonique* (Paris and Salonika 1935), vol. 2, pp. 39–42; my translation from the French – R.P.

Chapter Four
1. Cf. Patai, *Tents of Jacob*, p. 200.
2. I. Ben Ami in *Scripta Hierosolymitana* (Jerusalem 1971) vol. 22, pp. 1–18.
3. Edmondo de Amicis, *Morocco: Its People and Places* (New York and London 1888), pp. 19, 246–7.
4. Edward Westermark, *Ritual and Belief in Morocco* (London, 1926), vol. 1, p. 275.
5. L. Voinot, *Pélerinages judéo-musulmans au Maroc* (Paris 1948); cf. also André Chouraqui, *Les juifs d'Afrique du Nord* (Paris 1952), pp. 293–4.
6. This description of the Marrakesh *mellah* is based on Pierre Flamand, *Les communautés Israélites du Sud-Marocain* (Casablanca, n.d., ca. 1956).
7. The Jewish men and women aged twenty years or over who donated a minimum of 50 francs (about the price of one kilo of cereal) had the right to vote; cf. Flamand, *Les communautés*, p. 234.
8. Flamand, *Les communautés*, pp. 250, 298–301.
9. Lloyd Cabot Briggs, *Tribes of the Sahara* (Cambridge, Mass. 1960).
10. Briggs, *Tribes of the Sahara*, pp. 92, 104.

Chapter Five
1. This sketch of Kurdish life is largely based on Erich Brauer, *Y'hude Kurdistan: Mehqar Ethnologi*, completed, edited and translated from English to Hebrew by R. Patai (Jerusalem 1947).

Chapter Six
1. Louis Rabinowitz, *Far Eastern Mission*, Johannesburg, 1952, pp. 71–72; as quoted by Schifra Stritzower, *The Bene Israel of Bombay*, New York, 1971, p. 47.
2. The above summary is based on Stritzower, *op. cit.*, pp. 75ff.
3. Marcus Nathan Adler, ed., *The Itinerary of Benjamin of Tudela*, London, 1907, p. 59.
4. Cf. Walter J. Fischel, 'Early Zionism in India', in Raphael Patai, ed., *Herzl Year Book IV*, New York, 1961–62, pp. 309ff.
5. H. G. Reissner, 'Indian Jewish Statistics (1837–1941)', *Jewish Social Studies*, 1950, 12:4:350.

Acknowledgments

The pictures in this book are reproduced by kind permission of the following (numbers refer to pages):

Alliance Israélite Universelle, Paris: 146–7, 148, 149

Leo Baeck Institute, New York: 53, 56 top and bottom, 57 top and bottom

Ben Zvi Institute, Jerusalem: 144, 165

Beth Hatefutsoth, The Nahum Goldmann Museum of the Jewish Diaspora, Tel Aviv: 52, 89, 90, 91, 93, 94–5, 97 left, 108 left, 108–9

Jacques Boyer, Paris: 16

Brauer: 164

Central Zionist Archives: 126

Cultural Research and Communications Inc, New York: 25 bottom, 31, 66, 70, 86 (photo RAP, Paris), 106 left, 136

Field Museum, Chicago: 152, 154, 155 top, 155 bottom, 156, 157 left and right, 158, 160, 161

Moses Gans/Bosch & Keuning, Netherlands: 72, 75, 76, 77

G.D. Hackett, New York: 69

Israel Museum, Jerusalem: 98 (photo Bouhsira), 100, 104, 105, 106 right, 107, 109 right, 112, 113, 116, 119 top, 142, 162

Janet Naim (Associazione Ebrei di Libya, Roma): 122, 124, 125 left, 125 right

Magnes Museum, California: 110–1, 172 (photo Professor David Mandelbaum), 174, 176, 177 top and bottom, 179, 180, 185

Musée de l'homme, Paris: 118 bottom, 119 bottom, 166, 168, 170, 171

Catherine Noren: 54–5

Professor Raphael Patai: 64

Lazar Ran: 34, 36, 37 top and bottom, left and right, 38 top and bottom, 39

Moshe Raviv: 18

Victor Sanua: 127, 130, 131 top left, 131 top right, 132, 132–3, 135

Alexander Scheiber: 67 left and right

Union Theological Seminary, New York: 138, 140, 141

Roger Viollet: 30, 32, 48, 62–3, 102, 103, 114 left, 114–5, 118 top

YIVO, New York: 2, 21, 22 (Abramovitch Collection), 22 left (Abramovitch), 22 right (photo R. Przedecki), 24, 25 top, 26 top, 26 bottom, 27 (photo Vishniac), 28, 29 (photo A. Kacyvna, Abramovitch), 33, 40, 42, 43 (Abramovitch), 44, 45, 46, 47 (Abramovitch), 50, 58, 59 (photo Vishniac), 60, 61, 62, 74, 78, 81, 83, 84, 85, 92, 97 right, 131 bottom, 134

Index